My 1961

D1452550

MY
1961

Andy Strasberg

August Publications

To Roger Maris.

CONTENTS

My 1961

August Publications
3543 John Muir Dr.
Middleton, WI 53562
608.836.3730
augustpublications.com

Cover by Todd Radom.

ISBN 978-1-938532-59-7 (Print)
ISBN 978-1-938532-60-3 (eBook)

9 8 7 6 5 4 3 2 1

INTRODUCTION

On occasion, when I run into people I grew up with but haven't kept in touch with over the years, they aren't surprised to hear that the National Pastime has been my professional pastime for the past 45 years.

The first phase of my baseball career was a 22-year tenure (1975-1996) heading up the San Diego Padres' marketing department.

Then in 1997, I began my own consulting firm for a diverse list of clients in the baseball sphere that included successful year-long Hall of Fame campaigns for Ozzie Smith (player), Jerry Coleman (broadcaster), and Doug Harvey (umpire).

Other baseball credits include:

- Contributing participant on Ken Burns' award-winning PBS-TV documentary, *Baseball*;
- Consultant to Billy Crystal's HBO movie, *61**;
- Staging a baseball exhibit at the Lincoln Center for the Performing Arts;
- Originator and consultant for the 2008 U.S. Postal Service stamp based on baseball's anthem, "Take Me Out to the Ball Game";
- And advisory board member for the National Baseball Hall of Fame.

My writing credits include a feature in the 1978 and 2016 Major League Baseball All-Star Game programs; co-author of the book *Baseball's Greatest Hit: The Story of Take Me Out to the Ball Game* (Hal Leonard Corp., 2008); *The Famous Chicken's Baseball Quiz Book*; *Baseball Fantography* (Abrams Images); and *San Diego Baseball Fantography*.

Additionally, I wrote and performed a one-act/one-man play titled *That's Baseball* in 2012 at the Lyceum Theatre in San Diego.

Along the way, I secretly smiled every time while attending more than 1,760 Major League Baseball games in 50 different ballparks, knowing that I was being paid to be there.

For all of that and more, I cherish my good fortune.

This is the story of my greatest year of growing up—1961—when I was 13 years old.

That year tells the tales of my awkward transition from childhood to adolescence, as a young boy so deeply influenced by the nation's pastime that I made baseball my life-long career.

Summer Fun—When the Camp Kiowa photographer came around to shoot a photo of us playing softball in the summer of 1959, it was my lucky break because I was at bat. The photog asked for everyone to freeze as if we were actually playing. Pretty hokey, if you ask me.

Brilliant, reddish-orange flames were burning up the front of my shirt.

I was on fire.

I twisted and spun around, waving my hands, desperately trying to get the fire off me as if the flames were a swarm of bees.

I looked skyward to keep my face from burning, or was I instinctively looking for divine help?

For a moment, I was certain that I was going to be burnt to death because nothing I did would stop the fire on my chest.

But I'm getting ahead of myself, as I have a tendency to do.

Have you ever been twelve years old?

Well, I was.

In 1961.

The year that changed my world forever.

But I need to give you the background leading up to that fire, and the life-altering year that followed…1961.

In 1960 I spent July and August in the Pocono Mountains of Pennsylvania at Camp Kiowa. While I did enjoy camp, going there meant I'd lose access to my life's essentials, such as Yankee games on radio and TV, my mother's cooking—especially her lamb chops—sleeping late in my own bed, and watching *The Rifleman* on TV.

As September approached, I knew my summer-camp activities of swimming, playing baseball, making plastic-lace keychains in arts and crafts, sitting around a campfire cooking hot dogs on a stick while getting eaten alive by bugs—including the time a moth flew into my mouth—and competing in tetherball were just about over.

It was almost time to go home.

My last day of camp was August 26, 1960. Along with my sister, Bobbi, who is six years older than me, we were waiting for my dad to pick us up and drive us the two-and-a-half hours back home to White Plains, New York.

An hour before he arrived, there were only a handful of campers, including me, each patiently waiting for their ride to arrive. To pass the time, we hung around the smoldering bonfire from the evening before.

I was the oldest kid among the group and thought that, for safety's sake, it was time to put out the fire. I looked around and found a glass container that had an apple cider label on it. About one-third of its contents remained.

I pulled it out of the trash and unscrewed the top. Then I walked over to slowly pour the contents over the smoking embers to extinguish them.

As the liquid hit the ashes, I heard a hiss and was shocked as the ashes jumped toward me in an explosive, fiery flash. I dropped the container and turned around. My body was a human torch. My sister, Bobbi, a hundred yards away, saw the explosion and watched in horror.

I began twisting and turning to escape the inferno, all the time furiously patting myself, trying in vain to smother the flames.

At that moment, I recalled what I had learned in school to extinguish the flames if someone catches on fire: Roll on the ground, throwing dirt on yourself. So I dropped to the ground and did just that.

All this happened in a mere matter of seconds. When the fire was out, I stood up, looked down at my chest and realized that my shirt had totally disintegrated in the flames.

I was in disbelief—my skin appeared to have melted away as if it was flesh-colored candle wax. That was when I realized in the few seconds I was engulfed in flames, I had peed in my pants.

Twenty percent of my body was burned. I was bedridden and unable to start junior high school on time, which didn't bother me because I had a history of not doing so well in school.

Since my name starts with the letter S and seat assignments in class are done alphabetically with the A's and B's upfront, and I am not a "Go to the Head of the Class" winner, I sat in the back of the classroom, both figuratively and literally.

However, since I wasn't going to start school when every other kid I knew did, the good news was that I'd have more time to catch the New York Yankees on TV. As everyone knew, they were trying to return to the World Series after a dismal 1959 season when they finished in third place.

Back then, trying to turn things around, the Yanks made a humongous trade with the Kansas City Athletics after the '59 season, which for years, according to my know-it-all baseball friends, was nothing more than the Yankees' farm team.

I didn't know it at the time, but that December 11, 1959, trade would change my life. The Athletics swapped Roger Maris, Joe DeMaestri, and Kent Hadley to the Yankees for Don Larsen, Hank Bauer, Norm Siebern, and Marv Throneberry.

Place of Worship—The first World Series game I ever attended was in 1957 when the Yanks met the Milwaukee Braves in Yankee Stadium. It was then I realized that The Stadium is truly a place of worship. *Photo courtesy Don McNeish.*

Being a smart-ass, I offered my expert analysis when my friends and I discussed the trade. I said to seal the deal the Bronx Bombers should have tossed in a left-handed Yankee batboy, plus a roll of Indian-head nickels to buy that scrumptious apple pie desert at the Horn and Hardart Automat restaurant across from Yankee Stadium on the corner of River Avenue and 161st Street.

"That guy Roger Maris must be a little cuckoo," I told them. "He must have rocks in his head."

That's what I believed after reading what he said when he was traded from the A's to the Yankees: "Believe it or not, I had rather stayed with the Athletics. But I'll do my best for the Yankees."

Speaking out of the side of my mouth like a tough guy, while gesturing with my thumb on my right hand as if I was a hitchhiker, I told my buddies, "Hey, Maris, it's the Yanks, for God's sake, not Cleveland."

I always got a laugh when I did my gangster voice. But for months, I couldn't get Roger's quote about the multiplayer swap out of my head.

While I was growing up, all my friends, without exception, were baseball fans. Their favorite player was Mickey Mantle, or as my father enjoyed calling him, "Moishe Mandel," because he desperately wanted him to be Jewish.

Not really, but I think really.

I, however, was not a Mickey Mantle fan. Don't get me wrong. He was a great player—but I didn't want to be like everyone else who idolized him.

Plus, I admit it: I'm not good when it comes to sharing food, toys, or baseball idols with other kids.

Ever since I was nine years old back in 1957, I had been searching for a player I could call my own. Maybe Maris would be that player.

Maris's first game with the Yanks was Monday, April 19, 1960, in Boston against the Red Sox. He batted leadoff and went 4-for-5 with two homers, a double, and a base knock (single). The Yanks creamed the Bosox, 8–4. I loved saying words like "Bosox" because it made me sound more baseball savvy.

After ten games of the 1960 Yankee season, Roger was hitting over .400. I know, I know, it was just ten games. But as a result of those ten games, I was now a devout Roger Maris fan.

The new Yankee right fielder impressed the dickens out of me during the first three months of that 1960 season.

So while lying in bed as my burnt skin slowly healed, I would watch Yankee games televised on WPIX. The Yanks won the 1960 American League pennant on Sunday, September 25, edging the Red Sox by a score of 4-3.

But as everyone knows, the Bronx Bombers would go on to lose the 1960 World Series to the Pirates in seven games…but don't get me started.

Now don't get your skivvies in a bunch, this isn't just a baseball book. It's much more.

It's time for me to share everything in my life from 1961.

How will I do that?

Well, you can thank Miss Cramer, my English teacher. In January of 1961 she assigned everyone in class to write their autobiography. I made notes on everything that I could remember before 1961 and everything that was happening in 1961.

Practically everything, except my daily visits to the can.

In these pages, you will get the inside skinny on my life in the year 1961. Included is a lot of inside information that I didn't hand in to Miss Cramer because she would have had a shit fit reading some of my stuff.

That year of 1961 was at times crazy, scary, wonderful, funny, embarrassing, horrifying, titillating (hey, wipe that smirk off your face), but always memorable and enlightening.

The stories are from my private world inside and outside Yankee Stadium.

My obsession with baseball exploded in 1961, with numerous once-in-a-lifetime experiences. No longer was I just a thirteen-year-old fan who sat and watched a game at Yankee Stadium.

Get this: I caught a ball off the bat of Nellie Fox, met Yankee coach Jim Hegan, and even dined with my dad next to Paul Richards, manager of the Orioles, in Paul Daube's Bronx steakhouse frequented by Babe Ruth—the Bambino himself—during his playing days.

As if that wasn't enough baseball, I had a chance meeting with the "Hebrew Hammer" himself, Mr. Hank Greenberg.

Not surprisingly, I possessed a relentless obsession with all things baseball. Ask any fan, and I guarantee they will explain how baseball in 1961 was different from any other season they remember. It was the "Season of the Home Run."

For me, it became very personal when the Yankees' Roger Maris competed in a home run race chasing, tying, and passing Babe Ruth's ghost for homers hit in a single season.

I kept a day-to-day eye on Maris, who was hitting homers at a record pace—no fan anywhere followed that chase more closely than me. I collected nuggets of information about the home run race between Maris and his teammate Mickey Mantle, no matter how trivial to others.

Just like an investigative sports reporter, I uncovered the "New York Yankee Bat Boy for a Day" contest screw-up. I also "exposed" the unfortunate story of Yankee Stadium's Polaroid Kid the day Maris hit his sixty-first homer.

I devoured newspapers as if my very existence depended on it.

That's also when my eyes wandered to other sections besides Sports, which is how I learned—with apologies to Lois Lane, Jimmy Olsen, Mr. Mxyzptlk, Luthor, and Bizarro—that there was more than just *Superman* comics out there to read.

There were stories about Russian astronaut Yuri Gagarin circling the Earth in outer space, traveling more than 27,400 kilometers per hour in a Soviet spacecraft and landing safely; the Freedom Riders courageously putting their lives on the line in the South during Civil Rights protests; the American hero Alan Shepard being shot into space; the Adolph Eichmann trial and his role in subjecting Jews to inhumane atrocities that resulted in the death of millions; President John F. Kennedy wanting to put a man on the Moon as if he was an actor in a *Twilight Zone* episode; the division of East and West Germany as the Berlin Wall was being erected on a daily basis for the world to see.

By September of 1961, things got very scary here in the United States. While gobbling down Wonder Bread baloney sandwiches for lunch in our junior high school cafeteria, my classmates and I talked about the unimaginable threat of Russia dropping deadly bombs on the United States.

We believed at any moment that before our next class we might have to choose whether we'd rather be Red or dead.

Those twelve months of 1961 had a profound effect on me. To begin with, before 1961 I wouldn't have used the word *profound* because I was just a kid. Kids don't say the word *profound* because they haven't experienced profound.

Not anymore. I grew up in 1961.

Specifically, I was twelve years old for seven-and-a-half months and then thirteen years old for four-and-a-half months.

The year posed challenges—and opportunities—I'd never imagined and placed me in situations where my intellect and nincompoop sense of humor alone wouldn't solve my dilemmas.

There were my daily classroom clashes with my junior high home-room teacher, Mr. Clements. He was a sharp, cool dresser, smart as a whip, and quick-witted. He played rock 'n roll on his sax with his band, and they even appeared on the *American Bandstand* TV show.

Not having school smarts, I searched for ways to get through each school day. Regrettably, capturing my schoolmates' attention as the self-designated class clown and daydreaming were not subjects I could be graded on.

In these pages, I will enlighten you with my brilliant, though failed, attempt at conducting my school science project on an ingenious baseball theorem I invented.

I share details of my first movie date, where contrary to rumors floating around the halls of Highlands Junior High, "nothing happened."

I document how rock 'n' roll was no longer merely background music to me. It was now driving me to crave more songs every day. With so many songs playing in my head, there were times I couldn't sleep at all last night.

At the risk of creating bedlam in candy stores around the country, I espouse my formula to beat the Topps Bubble Gum baseball cards packaging system so that without unwrapping a cellophane pack I could tell if it contained a Roger Maris card.

I also reveal my secret inner thoughts about a 21-year-old blonde dental assistant that got me aroused in a most embarrassing situation.

In order to avoid jail time after getting caught stealing a Roy Rogers Chuck Wagon from a local toy store, I explain how I came clean.

I touch upon repeating nightmares about my parents, who weren't really my parents, or so I dreamt.

And, unashamedly, I divulge the solemn day I quit Hebrew school while standing in front of Rabbi Schwartz, mere moments after my Bar Mitzvah service.

And here and now, I admit that on those hot sweaty 1961 summer nights in the empty high-school football field scoreboard, I secretly met with three girls and two boys for our social club. Aw, who am I trying to fool? It was a sex club. That's spelled *s-e-x*.

No sugar coating. It's all here. Cross my heart and hope to die, every word is true.

***

It's almost midnight, December 31, 1960. Get ready to bang your pots and pans. I'm watching Channel 2 on the tube. Times Square is jammed with knuckleheads standing in below-freezing temperatures.

There's only seconds left before the ball drops and Guy Lombardo plays "Auld Lang Syne" for the nine-millionth time.

Here's my countdown.

Five Mississippi...four Mississippi...three Mississippi...two Mississippi...one Mississippi...HAPPY NEW YEAR!

Hello, 1961.

FOREWORD

There was an old joke (or maybe it's a modern proverb) that basically said "You and I are so much alike, one of us is unnecessary."

I think about that when I contemplate Andy Strasberg and me. I thought I was the necessary one, but then I read this youthful diary of his and realized he's got a lot to offer.

This book takes place some 60 years ago, but this foreword is written today, with the luxury of hindsight. In many ways, Andy and I have managed to become adults. Seniors, in fact. Yet, there is always 1961 to bring us back.

The most common bond between us is baseball, and growing up in New York's northern suburbs accounts for a lot of the reasons we can finish each other's sentences.

Baseball's connection to fans is very much geographic, and the northern suburbs were New York Yankees country, just as Long Island was New York Mets country. I was in Rockland County, Andy in Westchester. We didn't know each other at the time, but we had the same experiences. I recognized many of them as being mine as I read this diary.

And if baseball was our most common bond, the 1961 season long ago became the go-to source of conversation. Those of us Baby Boomers, in our young teens that year, blessed with a remarkable Yankees season, **knew** we were experiencing history. We knew that season was going to take on historic proportions and become part of the conversation of "greatest teams ever." As we watched it unfold, we felt we were connected to something extraordinary.

I believe that it being John F. Kennedy's rookie season as president had something to do with this.

Having previously floated through the Truman and Eisenhower administrations, we only knew our presidents as grandfather-like. Now, with a youthful presidential family in the White House, people like Andy and me could better relate to events of the day, and even be inspired by history. Everything suddenly turned more interesting. The awareness of history took on a fresher appeal.

Andy and I were born the same year, 1948, a year in which the Yankees didn't win the pennant. We were apparently programmed to discover baseball at the same age, Chinese food at the same age, rock 'n roll at the same age, and then girls at the same age. After that it was sort of a blur; the important things were already covered.

Mickey Mantle had entered the stage first. For we post-Joe DiMaggio people, who didn't need to compare Mickey to Joe, Mantle was the perfect hero. He had the looks, the muscles, the name, and the results. No one wore a baseball uniform as perfectly as he did. No one ran out home runs as smoothly. His baseball cards were the ones you had to own. I can still tell you where I was when I opened a pack and got a Mantle. He had more of a national following than Willie Mays, because he played in 12 World Series in his first 14 seasons, and was thus a fixture on the NBC fall schedule, just like *Bonanza*.

Me, I needed my own favorite. Similar to Andy, I didn't want to share Mickey with everyone else. So in 1959, in his first year as a regular, I adopted Bobby Richardson, the second baseman. (When I went to work for the Yankees PR department in 1968, we reformed our friendship as adults and remain friends to this day.)

Andy, across the Hudson River, discovered Roger Maris when he was traded to the Yankees in 1960. It was a good choice for Andy and for the Yankees; Maris went out and won the MVP award. And then came 1961.

Lefthanders always look better swinging the bat than righthanders, because their follow through naturally guides them to first. Righthanders had to uncork themselves and change direction from the end of their swing. So a lefty would always have a more picturesque swing, and Roger Maris not only had that, but he had a wonderful Yankee Stadium swing. It was level and smooth and it made Yankee fans swoon. None more than Andy.

I think the first time I heard the term "anti-hero" was in relation to Dustin Hoffman's character in the 1967 film *The Graduate*. But it would be retroactively applied to Maris for a variety of reasons, first of which was his having no desire to be a hero. Actors want to be beloved. Athletes mostly just want to play. Mantle would be the hero in the 1961 drama, and the word we were missing for Roger was anti-hero.

As for the home run race itself, it captivated the nation in the summer of '61. Both Mantle and Maris were taking aim at Babe Ruth's wonderfully symmetrical total of 60, accomplished in 1927. As the two of them continued their chase, newspapers (then the primary source of sports news), easily settled on the concept of "61 in '61," and began running charts showing how many games ahead they were of Ruth's pace. The charts began appearing in June, *Life* Magazine put them on the cover, and it seemed the whole world began watching. That may not have been true, but certainly Andy in White Plains and me in Spring Valley were riveted to every game. Channel 11 broadcast a remarkable number of games that year, and so we saw a lot, and had Mel Allen, Red Barber, and Phil Rizzuto to guide us through it. It was like having Washington, Adams, and Jefferson teach us democracy. Mel, who first broadcast Yankees games in 1939, was a fount of information on the "old days," and I think we found that going back 60 years in baseball history, with just 400 players a year, was not an insurmountable task. We came to know Tris Speaker and Al Simmons, Pie Traynor and Frankie Frisch. (I think for today's young fans, learning the last few decades of over a thousand players a year is an impossible task and they shouldn't be scorned for passing over the assignment).

The general public would turn against Roger, not so much for who he was, but rather, because Mickey seemed like the "chosen one." He'd been a Yankee for 11 years, had hit 52 five years earlier, was the more logical record breaker, and was a much beloved figure. Roger, the newspapers like to remind us, was this young upstart who could be grouchy or surly on occasion. Of course, we had to look past that to discover the real Roger. Andy did that. (The two of us wound up being consultants on Billy Crystal's HBO film, *61**, in which Andy primarily advised on Roger and me on Mickey. What a kick that was.)

Not all of us were smart enough to keep a diary like Andy did. (I kept a Richardson scrapbook). Hooray for him, because not only is it precociously insightful and full of forgotten moments, but it's also a wonderful look into what it was like to be 13 in the happiest summer a young baseball fan in New York could enjoy. Even without being able to ask the man for Ballantine.

Andy and I came out okay, both landing jobs with Major League Baseball and with it, a lifetime's worth of friendships and stories.

So thank you Andy for what you did in '61, how you've lovingly saved it, and how you developed a loyal friendship with the Maris family through the years. That love comes through here, and it is a gift to all who shared some piece of that magical year, in body or in spirit.

Marty Appel
September 1, 2020

Marty Appel is the author of 24 books including Pinstripe Empire, Casey Stengel, Munson, *and* Now Pitching for the Yankees. *He served the Yankees in PR and television production between 1968-92 and is generally considered the leading historian on the team.*

JANUARY 1961

"Here's a dime, kid...go call someone who cares."

January 2

Mondays are not my favorite day of the week during the school year. I dread Mondays. Instinct told me that I should have stayed home instead of going to school today.

Now before you call me a school crybaby, you have to understand that this Monday, January 2, is the absolute worst. Reason? Christmas vacation is over.

For the past few weeks it's been colder than a witch's you-know-what. Today the dark, cloudy gray skies hanging over my neighborhood look like they're about to snow enough to fill Yankee Stadium to the lights. Maybe enough for the Polo Grounds, too.

As I walk the four-and-a-half blocks from my house in White Plains, New York, to Highlands Junior High School, I figure that the next time I won't have to attend school legitimately will be Lincoln's birthday, which I'm pretty sure is sometime in February.

Unless, of course, I'm lucky—real lucky—and we have a mammoth blizzard in the next couple of hours that results in everyone being sent home from school.

Wouldn't it be something if all the New York radio stations announced that the twenty-one school days during January will become twenty-one snow days, with all schools closed in the tri-state area?

A boy can dream, can't he?

I'm gonna level with you, this school year has been difficult. The main difference from sixth grade last year is that instead of one teacher, now I have many teachers. There's a different teacher for each class, and classes are held in different rooms.

Seventh grade is a lot harder. There's a boatload of more facts to learn. For the first time in my life, I am being taught by a few male teachers. Which means I can't pretend to be that little freckle-faced kid that women teachers sometimes like to take care of as if I was their own.

Sure, women teachers can be crabby sometimes. But more often, they are sensitive, caring people, while I was afraid that men teachers would be mean and never smile.

Every school day begins with homeroom. Mr. Zach Clements is my homeroom teacher. So far he's the only real person I know whose first name begins with the letter Z. It was back in second grade when I read the *Friends and Neighbors* book that I became aware of a person whose name began with a Z. The story on page 179 was about a gardener named Zeke who tended to the gardens on Pleasant Street where Dick and Jane lived. So now here's a Z name again, but this time it's my teacher.

Mr. Clements takes attendance every morning like he's a prison guard taking roll. I think he's in his twenties. I'm pretty sure this is his first teaching job.

He's a smart-aleck teacher, but not in a bad way. Anytime a student tries to pull a fast one on him, Mr. Clements says, "Here's a dime, kid…go call someone who cares."

He's quick with the funny lines when a student asks if he can go to the school nurse when obviously nothing is wrong. He answers in a calm voice, "You can, but you may not."

He doesn't take guff from anyone, using the same street chatter as my friends by ending complaints with his favorite put-down: "Put a sock in it."

For those who try to get his attention by saying, "Hey, Mr. Clements," he responds with, "Hay is for horses." If he wasn't so old, he would fit right in as a pal.

He is without question my rival for the class's attention, and a most worthy opponent. "Worthy opponent" is my favorite current saying. I picked it up from reading newspapers when John F. Kennedy was running for president, and he was described as a most worthy opponent.

I'm not bragging, but I'm a pretty darn good class disrupter. Maybe one of the best. To get a laugh from my classroom audience I can imitate teachers, crack jokes, and do physical comedy bits.

Mr. Clements is "smart" funny. He doesn't do any of those things I do because he doesn't have to. He says things that are clever and is lightning fast with a one-liner.

When I get caught clowning around, I pay the price. Instead of writing, "I will not clown around in class," five thousand times on the blackboard or a report on "Why it's not funny to be funny in class," Mr. C makes me the center of attention, but not in a good way.

His favorite is making me hold a chair above my waist in the front corner of the classroom. That always comes with a warning to the other students: "Don't look at Mr. Strasberg unless you want to join him."

There's no question that Mr. C is the hippest teacher at Highlands. Compared to other male teachers, he's younger, wears stylish clothes, and has no competition when it comes to his sense of humor. As if that's not enough, he's in a rock 'n' roll band. I swear it's true. The band is called The Sherwoods. Mr. C plays the sax.

This is not just any run-of-the-mill band that plays at church socials. The Sherwoods have made real records. His 45 rpm record, "El Scorpion," is for sale at Kresge's. Now get this: the group actually appeared on TV's *American Bandstand* with Dick Clark.

No lie. How boss is that?

I hate to admit it, but I kinda look forward to homeroom, where I can do some joke-jousting with Mr. Clements. I never win but have a good time trying.

Right after my homeroom antics, real school begins, which is not easy for me nor do I enjoy it.

My problem is that I can't remember historical facts, have trouble with math, am bored reading long paragraphs, and I am the worst speller in the Western Hemisphere.

Pop quizzes make me cringe, and I'm a lost cause when it comes to homework...."*Work?*"

That's my Maynard G. Krebs impression, but you have to know the TV series *The Many Loves of Dobie Gillis* to get it. You see, Maynard is a beatnik with a goatee. He's Dobie's best friend who doesn't like to work. So every time he hears the word "work" he always repeats it in a high voice as if he's scared. I do the same thing. By the way, if I have to explain every joke, you're not going to laugh.

If it wasn't for all the cute girls, gym class, and lunch periods, there wouldn't be any incentive for me to attend school 'cause I know I ain't going to get smarter. And that's a fact.

The first day I'm back at school, Miss Beatrice Cramer, my English teacher, gives us an assignment. She wants us to write our autobiographies.

Shit (excuse my gutter talk), this ain't gonna be fun or easy because, like everyone else, I have twelve years to cover. The Civil War was shorter, and there's been whole books written about that.

She hands out a mimeographed sheet with an outline of what she wants us to include. She must have had the sheets printed before the Christmas holidays because I can't smell the light blue ink, dammit.

Nowhere in her instructions of what should be included is the word *baseball* or *Superman, food,* or *girls.* Therefore, my autobiography is going to be a short one-pager.

Before every other sentence Miss Cramer delivers, she clears her throat as if she's trying to hawk up a loogie. Man, that's annoying.

As my mind starts drifting, an imaginary daydream light must have started blinking over my head because Miss Cramer says, "Excuse me, Mr. Strasberg, *ahem,* do you mind coming back to earth and joining the rest of the class, *ahem,* as I go over the assignment?"

I'm now listening and get the feeling that Miss Cramer will not allow a lot of wiggle room. She provides a checklist of what should be included in our autobiography: Date of birth. Location of birth. Names of siblings. Family tree. Hobbies. Vacations. Pets. Future ambitions.

This is boring with a big fat dullsville capital *B.*

Miss Cramer finishes up by explaining, "Your autobiography is due the middle of March, *ahem,* so you have more than enough time to do the research and, *ahem,* interview family members."

To me that means I'll start and finish my autobiography the Sunday before it's due.

With the help of my sister, Bobbi, who's six years older than me and knows shorthand and can type fast because she's going to Claremont Secretarial School in Manhattan, I change my mind and decide to begin working on my autobiography right away.

The beginning is easy. I list information similar to what you find on the back of a baseball card, but add a couple of things so I'll have more words:

Born: July 17, 1948; Weight: 120 lbs; Eyes: Hazel; Sex: Male; Telephone: WH6-2062; Address: 135 Old Mamaroneck Road, White Plains, New York; Hair: Blondish Red; Height: 5'1"; Alias: "Dusty."

If you are wondering why I didn't list "Pot" as my nickname, which everyone calls me, it's because I hate my protruding, accentuated belly. I wanted a cooler name so I decided that, henceforth, my new nickname will be "Dusty," which I borrowed from all those big-league ballplayers whose last name was Rhodes. Now all I need is for all my friends to call me "Dusty," but nobody does.

Look, I know I'm chubby. Everyone knows I'm chubby. While all my friends are wearing normal clothes, my mom buys my clothes from J.C. Penney that are labeled "Boys Husky."

This autobiography assignment is driving me crazy. I put together a checklist of what I'd like to include and run it by Bobbi. Unfortunately, she puts the kibosh on almost everything because, according to her, it's either not appropriate or doesn't work.

"*Work?*" Never mind.

She says "no" to writing about baseball, my favorite foods, my comic book collection, names of past girlfriends, the last time I threw up, the time I had my tonsils taken out (which was a big thing to me), sleeping, and how often I go to the bathroom.

Before Bobbi can say "no" to the sleeping part, I argue that I spend at least a third of my life sleeping and, therefore, shouldn't it be included in my autobiography?

Stop Action—There's no mistaking me for a real baseball player catching a line drive because I'm wearing cargo pants and a Hawaiian shirt. My outfit would've been more appropriate for a cameo role in Elvis Presley's Blue Hawaii.

She takes the bait and asks, "How would you write about sleeping?"

I quickly answer, "I'd just fill up a couple of pages with *Zzzz*'s." She doesn't laugh. Doesn't even crack a smile. I move on.

The bathroom part I understand, but I'll bet dollars to donuts that some guys will be so desperate to fill up their autobiography they'll include a chapter about going to the bathroom.

I start off by interviewing my mom. My parents thought I would be a girl and had selected my name as Anne, which was the same name as both my grandmothers. She tells me that the doctor—Dr. Goldblatt—delivered me at

4:30 in the morning of July 17, 1948. Once I was born a boy, they decided on Andrew instead of Anne, with a middle name of Phillip.

She tells me that my first tooth appeared March 25, 1949. Well, I gotta include that. Teeth are important, right?

My mom then smiles, remembering that my hair was Champagne color with curls. Soon after my first tooth came in, I had my first haircut.

I write a quick summary of my school years. Third grade meant a lot of changes. We moved from the Bronx to White Plains, New York. I included my third-grade report card that showed my best subject was elementary science (got an A). My worst grade was a D+ was writing. As Mel Allen would say, "How about that!" Overall, I earned a "Could do better" under the remarks heading.

The "Could do better" remark has been used by every teacher for centuries. Great Scott, everybody could do better. If I found Einstein's report card, I'm pretty sure his teacher scribbled, "Could do better."

Give me a break, will ya?

My mother hands me what she thinks is the first short story I wrote. I was a kid. I read it. It's not very good. It's about my family, ice cream, and baseball bats. It's dated March 6, 1956, when I was seven years old.

During my conversation with my mom, she tells me in a not-very-subtle way that she thinks my nose is too big. "Andrew, someday soon, while playing you are going to break your nose. When it happens, we will have your nose fixed."

No wonder I have a "schnozzola complex."

***

As a result of Roger Maris winning the 1960 American League Most Valuable Player award, he was, according to the newspapers, now on the "rubber chicken" banquet circuit, which didn't sound very appetizing.

Newspaper reports provided sketchy information of Maris's whereabouts between the 1960 and 1961 baseball seasons.

My favorite part of the *New York Daily News* sports section is the notes that appeared at the end of a story under the heading "Diamond Dust." Most often, the items weren't quite worthy enough to be a full story.

The *Daily News* often would run those obscure notes followed by three dots (. . .) which newspapers referred to as ellipsis. (Now honestly, am I ever going to use that in a conversation with someone when I'm grown up? How's your ellipsis? Excuse me miss, your ellipsis is showing. It was a knock-out, drag-out fight, and I cut my upper ellipsis).

JUN   57

Please Enter Here—In 1957, as I was about to step into the National Baseball Hall of Fame in Cooperstown for the first time in my life, my dad snapped this photo.

January 4

The Sporting News newspaper ran a silly article of predictions by Larry Middlemas of the *Detroit News* in their January 4 edition. With tongue firmly planted in cheek while making reference to the trade that brought Maris from Kansas City to New York, he predicted that KC exec Frank "Trader" Lane will be quoted as saying, "Norm Siebern will out-hit Roger Maris. Kansas City may have the better of the trade."

January 10

January was going to be a busy month for Roger. It began with his appearance for Spalding, the sporting goods manufacturer, at the sporting goods dealers' convention in Manhattan on January 10. Man, I would have loved to be there so I could smell those brand-new Spalding leather mitts and meet Rog. Although I have yet to meet Maris, I'm starting to think we are buddies, so, like his Yankee teammates, I refer to him as Rog.

January 15

A newspaper photo of Maris appeared of him sledding on a toboggan January 15 while relaxing at Grossinger's in the Catskill Mountains of upstate New York.

January 16

I read in the *New York Daily News* that on Monday, January 16, Maris was in Baltimore at the Lord Baltimore Hotel for the Maryland Professional Baseball Players Association eighth annual Tops in Sports banquet.

Because of his 1960 stats, he was there to received what appeared to be an elaborate decorative king's crown known as the Babe Ruth Sultan of Swat Award. There was a great photo of Frank "Home Run" Baker presenting Rog with the crown.

I looked up Baker's stats in my copy of *The Official Encyclopedia of Baseball*. Found out that Baker was the former Philadelphia Athletics third baseman who led the American League in homers four consecutive years beginning in 1911, while never hitting more than twelve homers. Baker then finished his career in 1922 after six seasons with the Yankees.

The Babe Ruth Sultan of Swat Award was created in the mid-1950s by the Maryland Professional Baseball Players Association to recognize the player with the greatest combination of home runs and runs batted in, while at the same time honoring Babe Ruth, who grew up in Baltimore.

The glorious, regal-looking crown is truly fit for a king with its six points displaying six bejeweled baseball diamonds. They circle the golden metal headband and a crushed-red-velvet center head-covering.

One newspaper noted that the award has become one of the most respected in baseball, likely due to its reverence toward Baltimore's favorite son, Babe Ruth.

January 18

On January 18 in Manchester, New Hampshire, Ted Williams was honored by the American Legion Junior Baseball Program as the Man of the Year in front of a record black-tie crowd of 2,340 on "Thumper Night."

Maris attended alongwith Whitey Ford and Mickey Mantle. The dinner was held at the Manchester National Guard Armory. It was noted in a newspaper that Robert P. Paine, of 61 Atherton Avenue, gave his eleven-year-old son, Robert Jr., an opportunity to chat with and obtain autographs from both Williams and Maris.

That Robert is one lucky kid.

January 19

The Yanks announced that there was a press conference scheduled for the next afternoon. The *Daily News* jumped to the conclusion that it was—according to them—an expression of sublime confidence on the part of general manager Roy Hamey that he will be able to sign Roger Maris quickly as a result of their meeting scheduled for the following morning. It was pointed out that on the chance it doesn't come to fruition, the Yanks have a lesser player's contract signed and locked in a safe.

I wondered: Was this confidence or a tactic to get Roger's autograph on the 1961 contract? As it turned out, nothing happened as a result of a snowstorm, which hammered the northeast. The blizzard marooned Maris, along with Mick and Whitey, in New England.

January 20

On Friday, January 20, along with my junior high seventh-grade homeroom classmates, we watched John F. Kennedy's presidential inauguration on a portable black-and-white TV. At twelve years old, I wasn't into politics, but John F. Kennedy triggered something in me. It could have been his age, looks, or personality. I wasn't politically motivated and didn't have allegiance to the Democrats or Republicans.

During JFK's speech he said, "We shall pay any price, bear any burden, meet any hardship, support any friend or oppose any foe, in order to assure the survival and success of liberty."

I know what that means. The president was warning the Russians that we are not afraid to go to war, and will not be pushed around.

Them's fighting words.

I needed to think about things other than an eventual war with Russia. My thoughts started to drift from Washington, D.C., to Florida. While everyone was focused on the TV, I looked out the window at the snow-plowed streets, daydreaming about the Yankee spring training report dates—February 19 for battery men, February 28 for all others.

In my heart I felt that the 1961 Yankee season was going to be "boss."

January 21

In front of seven hundred people who paid fifteen dollars each, Maris was one of thirty honorees at the Columbus Touchdown Club in Ohio at their sixth annual awards dinner on January 21. For that price, I figure they had to be serving steak, not chicken. According to one newspaper account, the dinner went on for more than three hours.

January 22

Rog was given a plaque for "high principle and achievement in sports" at the Bill Corum Memorial Dinner sponsored by the Sports Lodge of B'nai B'rith on January 22 at the Roosevelt Hotel in New York City.

***

The winter is the ideal time to meticulously go through my Topps baseball card collection, making doubly sure I got 'em all.

Unfortunately, the sweet smell of gum that permeates each pack of that gum—each piece a bit larger than litmus test paper, but just as thin—has long dissipated.

Instinctively, while sorting my cards every few minutes, I pick up one that might still have the bubble gum's sweet aroma and I smell it, hoping to catch one more whiff of the remains of the sugary pink slab of gum.

While going through my baseball card set, I find myself spending a lot of time looking at the cartoon drawings on the back of the cards below a player's stats. It's obvious that some of the highlights in a player's baseball career don't provide much fodder for the artist doing the drawings.

A perfect example would be the back of Boston Red Sox middle infielder Pumpsie Green's card No. 454. The artist went overboard drawing a player in water wearing a baseball cap with the caption: "He enjoys swimming on a day off."

Then there's card No. 18 of Cleveland Indians pitcher Jim Grant. The back of his card has a cartoon of a player sitting next to a record player and wearing a beatnik-style beret with the caption: "He enjoys listening to progressive jazz."

January 23

On January 23, Maris was a guest at the Rochester Press and Radio Club Dinner where Arnold Palmer was awarded the Hickok Belt for 1960, a big sports prize. Murray Rose's article is headlined: "Homer Mark Will Stand, Says Maris." Rog is quoted as saying no one one will touch it: "Look up the records and you'll see that it's a rare year when anyone hits fifty homers, let alone sixty as Ruth hit in 1927."

January 25

Paying close attention to minuscule Maris mentions, I read that the next day, Maris—along with sportswriter Dick Young, players Roy Face, Jim Bunning, and Hal Smith—attended the New York Men's Club of Temple Hesed Abraham Sports Night Dinner in the Crystal Ballroom in Jamestown, New York, on January 24. The dinner was open to the public with the cost of tickets at eight dollars each. Eight bucks?

Immediately after the dinner Rog was able to catch a midnight plane to New York City so that he could meet with Yanks general manager Roy Hamey about his 1961 contract.

January 26

Roger was photographed while waiting in the Park Avenue Yankee offices on January 25 to meet with Hamey. The picture appeared the next day on the back page of the *New York Daily News*. He left without signing his contract. The inside story revealed that Hamey's concern was this: "If Maris had a good season in 1961, he might demand 50 grand for 1962...and in these inflated times, probably be worth it."

January 27

Maris was in attendance for the Boston Baseball Writers Dinner held at the Statler-Hilton Hotel on January 26. It was there that Pittsburgh Pirates manager Danny Murtaugh disclosed that when Maris was with Kansas City he almost traded Dick Groat for Rog. Asked why he didn't, Murtaugh he replied, "Stomach trouble," then elaborated, "no guts."

Sportswriter Ray Gillespie noted after one banquet in New England banquet that Maris was confronted by an impolite guest who told him, "You're a horrible speaker, chum!" The outfielder considered the insult briefly, then replied, "Mister, I know a lot of spellbinders who can't even hit their weight."

This was Maris's ninth of ten banquets over a two-week period. He announced that after the New York Baseball Writers' Association of America annual winter dinner he would fly home to Raytown, Missouri.

January 30

On January 29, the day before Maris was to meet again with general manager Roy Hamey to discuss his 1961 contract, he attended the New York Baseball Writers' Association of America annual dinner. It took place at the swanky Waldorf Astoria. The newspaper account revealed that Maris sat at Table 55 with teammates Whitey Ford, Bill Skowron, and Elston Howard, while comedian Phil Foster's baseball routine shook the house with laughter.

As had been the custom for years, the baseball writers acted out skits, one of which lampooned Maris. They rewrote the words to the popular song "I Love Paris" and sang it (more than likely off-key).

I love money in the springtime,
I love money in the fall,
They love Maris in the summer, when they play me,
But in winter I must fight for, what they pay me,
I want 50 thousand this year
'Cause I didn't get it last year
If they cut me, they can take their stinkin' contract
And shove it up their....

"Just a second," interrupted a man playing the part of Roy Hamey, the New York general manager, "just a second. Listen to our side of it." And he sang:

We love Maris in the springtime, when he sizzles,
Maris in September, when he fizzles,
We love Maris every moment,
Every moment of the year,
We love Maris,
Boy oh boy, do we love Maris,
But not for 50 grand.

***

Finally, on January 30, after twelve long weeks of dragged-out negotiations, Maris met with Hamey at the Yankees' august Squibb Building offices on the twenty-seventh floor of 745 Fifth Avenue and penned his 1961 contract for a reported $37,000. This was a hearty but well-deserved raise from his $18,000 salary for 1960.

Whew, what a relief. He earned it.

FEBRUARY 1961

"Okay, let's see how Pot can do."

February 1

On page 25 of the February 1 *Sporting News* was a Spalding glove ad featuring Maris. The prices ranged from $12.45 to $31. Honestly, who has that kinda money? (I wish I did.)

February 3

A space chimp named "Ham" took a 150-mile-high test ride in a Project Mercury space capsule on February 3.

***

I have a cuddly soft spot in my heart for monkeys. As a little kid, before I was old enough to attend school, I organized a "Monkey Club." The Monkey Club was an exclusive group whose membership consisted of my stuffed animals, not all of whom were monkeys. The president of the Monkey Club was Smokey Bear, who received the necessary votes to be the leader.

Other members included Throw-Up Monkey, Sleepy Monkey, Jocko, Smiley Monkey, Froggy the Gremlin—from the "Andy's Gang" TV show—and Teddy Snow Crop Polar Bear hand puppet.

We would have meetings and discussions, but mostly we watched TV and slept in the same bed. I still have all the members, but they now reside in my closet with the exception of my pal Smokey, who still sleeps with me every night.

Monkeying Around—Members of The Monkey Club that I proudly belonged to assembled for a group photo. I wish I could have been in the shot but I was the only member who knew how to use a camera. (L to R): Throw-Up Monkey, Teddy Snow Crop Bear, Sleepy, Jocko, Smokey Bear, J. Fred Muggs, Smiley, and Coco.

February 6

One of Maris's February stops took place on the fifth of that month when he attended the *Post-Gazette* twenty-fifth anniversary Dapper Dan Dinner at the Hilton Hotel in Pittsburgh. According to newspaper reports, 2,186 fans paid fifteen dollars each to attend. That dinner most definitely had to include steak.

February 7

On February 7, JFK sent Congress a proposal to raise the minimum wage from $1 to $1.25 an hour.

I know all about the challenges of earning a buck. At a very early age, my motivation was driven by my intense desire to purchase baseball cards.

Because my résumé qualifications were slim to none, the ways in which I thought I could earn money were limited. At nine years old, unlike a number of my contemporaries, I decided not to get into the firecracker business. Their operation was largely predicated on stopping at roadside fireworks stores to purchase a brick of firecrackers when their families drove back from vacationing in Florida. They would then break down the brick and sell packs with a considerable profit margin.

For me, there were too many risks. Besides, I didn't have the upfront money to purchase a brick. The most common and legitimate way to earn dough at my age was delivering newspapers. That wasn't for me. I'm not an early riser, and the money was not that great for time and effort expended.

Similar to legions of kids before me, I began searching for discarded glass soda bottles in the neighborhood so I could return them for money at nearby candy stores.

Admittedly, in the beginning, I was as green as a Canada Dry Ginger Ale bottle. I didn't know the ropes of bottle retrieval. However, after roaming the streets I began picking up tips (not money) on where and when to look for bottles. Off the record, here's my advice: Search alleys during the summer months. But, wink, wink, you didn't hear that from me, okay?

Unfortunately, I was at summer camp in July and August, which is the hay-making, peak bottle-collecting season. Plus, the competition was furious. I think every kid was doing the same thing. As a result, my career as a bottle returner was short-lived.

The next entry on my résumé came in 1958 when I was ten years old. I would occasionally find loose change on the ground near parking meters. I stood face to face with a parking meter, trying to understand the process of putting a coin in the meter and, more importantly, why there was change on the ground.

I surmised that when men pulled change from their pants, they would occasionally drop a coin trying to put it in the slot or extracting it from their pocket. In either situation, they would not bother to pick up the change, which is where I think the term "finders keepers, losers weepers" originated. The same dropsies would happen to women when they dug into their change purse.

I stared at the parking meter and the slot for the nickel. Although physics was not my strong suit, I calculated that the nickel inserted into the meter was resting inside on a sloped angle. My inner voice of reason and risk told me that if I hit the meter from the opposite side of the coin slot with an upward motion using the palm of my left hand, the nickel would pop out.

I put my theory to practice. It worked. I was now thinking that I was the richest kid on the block. This was an untapped gold mine of nickels.

Now, I can only imagine what you're thinking, that I was involved in a petty theft scam, right? Well, I'm not going to deny it. Let's just keep it between us.

After a few weeks of hitting parking meters in 1958, I had collected almost five bucks. Yet I was paying a physical price for my newfound riches. My left hand was bruised black and blue, and it hurt.

Instinctively, I decided to change career paths.

I positioned myself outside the local Finast grocery store's front door. As women shoppers exited, I would politely greet them: "Good afternoon, ma'am, could I assist you with your packages to your car?"

Honestly, what woman could resist the help of an adorable, freckle-faced, respectful ten-year-old kid with reddish brown hair?

If she were carrying a grocery bag, she would hand it over to me. If she was pushing a shopping cart, I'd take over steering. Once they agreed, I'd ask the location of their car. Then, during our walk, I'd charm them with small talk.

"Beautiful day, wouldn't you say?" Looking at the groceries, I'd exclaim with sincerity, "My, everything looks delicious. You must be an excellent cook. Do you have a large family?"

Once we arrived at their car, but before I unloaded the bags of groceries, I would pay another compliment: "Now, that's a beauty of a car. What year is it?"

Needless to say, business was good. I received at least a quarter tip for every load of groceries. There were days that I could make two, maybe three bucks...no lie.

Unfortunately, after months of success, one of the store's clerks caught on to my scheme and assigned a grocery bagger the task of assisting women customers to their cars. Rather than quit, I opted to retain my dignity and simply retired.

February 12

I read that sportswriter Jim Murray joined the *Los Angeles Times* and his first column would appear on February 12. I'm thinking that after my career as a Major League Baseball player, I could always become a sportswriter.

***

Coach DeNike, the gym teacher for Mamaroneck Avenue Elementary

School in White Plains, New York, was beloved by his students. His class was fun because it didn't involve reading, writing, or arithmetic. There were no tests. It was all playtime all the time.

He appeared to be larger than life, a man who wasn't really a teacher because he never dressed up in business-like clothing. He wore khakis, sneakers, and a sweatshirt. He ran his gym class with discipline. He wouldn't tolerate students who did not pay attention when he was talking. But rather than yell, he would fold his arms and abruptly stop talking. The silent treatment always worked.

As a sixth grader, I had come to the attention of Coach DeNike when he noticed that my body was changing—not in height, but in width.

So, naturally, Coach DeNike, the ever-sensitive and ultra-understanding influence over grade-school boys, dubbed me "Pot" in obvious reference to my stomach.

The nickname stuck, as did my pot-like belly when I entered junior high in September 1960. Coach Cropsey was the physical education teacher at Highlands Junior High School. Once he heard that my buddies called me Pot, he loved the nickname so much that he used it every five minutes of gym class.

Way to go, Pot....Hang in there, Pot....Pot, you're up first....Okay, let's see how Pot can do....Pot, what's the score?

As if there wasn't enough going on in my life, by February of 1961 I had, thanks to my mother, ongoing appointments with an orthodontist who was measuring the movement of my crooked teeth.

Those visits to the orthodontist placed me in a most embarrassing predicament. The orthodontist's assistant was a very attractive, buxom blonde in her early twenties who, I swear, my hand to God, could have been a Playboy Playmate. Her smile was perfect, as were her white teeth.

As I sat in the dentist chair, while the orthodontist examined me with dental instruments that appeared to be a pair of pliers, I couldn't keep my eyes off my gorgeous, calendar-girl dental assistant. She was especially nice to me, always reassuring me that everything would be okay by placing her hand gently on my forearm.

Her looks, that touch, and my dirty twelve-year-old mind resulted in me getting a boner religiously every appointment.

February 11

Then, on Saturday, February 11, my classmate and buddy Ray Simons and I were talking about an upcoming Church in The Highlands dance, knowing girls would be there. For both of us, girls were becoming more important in our lives with each passing day.

A Ray of True Friendship—I'm a lucky stiff. Ray Simons is my best friend. He's a great guy. We did everything together.

During our conversation, I felt an itch on my chin that I began to scratch. I thought it was a mosquito bite. It must have been a big one that got me because I could feel the bump with my fingers. It kept getting bigger as Ray and I gabbed on about certain cute girls.

A day later I looked in the mirror and, for the love of God, it wasn't a mosquito bite. It was a goddamn pimple! My first. That was almost impossible because I didn't even have any pubic hair. How could I be cursed with a zit?

My life was over.

Besides being teased for my pot belly, I was, according to my mom, to start wearing *glasses* after my September Bar Mitzvah. My teeth were already covered with shiny metal braces. Now my face was sprouting pus-filled, humongous freaking zits. Oh, I left out the fact that my hair was impossible to comb because it was a mass of kinky curls.

I'm a complete mess.

Well, I knew one thing for sure, I wasn't going to the next Church in the Highlands dance—or for that matter, any dance ever again.

February 15

The *Bob Hope Buick Show* TV special aired the evening of February 15 at 10 p.m. on NBC, Channel 4. The show featured eleven 1960 Athletes of the Year. Movie star Jane Wyman, who had been married to Ronald Reagan from 1940 to 1949, presented Maris with his award.

Other honored athletes included Heisman Trophy winner Joe Bellino, basketball star Wilt Chamberlain, tennis champion Pancho Gonzalez, National League MVP Dick Groat, Olympic star Rafer Johnson, National Basketball Association great Jerry Lucas, tennis French open–winner Barry

MacKay, golf great Arnold Palmer, heavyweight boxing champ Floyd Patterson, and National Football League fan favorite Norm Van Brocklin.

On a lark I asked my friends who the Heisman Trophy was named after. No one knew the answer. I still don't know.

February 18

In Jimmy Cannon's February 18 column in the *New York Journal-American*, he boldly wrote a prediction: "Guaranteed to happen in '61; In June a batter will threaten Babe Ruth's home run record, but will fold in July."

February 22

That prediction just might have been what prompted Ray Gillespie to quote former Yankee manager Casey Stengel in his February 22 *Sporting News* column, saying that Mantle would break Ruth's sixty homers.

***

A half-page Spalding ad for Maris gloves appeared on page 29 of the February 22 issue of *The Sporting News.* It repeated the familiar promotional line, "These Maris model gloves are sure to help your game no matter how good you are."

The gloves and prices were listed:

Model # 42-107 $31.00
Model # 42-233 $18.50
Model # 42-137 $12.45

I lost count of how many soda bottles I'd have to return at a nickel apiece to afford the $12.45 model.

February 28

The February 28 *Sporting News* attempted to be cute in their notes column explaining that the last two "Yanquis" had arrived in spring training camp: Luis Arroyo from Puerto Rico and Hector Lopez from Panama.

The same issue had an item that Hub Hose (which means Boston Red Sox) right-hander Tracy Stallard said he would be happy to pitch in relief. He grew up rooting for the Yankees, but stated, "The Yankees were my favorites when I was a kid…Now they are my enemies."

MARCH 1961

"There goes the Strasberg kid again, dancing by himself."

March 1

By March 1961, I was a measly five months from becoming a teenager, yet my world was beginning to turn upside down. How did I know that it was turning upside down?

Easy. I read it on the cover of the March issue of *MAD* magazine. The cover was divided in half. The horizontal top half had the headline, "No matter how you look at it....It's gonna be a MAD year."

To the right of those words was freckle-faced, guttersnipe urchin Alfred E. Neuman's portrait: unusually large protruding ears, uncombed red-headed mop of hair, a "normal" right eye slightly higher than his left, and his gap-toothed, apple-cheeked, cock-a-hoop grin.

Below Neuman was a red banner with the numerals 1961 in white, which appeared the same when turned upside down.

Also, on the cover was the historical note that this was the last upside-down year until 6009, and the first upside-down year since 1881.

The bottom half of the cover was printed upside down, so if you turned the magazine upside down the cover design appeared the same.

Since everything in my life was and is baseball-related, I looked up who the home run champ was in 1881. Turns out it was Dan Brouthers, the left-handed Buffalo Bisons first baseman of the National League (there was no American League yet), who led the league in round-trippers with the appropriately strobogrammatic total number of eight.

Spring Wing Thing—After a few months of not playing baseball, Rog slowly begins to develop his arm strength in spring training. In 1960, Rog won the Rawlings Gold Glove Award for fielding excellence.

I threw in that big word *strobogrammatic*—which means that the number reads the same if turned upside down—just to impress myself and will probably never use it again for the rest of my life.

Obviously, it was a different game way back then, when dinosaurs inhabited the earth. Ever hear of the plant-eating baseballasouras? Didn't think so.

***

After the 1960 season ended, it was clear that the '61 Yankees would make lots of changes.

To begin with, the Yankees' radio broadcasts switched from WMGM to WCBS. WMGM plays Top 40 records while WCBS is filled with old guys jabbering about stuff that is of no interest to me and hurts my ears when they aren't broadcasting the Yanks' games.

And after twenty-six years, the upcoming 1961 season would be the last year the Yanks would train in St. Petersburg, Florida. The biggest concern I read about was the housing for Negro Yankee players in Florida. Seems the McAllister Hotel in Miami wouldn't allow black players to stay there, which upset Yankee players, coaches, and front-office management.

But the most obvious change was that Yankee manager Casey Stengel would be absent. He was fired after twelve years for being too old (seventy) in addition to losing the 1960 World Series to the Pirates. Maybe when I'm older I'll understand how the Yanks could give Ol' Case the heave-ho. Sure, he's ancient, but the Yanks won the pennant last year. Doesn't seem fair to me. No. 37 is a proven winner in my book.

Former Yankee coach Ralph Houk took over the managerial reins, which made him the sixth former Yankee player elevated to skipper. None lasted more than a year and a half, so good luck, Ralphie.

The only thing I knew about Houk was what I read in Yankee year-books—that he was a former Yankee catcher starting in the late 1940s who didn't play much and was finished as a player after the 1954 season. From 1955 to 1957 he was the Denver Bears manager in the Yankee minor league farm system, while for the last three years he'd been the Yanks' first-base coach.

His nickname was "The Major" because he rose from private to major during his four years in military service in World War II. He fought in the Battle of the Bulge and in the Remagen crossing of the Rhine. He was awarded the Bronze Star, Silver Star, and Purple Heart.

One of the mysteries of life for me is the military. Specifically, I'm refer-ring to the different ribbon colors soldiers wear on their uniforms. Each one is a secret code that means something. There must be some great story behind it all.

I asked one of my buddies if he knew why the heart is purple. His answer kinda made sense to me: "It's worse than a bad bruise, you know, that turns purple." I still think he's an imbecile. No, I'm *sure* he's an imbecile.

I remembered that Houk did have major-league managing experience. He took over for an ill Stengel in 1960 on May 28 for twelve games. The Yanks won six and lost six.

Interestingly, Maris hit six homers during Houk's first crack as the Yankee skipper. Houk toyed with Roger's place in the lineup.

Six times Rog batted third, four times he batted fourth, once batted fifth, and once as a pinch hitter. He couldn't run well because he'd been hit in the ankle by a fungo bat that slipped out of the hands of the Senators' Pedro Ramos moments before the start of a game. *Ouch!*

Before spring training started, I read a newspaper article written by Dan Daniel of the *New York World-Telegram and Sun*. He reported that Houk had decided the Yankees' spring-training lunch menu was no longer going to be bologna, liverwurst, chicken, corned beef, and cheese sandwiches. Instead, it would consist of hot soup, raw carrots, celery, apples, and milk. Well, excuse me, but that doesn't sound so yummy.

Since everyone on earth and their cousin is making predictions about the upcoming baseball season, I will, too. As a result of the "rabbit food" provided to players, I'm going to go out on a limb by predicting the team will lose more total pounds than games this season.

Chew on this for a moment. I figure twenty-five guys on average will lose two pounds each for a total of fifty pounds, which means they could lose no more than 49 games. That figures out to the Yanks winning 113 games, which would put them in second place for all-time wins in a season after the 116 wins of the 1906 Chicago Cubs.

Oh yeah, things were going to be different, for sure. Personally, my voice is changing. While I'm talking in a normal tone, my voice goes into a higher pitch. It's embarrassing, especially when I'm talking to a girl.

Additionally, because of expansion, the 1961 American League schedule would in no way resemble the previous season. This was pointed out by a Mr. Smarty Pants nebbish ninth grader in our Highlands Junior High School cafeteria during lunch one day. He noted the obvious: "For the first time since Christ left Denver the American League will now have ten teams instead of eight."

Then he added, "Those knucklehead teams will play eight more games bringing the total to 162 games instead of the traditional 154 games."

Let's hear it for Mr. Smarty Pants who demonstrated his ability to state the obvious.

***

In early March, well in advance of my scheduled Bar Mitzvah in September, I began attending Hebrew school twice a week. Those ninety-minute sessions resulted in a large chunk of my free time evaporating. *Oy*, more time spent in a classroom.

March 2

Great picture of Rog, Mick, and Houk in the *Daily News* on March 2 noting that WPIX television will broadcast 130 Yankee games (46 from the road).

March 7

Interesting note on March 7: No segregation at Al Lang Field spring training games. Negro fans attending the game can sit anywhere their tickets indicate.

March 8

Statistics are at the heart of baseball, so I cracked up when I read a note in a March 8 *Daily News* that as a follow-up to the Yankees' new spring-training lunch menu, the final consumption tabulation was printed: 364 ounces of soup, five dozen apples, two bunches of celery and carrots. It also noted that Maris is the No. 1 user of sunscreen lotion.

Did I mention that I love reading this useless baseball information? I do.

March 9

It was reported on March 9 that for the first time since his retirement ten years ago, Joltin' Joe DiMaggio would return to spring training as an instructor at the invitation of manager Ralph Houk. Joe D. is Yankee royalty.

Joe mentioned that he was not being paid. The forty-six-year-old former Yankee center fielder said, "I would have been here before had I been invited."

Watch out, Casey, I'm pretty sure that ball was hit in your direction.

***

According to news reports on this same date, the Soviets launched into orbit a dog named Chernushka. Fortunately, the Russians successfully recovered the spacecraft and the Ruskie pooch.

March 10

Since the Yanks and Cardinals have for years conducted their spring training in St. Petersburg, the city's Chamber of Commerce welcomed the public to a special baseball breakfast March 10. A total of forty-eight players from both teams attended. It wasn't mentioned, but my guess is they served pancakes.

March 11

I noticed that for the Yanks' March 11 spring training opener against the St. Louis Cardinals, Maris was batting fifth behind Mickey Mantle. Already Houk and I are not seeing eye to eye. If I was managing the team Rog would be batting third.

March 13

My interest hardly ever wavered from the baseball diamond, but on rare occasions I would glance at other sports, such as when Floyd Patterson KO'd Ingemar Johansson in six rounds on March 13. I'm sorry, but two guys beating the crap out of each other is not a sport.

***

Houk is starting to get under my skin, because he had Rog, an established right fielder, playing center field on March 13. Rog went 1-for-4.

March 15

Combatting the discrimination faced by Negro Yankee players, team president Dan Topping announced to the beat writers covering the Yanks on March 15 that the team would no longer tolerate Negro players having to stay at different hotels when traveling in Florida.

He called it a "One Roof" policy, which meant that every player must stay in the same hotel. As a result, on a Miami road trip to face the Orioles the Yanks switched to the Biscayne Terrace Hotel from the McAllister because they agreed to take in the four Yankee Negro players in camp.

I knew about Jackie Robinson breaking the color barrier in 1947 and thought discrimination was a thing of the past. Obviously, for many people the Civil War isn't over. Aren't people just people? Why do others judge people based on the color of their skin or religion? I don't understand it.

A Bus Stop—Imagine for a moment after a spring training game that as you leave the ballpark a group of players still in uniform are boarding a Greyhound bus. You quickly notice that it's Mickey Mantle, Clete Boyer, and coming around the other side of the bus is Roger Maris. Is it a dream or have you just entered The Twilight Zone? *Photo by John Mattei.*

***

On March 15, Maris is nursing a strained left ankle but pinch hits and goes 0-for-1.

***

Photo of outfielders Hector Lopez, Mantle, and Maris in the March 15 issue of *The Sporting News* with the caption, "Yankees' Peerless Patrol," rated by respected sportswriter Dan Daniel as "far ahead of any rival group."

***

Thanks to my classmate Nancy Klein, who coincidentally was born the same day as me, my name appeared in the March issue of the Highlands Junior High School newspaper, *Blue and Gold.* She wrote in her column, "Did You Know?," that I loved to sit next to my favorite teacher, Miss Menaugh.

I got a kick out of seeing my name in print, which reminded me that when I was in third grade I wrote a paragraph about throwing snowballs that appeared in the February 18, 1957, Mamaroneck Avenue school paper, *This 'n' That.* I still have a copy.

Perhaps I'm a writer. Naw, couldn't be, 'cause I can't spell a darn and have no idea where to put punctuation in the appropriate places.

I need to make a point to thank Nancy next time I see her in the halls at school.

March 17

That autobiography that Miss Cramer assigned back in January was due today, March 17.

I must admit, I kinda enjoyed working on it. I found out a lot of things about me that I never knew, while other things were pretty obvious.

For my hobbies, I wrote about my baseball card collection, which is a really good collection. I also wrote about playing baseball.

For my future ambitions, I explained that I want to be a baseball player. I end that section by stating that I can't predict what I'm going to be but whatever it is, I hope I will be happy.

I also included a "Likes" page. For every category listed I end with the word "girls." Hey, I like girls. So shoot me.

For "Dislikes," I listed "Going to school five days a week." Honesty is the best policy, they say.

I conclude my autobiography with a "Thank You" page by listing every member of my family. I also write a thanks to anyone—with a notation to my older self (who might even be me someday when I grow up)—who had the patience to read my autobiography.

Rather than hand in the typewritten pages, I staple them to red construction paper and include different keepsakes for illustrations such as doctors' notes, hall passes, birthday party invitations, a newspaper clipping of Mr. Clements, get-well cards, my sister's high-school graduation ceremony brochure, some cartoon sketches I drew in 1959, a newspaper police blotter clipping from when my bike was stolen, and a caricature of me drawn by a street artist in New York City.

I'll betcha Miss Cramer takes forever to read all these student autobiographies. By then I will have a long beard and seventeen grandchildren.

***

Joe Falls of the *Detroit Free Press* has some fun looking into the future. He predicts that Maris will hit a homer in the Yanks' first game and as a result be four games ahead of Ruth's 1927 pace.

By May, Falls continued, Maris will hit his fourth homer and be seven games ahead of Ruth's pace. In July, when Maris hits his twenty-seventh homer, that will put him twenty days ahead of Babe Ruth. He foresees that in August Maris will be twenty-four games ahead of Ruth's pace. Come September, Maris will hit home run No. 48, and no more. Interesting, I guess, but like every other prediction, it's meaningless.

March 19

An article titled "Are Umpires Ruining Baseball?" appeared in *This Week* magazine, a supplement of the March 19 issue of the *New York Herald Tribune*. It was by Bill Veeck, as told to Bill Surface, a sportswriter. Veeck is the president of the Chicago White Sox. He's pulled off some crazy stunts such as sending a midget to the plate ten years ago.

He speculates that umpire blunders can mean as much to a team as winning or losing ten games.

Veeck offers solutions for improving umpiring. One of them kinda made sense to me. He suggested that, similar to ballplayers, umps are probably better working at a specific base. He compares them to players who excel at their position, which is why they play that position.

He reasoned that if an umpire is good at calling balls and strikes then he should be the home plate ump for every game. Same goes for those umps who are good at second base, first base, or the hot corner. In other words, umpiring would be specialized.

The other idea Veeck runs up the flagpole is what he calls "Eye-in-the-Sky." He suggests using electronic cameras for deciding close plays. He compares it to the finish-line photos in horse racing. Veeck explains that a camera with its thousand frames a second could catch every nuance of a situation if need be with on-the-spot photographic evidence.

For me, the ump working the same-base concept is a safe call, but that camera idea is unquestionably foul.

March 22

Hard to believe that in 1961 discrimination is still newsworthy. On March 22, the Negroes on the Yankees team didn't make the trip to Orlando because "there was no way of feeding them in that city," according to *The Sporting News*.

The Civil War has been over for close to a hundred years. Yet this story was in all the newspapers at the time.

***

A picture of Marilyn Monroe sunbathing at Redington Beach with Joe DiMaggio made the back page of the March 22 *Daily News*. The article explained that the couple had to leave after ten minutes before the crowd became too overwhelming. The actress and Joe D.—"erstwhile Yankee and erstwhile husband of Monroe"—shared a cabana, according to the photo caption.

Naturally, I had to look up the word "erstwhile" in the dictionary that day and found that it means "former." Man, I'm learning a lot of words this year.

Elsewhere in the paper, Monroe is quoted as saying that she was in Florida for sun, rest, and to visit Joe. Her latest movie, *The Misfits*, had been released six weeks earlier on February 1. Didn't see it.

I guarantee this will slay you. Marilyn Monroe is not my type. I'm a Bridget Bardot fan. But let me explain why. Monroe's hair looks like it's overly bleached, dry, and brittle. Bardot's hair looks to be soft, silky, and healthy. I'm guessing it smells good, too. I'm a BB guy, not MM.

That evening, the Yanks had a private party at St. Petersburg Colonial Inn that was attended by Joe and Marilyn. Think about it: a party with the Yanks, Joe D., and Marilyn Monroe. Bet they didn't play Spin the Bottle.

March 28

In columnist Gene Ward's March 28 *Daily News* "Inside Sports," a fan wrote that this is the year Mickey Mantle gives American League pitching and his critics their lumps. Ward responded, "The hot-hitting Mantle would cool off once the regular season began" and added, "I'm a Maris man, myself."

That Ward knows his baseball.

March 29

I was happy to read on March 29 that the Yanks are picked by the Las Vegas oddsmakers to repeat as American League champs.

My Uncle Louis explained to me that the only time to bet is when you can afford to lose the money you are betting. In other words, there are no sure bets.

March 31

For the second time since the 1960 World Series, the Yanks met the Pittsburgh Pirates in an exhibition game on March 31 in St. Petersburg—New York lost again. In front of 6,249 fans, Ralph Terry was the loser giving up all four runs. The final score: 4–2.

***

Story after story is being written about the possibilities of new records being set as a result of the schedule being expanded from 154 games to 162 games. However, I have yet to read anything about the players' contracts being raised for the additional eight games, which will provide additional income from ticket sales, concessions, and broadcasting fees for each team. *Hmmmmm?*

***

Of the eleven writers covering the Yankees, nine of them pick the team to repeat as American League champs. I hope they're right, but, with the team having an awful spring and a 8-14 record, it doesn't look good. I know, I know, it's only spring training and winning is not important…unless the team is winning.

***

Former Yankee second-baseman Jerry Coleman, now employed by the

Van Heusen shirt company, announced that the company would provide an award for outstanding achievement in sports.

The committee voting on the award would consist of Roy Campanella, Carl Erskine, James A. Farley (U.S. Postmaster), Frank Frisch, Pee Wee Reese, Jackie Robinson, Frank Slocum (sportswriter), Ted Williams, Joe Garagiola, C.C. Johnson Spink (publisher of *The Sporting News*), and Joe DiMaggio.

***

A *Daily News* "Diamond Dust" note appeared explaining that Baseball Commissioner Ford Frick nixed Mel Allen's idea to broadcast the Yanks April 11 home opener from a seat next to the dugout. His fear was that other broadcasters and reporters would want the same opportunity during games. I don't get it. Why is that a bad thing?

***

Sitting on my bedroom dresser is a black plastic Zenith table-top radio. It's a tad bigger than a loaf of Wonder Bread and probably built during World War II,

As I get older, my radio takes on a more significant role in my life. It's my companion. It fills my bedroom with sounds that make me happy.

When I'm not tuned into Yankee games, my favorite stations are WINS, WABC, and WMCA.

Certain disc jockeys make me laugh, and the songs they spin knock me out. It's not unusual, if the right song comes on, that I'll get up and dance by myself in my stocking feet or sing along with an imaginary mic in my hand, as if I'm on stage playing to a Christmas audience at the Brooklyn Paramount.

As I dance, I can only imagine Mr. and Mrs. Donnellan, our neighbors living directly under us, looking up at their ceiling with one of them saying, "There goes the Strasberg kid again, dancing by himself."

I have the volume turned down low so my bedroom is not filled with dead silence when I'm doing homework. Honestly, who can think with dead silence? Not me, that's for sure.

I turn the volume up a bit when I'm sorting baseball cards, assembling plastic models, working on my Maris scrapbooks, writing, or just thinking and looking out the window.

I'm envious of how quick-witted the jocks are and how fast they talk.

Even though they're much older than me, these guys are my friends. Or so it seems. I get their jokes, which I'm sure not everybody does.

Each morning, as I sit down to a breakfast of Thomas' English Muffins and a glass of milk, my mother has the kitchen radio turned on to Herb Oscar Anderson, or "HOA" as he is known on the airwaves.

And so begins my daily dose of radio.

HOA doesn't play the music I like and his show is filled with news, weather, and traffic reports. But I must admit it comforts me to hear him singing his theme song, "Hello Again," every morning.

During the day and early evening, I'm a member of a select group of radio listeners who enjoy the Swinging 77, the Good Guys, and the All-Americans with the All-American Sound.

The jocks that impress me include Scott Muni, who has a great voice and whose "Instant Sound Survey" confirms the best songs of the day are the ones that I enjoy.

Then there's fast-talking Bruce Morrow on WABC, who jumped over from playing the hits on WINS.

The new jock in town is Dandy Dan Daniel on WMCA, the Good Guys station. He's cool, but he needs to be cool all year before I include him with the bee-izz-ests. (For you unhip cats, that's Murray the K language for "best.")

Murray the K of 1010 WINS is by far the coolest cat on radio. He has so many unique bits on his "Swinging Soiree" show. He's always mentioning going to the beach with your date to watch the submarine races. Even though I'm thirteen, I know what he's talking about.

"Mee-izz-urray the Kee-izz-ay" has his own secret language, be-izz-aby.

My favorite bit is his occasional unique introduction to a song. He starts by narrating in a dramatic voice a short one-minute story like an old-time radio show with sound effects and foreboding music. Without warning, he stops in the middle of a sentence and plays a song whose first lyrics finish his sentence.

Like the time he told a make-believe story about WWII. He said he and a fellow GI were pinned down in a foxhole with enemy fire all around them. There was no way to escape. They both feared for their lives, with sickening knots in their stomachs, realizing the end was near. Tears formed in their eyes. Murray assured his buddy not to be afraid and that everything would be okay.

Heartfelt and trembling, his buddy said…and here Murray drops the needle on the record, "Runaround Sue." Listeners now hear Dion's song about a story that's sad and true. It has to do with a girl from his past and how she took his love yet dated other guys in town.

Just play the record and you'll hear how it works.

By far, my fave disk jockey is Dan Ingram. He's smart, funny, cool, hip, and makes fun of the commercials he plays, the songs he spins, the station breaks he mentions, and the other jocks. He's honest and real. I love it when he calls his listeners, "Kemosabe," Kemosabe.

APRIL 1961

"JFK's throw caught the players off guard."

April 1

While I waited in the barber shop not far from my house to get a haircut Saturday morning, April 1, a copy of the oversized 10″ × 14″ *National Police Gazette* was on top of an assortment of magazines available for waiting customers. You couldn't miss it because of its size and the cover, splashed with pink and red.

It was the April issue. It had a photo of Frank Sinatra and Jackie Kennedy on the cover with the headline: "The Real Reason for SINATRA'S STRANGE POWER in the WHITE HOUSE."

More prominent was the bold headline in larger type: "EICHMANN TRIAL: THE UNCENSORED FACTS" with a subheadline in smaller type: "WHAT ISRAELI SECRET AGENTS FOUND OUT ABOUT HITLER'S ESCAPE," with a small, square-shaped photo of Eichmann.

Yet in the lower bottom left of the cover was a small headline that caught my eye: "Real Lowdown on BASEBALL'S 1961 LOOK."

Since it would be a while for the next available barber to give me a ballplayer flattop, I read the baseball article that began on page 14.

Roger Maris was quoted: "Most major leaguers feel Ruth's record of sixty homers will survive."

He explained: "Those extra eight games will mean about twenty-seven extra times at bat." Roger then confessed, "So that means I should hit an extra three homers this year, but where am I going to get the other fifty-seven?"

Based on the fact that in 1960 he hit only thirty-nine homers, I couldn't understand why Maris was even quoted.

The *National Police Gazette* has little if any newsworthy stories, but a lot of provocative girlie photos. Check out page 9 about Zsa Zsa Gabor or page 10 for an article about belly dancers titled, "Lure For Tired Businessmen."

Is this magazine written by police or for police? I was going to ask the middle-aged guy sitting next to me, who was nervously jiggling his right leg, looking out the window and who smelled like an ashtray. Maybe he was on the lam from the cops. I cautiously kept to myself and avoided eye contact.

April 2

WPIX took out a gigunda ad in the April 2 *Daily News*, promoting the fact that they would televise all Yankee home games and forty-six road games.

April 5

By April 4, Maris continued to be in a god-awful spring training slump, hitting .211 with no hope of turning it around as time was running out. However, in the bottom of the eleventh on April 5, Maris delivered the winning hit against the St Louis Cardinals, driving in Clete Boyer. It was the last game the Yanks played at Al Lang Field this season.

The game article pointed out that Rog almost forgot to touch first base. I figured that he must be preoccupied with something else, or, God forbid, he lost his eye. Well, not actually. I'm saying that to make the point that hitters get in slumps.

***

Daydreaming is one of the major problems I have in school. Specifically, baseball daydreaming.

I'm not paying attention while the teacher goes on with a bad case of diarrhea of the mouth. I'm thinking about baseball. Sometimes I'll draw a baseball diamond, trying my best to re-create the Yankee Stadium field layout.

My baseball daydreaming most often happens for those classes I have in the back of the school. I can see the blacktop where we play kick ball in the spring.

More importantly, that's where my friends and I play baseball in February once the snow is plowed close to the fence, which then resembles a short forty-inch wall similar to Yankee Stadium's right-field fence.

Once my stadium drawing is completed with my mechanical drawing pencil, I draw a dotted line from home plate to the right-field stands as if I'm tracking the path of a Maris home run.

In my head, with each couple of dots, I'm also doing my best impression of Yankee broadcaster Mel Allen: "Here comes the pitch. Maris swings, and there it goes—dot, dot, dot—it is—dot, dot, dot—going—dot, dot, dot—going—dot, dot, dot—it is gone! How about that, fans!"

April 8

April 8 was the Yanks' last spring-training exhibition game. It was against the Cardinals in St. Louis. Rog hit a double and went 2-for-4, but the Yanks lost the slugfest 16–12.

Rough day for hurlers. The Cards had three pitchers toe the rubber, while the Yanks had five.

April 10

As the Yankees finish up spring training, New York Mayor Robert Wagner proclaimed that Monday, April 10, would be New York Yankees Day. There would be a twelve-car parade at noon starting at Bowling Green, up Broadway to City Hall, a Welcome Home dinner at Hotel Astor with 1,200 attending that evening, and Times Square would be renamed Yankee Square.

In spite of a horrendous spring training, I never lost faith in the Yanks. Okay, maybe a little. They stunk up the place big-time as they finished with a record of 10–19, which placed them tenth in the new ten-team American League standings.

***

Before the season begins, the *Daily News'* Jimmy Powers predicts Mantle will shatter Ruth's sixty home run mark. Next to the article is a cartoon of Mantle swatting the number and letters "61 HRS."

***

Another three-dot newspaper note points out that when on the road, Yankee players' meal money for the 1961 season was now at ten dollars a day. My weekly two bucks allowance pales in comparison. I'm just saying.

***

The New York Times has a full-page ad from the *New York Daily News* that has the headline, "An urgent message about the Eichmann trial to every responsible person in the United States."

This caught my attention because a newspaper ran an ad in a competitor's pages. This would be like Al Kaline of the Tigers playing one game in the outfield for the Yankees at Yankee Stadium while still wearing his Detroit uniform.

The ad on page 17 referenced Eichmann, stating, "His crime is a crime against the whole human race." It went on to encourage everyone to read details of the trial and discuss it with every member of their family.

While I sorta understood crimes against individuals, frankly I couldn't comprehend the magnitude of "a crime against humanity."

The chatter in school about Eichmann included the two girls who read *The Diary of Anne Frank* and the newspapers' horrifying pictures of Jews executed in German concentration camps who were so skinny they looked like skeletons.

I overheard that some seventh-grade theorists found it ironic that Eichmann was born Jewish, similar to Hitler. Was that true? I just took it all in and listened. I'm not a reader unless it's a school assignment, but I am starting to read more than just the sports section in newspapers.

April 10

I love all baseball traditions. Certain ones are unique to the sport.

Yes, the seventh-inning stretch is one of them, and it's a big one. But because it's about airing out the fans' butts, you have to know when it's your time to stretch. Most fans don't know that, by tradition, the visiting team's fans are supposed to stretch in the top of the seventh inning as their team comes to bat, while the home team's fans should stand in the middle of the inning.

As the 1961 baseball season gets underway, one baseball tradition is interrupted while another one continues, this time with a newly elected "player."

On April 10, the Washington Senators opened the season against the

Chicago White Sox at Griffith Stadium. This was a break from the tradition by which the Cincinnati Reds played the opening-day game of the season because they were baseball's first officially recognized franchise.

Presidential Bunting—President Kennedy is the youngest man to be elected president in my lifetime. As he throws out the ceremonial first pitch of the season at Griffith Stadium, I swear he looks like he can make the throw from deep centerfield on a bounce to relay man Bobby Richardson to nab the runner attempting to stretch a single into a double. *Photo provided by John F. Kennedy Presidential Library and Museum.*

Newly elected President Kennedy had the honor of throwing out the ceremonial first pitch in the nation's capital. The right-hander, who resides at 1600 Pennsylvania Avenue, made the throw from his box seat in the stands to the players who assembled as a group on the field.

As described by the Associated Press, JFK's throw caught the players off guard with a high hard peg instead of the traditional presidential soft toss. The throw bounced off two players' hands and was grabbed by the left-handed outfielder Jim Rivera of the White Sox.

Then, to accommodate the photographers, JFK made a second toss. This time, Hal Woodeschick, a left-handed pitcher for the Senators, came up with the ball.

I love this tradition because players are acting like little kids as they scramble trying to catch the baseball.

The Senators lost 4-2, and I'm sure someone will write, "Washington—first in war, first in peace, and last in the American League."

The Senators have 161 games left in their schedule to redeem themselves. Don't hold your breath.

April 11

The Yanks were set to open the 1961 season at Yankee Stadium on April 11 against the transplanted Washington Senators, now the Minnesota Twins.

The pregame ceremonies began at 1:25 p.m. with Mel Allen as emcee. "The Star Spangled Banner," usually sung by Lucy Monroe, was, according to Jim McCulley of the *Daily News*, sung by Stuart Foster of TV and radio fame. But *The New York Times'* John Drebinger had Gordon MacRae singing the national anthem.

As a result of the conflicting newspaper reports, the two writers could have made an appearance on the popular TV show that features contestants with conflicting and misleading stories—*Who Do You Trust?* with host Johnny Carson.

The Yanks' 1960 pennant, a gaudy red, white, and blue job, was run up the flagpole with the 1921 pennant, the first ever won by a Yankee club.

Back at the home-plate ceremony, Yankee players were presented with their 1960 championship mementos...as per their requests, some received watches, others silverware of one variety or another. The *Daily News'* Dick Young, chairman of the New York chapter of the Baseball Writers Association of America, with the assistance of American League President Joe Cronin, presented the American League's Most Valuable Player award to Roger Maris. Bronx Borough President James J. Lyons tossed out the ceremonial first ball to start the Yankee season.

Arthur Daley of *The New York Times* wrote in "Sports of The Times" that Maris was the first player to emerge from the dugout on Opening Day. He noted that "the flags atop the Yankee Stadium ramparts crackled like bullwhips in the wind and Maris shivered."

According to Daley's article, Maris called back into the dugout runway to his teammates, "Bring your overcoats, fellows."

One of the newspapers noted the number of different nationalities on each team: The Yankees had Hector Lopez from Panama, Luis Arroyo from Puerto Rico. The Twins had Elmer Valo, born in Czechoslovakia; Reno

Bertoia, born in St. Vito, Italy; and four Cubans—Camilo Pascual, Pedro Ramos, Jose Valdivielso, and "Zorro" Versalles.

The other tidbit I found of interest was that fifty times as many fans will see the Yankees on television than will ever see them in person at The Stadium.

The first game score: 6–zip. Yanks lose in front of a little more than 14,000 fans that included Joe DiMaggio and Marilyn Monroe. Losing the opener meant every guy at school the next day would repeat the same tired wisecrack: "Beer will not be sold at Yankee Stadium this year 'cause they lost the opener."

Since the Twins were an old team with a new name, one writer cracked that had the Yanks won, they would get credit for two wins.

***

No Beer Sales—When the Yankees lost their season opener, every wise-ass at school announced that the Yanks wouldn't be selling beer at The Stadium this season because...wait for it...they lost the opener. Hardy har har.

The April 11 issue of *Look* magazine contained a 1961 baseball preview written by Tom Meany. The article began, "There has never been a baseball season comparable to the one that is coming up, and it is unlikely that there ever will be again." Does Meany know something more than the rest of us?

April 12

Reading through the April 12 newspapers the day after the first game, I found articles about the Soviet Union. The *Daily News* headline: "REDS CLAIM MAN IN SPACE."

Science fiction has become a reality in 1961, thanks to the Russians putting a man in orbit—Major Yuri Alekseyevich Gagarin. The *New York Daily News* article compared the celebration of the Russian people in the streets of Moscow to that of baseball fans in Pittsburgh after last year's World Series.

The front-page picture is of Adolf Eichmann, who is being tried in Jerusalem as the Nazis' chief exterminator of millions of Jews. The newspaper account explained that Eichmann spoke only one word all day. The presiding judge, Moshe Landau, asked: "Are you Adolf Eichmann, son of Karl Adolf Eichmann?" "*Jawohl,*" was the reply, a German military way of saying *yes.*

I'm horrified and scared. Are the Germans and Russians our enemies? Could history repeat itself someday? Am I, along with my classmates and family, going to die a horrible death in a concentration camp or as a result of the A-bomb being dropped on New York City?

***

The Sporting News noted that three American League ballparks moved fences back, making it more difficult to hit homers.

The new Senators removed the inner fence in left field at Griffith Stadium, which makes the distance down the left-field line 388 feet instead of 350 feet.

Kansas City moved the left-field fence back and it is now 370 feet down the line instead of 350 feet. Additionally, the left-field fence is only 10 feet high instead of 38 feet.

Detroit erected a 20-foot screen in front of the lower right-field stands extending 101 feet from the right-field foul line.

***

The Yankees have an off-day April 12, but as a result of the lackluster bats for the opener, Houk called for a two-hour workout at The Stadium. *The New York Times* acknowledged how Lee Thomas and Jack Reed pranced under fungoes while Duke Maas, Ted Wieand, Art Ditmar, and Danny McDevitt served up fat batting-practice pitches. It was curious that these players were mentioned and not the Yankee stars. Maybe their days on the club are numbered? After all, how can any player break into this Yankee lineup?

April 13

Rain, rain, go away, come again another day. The April 13 game vs. the Twins was rained out.

April 14

The Yanks traveled up the Hudson River on April 14 to play a three p.m. game against the West Point Cadet baseball team.

The cadets treated the Yankee team to lunch, but as lunch was ending the cadets began the cadence of, "We want Mantle, We want Mantle."

Mantle obliged the cadets by reading the "Order of the Day." He announced that the physical fitness test operations of the day are postponed in honor of the Yanks' visit. In his slow Oklahoma accent, Mick read the word *corps* by pronouncing the *s*, which got the cadets laughing.

Eric Tipton, who played for the Philadelphia Athletics and Cincinnati Reds back in the 1940s, coached the cadets. According to the newspaper report, it was the first West Point exhibition game since 1944. Attendance was listed at 6,000, but that was unofficial since there was no admission charge. In the sixth inning, while Maris was batting, the game was briefly suspended when a cannon went off, and the crowd stood in silence as a bugler played "Taps." The flag was lowered at 4:28 p.m.

Final score of the West Point game, which was cut short after seven innings because of the cold weather, was 14–0 in favor of the Yanks.

April 15

The Bronx Bombers won the next four home games, but the fans pretty much stayed home because of the crappy weather. The second game of the season was played against Kansas City on April 15, but drew only 11,802 fans. Yanks won 5–3.

April 16

The April 16 game against the Athletics at Yankee Stadium was rained out. I guess because of that April shower the only positive outcome of the cancelled game would be those flowers due in May that I have always heard so much about.

April 17

When I checked the paper for stories of games played on April 17, I saw that 1,947 fans showed up as Yanks won 3–0 with Ford getting the victory over Kansas City. That had to be a typo. It was probably 19,470. So I checked other papers and discovered it was true. This was the smallest crowd since September 21, 1954, when 1,912 fans attended a game at Yankee Stadium against Washington.

***

According to the *Daily News*, Mantle started the season with a severe reaction to a hay fever shot in his left arm, which swelled up to the size of a baseball. I'm now thinking this 1961 Yankee team is cursed and may not win another game all season.

***

Now that I am a Maris fan I should point out that after the 1960 Yankee season, hoping that I'd be fortunate enough someday to have my picture taken with Roger Maris, I went into a "four-photos-for-a-quarter booth" with a magazine that had a picture featuring his mighty swing.

I just wanted to see what I'd look like in a photo showing me and Roger's image together.

The seat inside the booth was round with arrows indicating which way to turn it to make it higher or lower. I spun the seat so that my eyes were at the same level with the red-line eye level marked on the back wall. It was next to the glass through which the camera would take the photo.

With my left hand, I pulled the booth curtain closed, making sure that no one could see inside. I folded over the page in the magazine where Rog was pictured wearing a long sleeve undershirt in his extended swing. I held the magazine in my right hand under my face to make sure it would be in the photo.

I held my breath.

The flash went off, filling the booth with a blinding white light accompanied by a quick, stifled thump sound. A few seconds later it happened again, a burst of white light and a muffled thump. Then again. And again. I stepped out of the booth wondering if it worked.

The frustrating part of this photographic marvel is the "photo booth wait" as it processes the narrow strip of four photos. I could hear the gears turning, the whining of the contraption as if actual elves were feverishly working to develop and print the photos.

After a few minutes that felt longer, in a process oddly similar to someone slowly sticking out their tongue, the photo booth just as slowly spat out the strip of four postage-stamp-sized photos.

I removed the strip to examine it. Everything was in focus. Guess I should've smiled. No, a smile would have ruined it. It was what it was.

Honestly, I thought that was probably as close as I'd ever get to having my photo taken with Maris. But a kid can dream, can't he?

These days, every time I look at those photos of "Roger" and me, "pathetic" is the word that comes to mind.

***

It appears that baseball is spinning out of control because Dodger coach Leo Durocher and umpire Jocko Conlan have, without a doubt, lost their marbles. There was a photo in today's April 17 newspaper that showed the two of them exchanging shin-kicks in the fourth inning of yesterday's game in Los Angeles. With the score Pirates 3, Dodgers 2, the caption read that Leo was upset with Conlan for blowing the call of a pop-up foul off the bat of Norm Larker. After Conlan ejected Durocher from the game for throwing a towel, Durocher ran onto the field and kicked dirt on the umpire. Conlan then kicked Durocher in the shin. Has baseball been reduced to old shin-kicking men?

April 18

I read in the newspaper on April 18 about the *Bahía de Cochinos* invasion, which translated means Bay of Pigs. I read it, then reread it, but frankly didn't understand what was going on. But thanks to a map, I knew it happened in Cuba, which is pretty damn close to Florida.

April 20

WPIX tried something that didn't make sense to me. For the April 20 doubleheader with the Angels, the first game would be broadcast but the second game would be recorded and shown starting at eight p.m., which meant that if you listened to the radio broadcast you knew what happened before it aired on TV. In any event, the Yanks were probably the first team in baseball history to broadcast a day game later that night on TV.

April 21

Shitola. The January 1–April 17 report cards were handed out today,

April 21. Once again, Sid and Helene are not going to be happy with their son when they get their mitts on my report card this weekend.

In addition to me being absent five out of the fifty-six days, my grades stunk up the place. Honestly, after eight years of public education, am I the only one who realizes that school is not something I'm really good at?

Getting exceptional grades is for kids with photographic minds who can "ace" a test by remembering historical dates, names of people, places, and wars, plus something else...but I don't remember what the other thing is.

If you're wondering how I did grade-wise, I was awarded a C in English and a C in Mathematics, obviously meaning that "this Strasberg kid is just average."

So shoot me.

What torpedoed my report card was General Science. My grade was a D, as in "disgusting," but, in my defense, that grade requires an explanation.

We had a science fair, for which each student needed to construct a science-subject diorama. Naturally, I decided that mine would be about baseball, complete with photos of ballplayers and ballparks.

You see, I came up with my Einstein-like theory of baseball relativity. Stay with me, people, as I explain, because this may be complicated.

As we all know, the most homers in a season is sixty, a record set by the left-handed hitting Babe Ruth in 1927.

With equal amounts of deliberation and consternation, I developed a formula that Ruth's outstanding homer productivity was in large part a result of him facing right-handed pitchers who are in the majority in baseball, while hitting from the left side of home plate. This provides Babe an advantage because a left-handed swinger's natural first step after connecting is toward first base. Unlike right-handed swingers, left-handed swingers don't have to reverse direction after swinging the bat.

Furthermore, if the batter combines the appropriate hitting ability, swing, and strength, the result equals a bushel of home runs.

Next step to proceed with my theorem for the science fair project, I needed the approval of my science teacher, a pleasant, middle-aged fellow who was maybe an inch taller than me at five foot two. His face was gaunt, without color, as if it lacked proper circulation or, more than likely, had never been exposed to sunlight.

His brow was constantly wrinkled with thoughts. He was a fast eye-blinker, which was a distraction when you looked at him. He spoke with an annoying gravelly rasp and always wore a frown, along with a white knee-length smock so as to resemble a scientist.

His science classroom was way different than other classrooms in school. To begin with, instead of white plaster walls, the science room walls are uniquely dark-wood paneled.

The overhead lighting was dimmer than other classrooms, and the room was never illuminated with bright, cheerful afternoon sunight. The telltale signal that his room was all about science, however, was the aroma of formaldehyde. It rose from the dead frogs floating in dozens of jars situated in back of the room on shelves originally meant for books.

One day after science class, I proceeded to explain to my teacher in great detail how I'd like my science project to be a graphic explanation of my home run theory.

His initial reaction was a short *"Hmmm,"* which I took as "intriguing," so I proceeded. I began by swinging an imaginary bat from the right side of a make-believe home plate situated in front of the classroom's rows of student desks.

To drive home my point, I then crossed over to the other side, making sure not to step on the invisible home plate, and took a swing from the left side. After my follow-through swing, I headed in the direction of first base in slow motion while doing the play-by-play explanation.

It was at this point that I put on my rarely worn horn-rimmed tortoiseshell eyeglasses so as to appear smarter. Then, I quickly removed from my pants pocket a thick, oversized piece of chalk, the kind that's normally used to draw sidewalk hopscotch games.

To draw attention to my "cheaters," I kept poking my glasses higher on my nose with a forefinger while I wrote my theorem in large letters on the blackboard:

LHH + UCS + S / A vs. RHP = AAHRT

My science teacher appeared to listen patiently because he placed the index finger of his right hand to his chin as I spoke. I briefly explained what each notation meant:

LHH (Left-handed hitter) + UCS (Upper-cut swing) + S (Strength) / over A (Ability) versus RHP (Right-handed pitchers which outnumber left-handed pitchers 3-1) = AAHRT (Above average home-run total).

Once I completed my presentation, my teacher gave a singular clap of both hands, which was not applause, but rather his exclamation that I was done. He then politely and diplomatically said, "Interesting, but not appropriate."

"Andy," he offered, "I think you should consider doing a traditional science diorama that is more of archeological significance rather than about baseball."

Well, for those of you scoring at home, that's a swing and a miss for Strasberg, strike three. The game was over. I lost.

WHITE PLAINS PUBLIC SCHOOLS
HIGHLANDS

PROGRESS AND JUNIOR HIGH SCHOOL		217 H.R.
Report of Andrew Strassberg Grade Eight		Seven 1 1A
From January 1961 To April 14 1961		

Academic		Citizenship
A - Excellent B - Good C - Fair		E - Excellent G - Good
D - Unsatisfactory F - Not Passing		P - Passing U - Unsatisfactory

Subject	Period	Mark Term or Year	Class Citizen- Ship	Remarks
English	C			
Spelling				
Reading				
Speech				
Mathematics	C			low
Social Studies	C			
Library Instruction				
Communications				
Art	A			
Music	C-			
Gen. Science	D			
Home Making				
Shop	B			
Health				
Mechanical Drawing	B-			LOW
Home Room				
Instrument Inst.				
Band				
Orchestra				
Glee Club				
A Cappella Choir				
Boys Chorus				
Physical Educ.				
General Citizenship	B			

DAYS PRESENT ...51... WHOLE DAYS ABSENT ...5...
TIMES TARDY ...0... PART DAYS ABSENT ...6...

LHH + UCS + S / A vs RHP = AAHRs

D Grading—This science project was not my first subject choice for a diorama, which explains my report card grade. Honestly, why am I subjected to doing things like a school science project, which I have little or no interest in.

I dutifully picked up the blackboard eraser and painfully removed my freshly chalked baseball formula from the black slate board. With each erase stroke, the inscription began to disappear and turn into what appeared to be a bad case of powdered dandruff flakes floating slowly in the air. Some of the white chalk dust settled on my dark sweater. Rather than cause the dust to become airborne again, I decided not to swat it away until I was in the hallway.

Soundly defeated, the next day I began to construct a more science-friendly display that was a smorgasbord of archeological Dullsville topics: The Fall of Pompeii, the Dead Sea Scrolls, and Mastodons.

Let's be perfectly honest. The *D* I received in General Science was a "pity gift grade," proving once again that, unlike Jellystone Park's Yogi Bear, I am not smarter than the average bear.

April 22

On April 22, New York Governor Nelson Rockefeller authorized the building of a ballpark in Flushing, Queens. This will eventually be the home of the new National League baseball expansion team. Let's be honest about this. Nothing will replace the Giants and Dodgers in this town. Nuttin', period.

***   .

The weather is beating the crap out of the Yanks this season. On April 22, the second game of a Yankees-Orioles doubleheader was played to a 5–5 tie when the game was called in the seventh inning on account of rain.

The umps waited thirty-two minutes before calling the game off. The game officially goes into the records as a tie game and will be replayed as a completely new game at a later date.

April 23

The April 23 *Daily News Sunday Coloroto Magazine*—you know, the newspaper magazine that has great color photos of baseball players every so often—has shots of the Yanks and their families sitting in bleachers during spring training. Rog is in the front row with his wife, Pat, along with son Roger, Jr., and daughter Susan.

April 24

On April 24, the Yanks and Tigers attended a charity dinner staged by Capuchin fathers in Detroit. Film star and comedian Joe E. Brown was the master of ceremonies. Joe's son, Joe L. Brown, is the general manager of the 1960 World Champion Pittsburgh Pirates.

April 25

Remember Miss Cramer? She's the teacher who assigned the students to write their autobiography five weeks ago. Today, April 25, forty-five years ahead of my prediction, Miss Cramer returned them to the students.

She wrote in the red ink that teachers use when grading papers, the following notation:

This is a magnificent piece of work, Andy! Congratulations and best wishes for success and happiness through all the years to come. Beatrice E. Cramer 4/25/61

On the off-chance that this autobiography assignment comes up again when I'm older, I'm going to start keeping notes. Not a diary, but notes, because you never know.

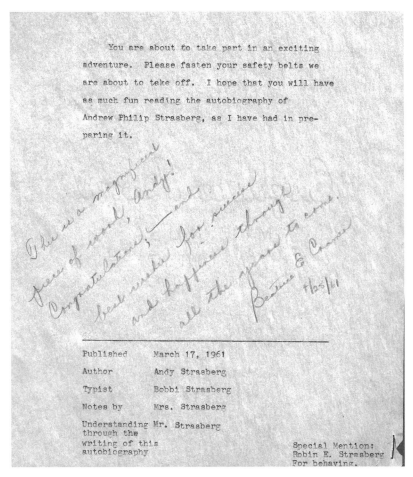

You are about to take part in an exciting
adventure. Please fasten your safety belts we
are about to take off. I hope that you will have
as much fun reading the autobiography of
Andrew Philip Strasberg, as I have had in preparing it.

Published	March 17, 1961
Author	Andy Strasberg
Typist	Bobbi Strasberg
Notes by	Mrs. Strasberg
Understanding	Mr. Strasberg

through the
writing of this
autobiography

Special Mention:
Robin E. Strasberg
For behaving.

Take Note—Miss Cramer's class assignment was to write our autobiography. I waited and waited. Finally, after five weeks, she handed them back along with this note.

April 26

Sportswriters speculate on April 26 that the Yanks will trade for Bronx-born-and-raised Rocky Colavito of the Tigers. I'm excited. The Rock would be a dream come true as the Yankees' third outfielder. He has, in my opinion, the strongest arm in the league and can crush the ball.

April 27

The *New York Daily News* had a photo of Maris talking to Rocky Colavito in the April 27 edition. It's going to happen. I just know it. The Yanks are going to pull the string and make a deal for Colavito. Here's why I know it will happen. Rog and Rocky were teammates back in 1957 when they played for the Cleveland Indians, and I'm guessing they are as excited as I am. Wowie, what an outfield! Rock-Mick-Rog.

April 28

Meanwhile, talk about a slump. Maris is batting .216 with only one homer on April 28. Unfortunately, his spring-training hitting woes have carried over into the season. I read where Rog has been ordered by Houk to come in an hour early for batting practice. Maris hits for forty-five minutes against the Johnnies—Sain and Blanchard.

April 30

Unbelievable. I was "a Mays'ed" to see splashed all over every sports section that San Francisco centerfielder Willie Mays hit four homers in one game on April 30 against the Braves. I checked the box score and noticed that lost in the shadow of Mays' four clouts were Hank Aaron's two four-baggers.

Mays became just the seventh player since 1900 to accomplish the feat. The last player to do it was soon-to-be Yankee and former-Cleveland-Indians-outfielder-now-with-the-Tigers Rocky Colavito back on June 10, 1959. The last National Leaguer to poke four in a game was the Braves' Joe Adcock on July 31, 1954.

One newspaper account pointed out that Willie didn't know that he'd tied the record until he heard it over the public address system.

The New York Times reported the distance traveled for each blast: No. 1: 420-footer; No. 2: 400-footer; No. 3: 450-footer; and No. 4: 430-footer, which adds up to more feet than you would find in a Buster Brown shoe store on any given Saturday.

Final score: San Francisco 14, Milwaukee 4.

***

Is anyone on the Yanks paying attention? After the Senators' Marty Keough popped out to Kubek for the third out of the third inning of the second game against Washington on April 30, the Yanks tossed the ball around the infield not realizing that the Nats were retired.

MAY 1961

Life is unfair, especially if you are a girl.

May 2

The day after the eighty-fifth anniversary of the day that the Chicago White Stockings' Ross Barnes of the National League hit the first home run in major-league history on May 2, 1876, Rog hit his second homer of 1961. It was a three-run job off the Twins' Pedro Ramos in the seventh inning in Minnesota on May 3. Yanks win 7–3.

May 5

Former Yankee manager Casey Stengel sat in the stands watching the Angels play the Yanks at Wrigley Field in Los Angeles on May 5. The Yanks won 5–4, but it must have been odd to have Casey in the ballpark. Kinda like watching your sixth-grade girlfriend at a seventh-grade social event slow-dancing with her new boyfriend. (You know who I'm referring to, Bobby S and Cathy U.) My heart goes out to you, Casey. I know the feeling.

By the way, for those of you who think I have lost my mind as to where Wrigley is located, there are two Wrigley Fields. One is in Chicago, the other in Los Angeles.

***

The front-page news was all about NASA Navy commander Alan Shepard, an astronaut aboard the Freedom 7 spacecraft, becoming the first American to travel in space, which instantly catapulted him into hero status.

In a moment's flash all my buddies who wanted to be professional baseball players now wanted to be astronauts. Well, at least the haircuts are the same.

Oh, did I point out that the Yanks are sitting in second place and it's the fifth of May, ferchrissakes?

***

Noticing everything "Maris" in the newspapers, I came across a Channel 4 NBC-TV show that airs at 7 p.m., Friday, May 5, called *Lock Up*. It's a crime drama. Macdonald Carey plays the role of Herbert L. Maris, a Philadelphia defense attorney who defends those who are unjustly accused of a crime. I didn't watch it.

***

As often as possible, I watched Yankee games on WPIX Channel 11 or listened to the games on my radio. This presented a problem, especially when the team was in California to play the Angels with the three-hour time difference. In other words, the games would start at eleven p.m. in New York, which was eight p.m. in California, which is exactly what's happening tonight, May 5.

I sneak my transistor radio into my bed with lights out, tricking my parents who thought I was asleep.

May 6

Sure, there were a few times I would fall asleep listening to Yankee games. The Yanks were playing the second game of a three-game series against the Angels. It was May 6. In the fifth inning, Rog hit his third homer of the season off Eli Grba, a right-hander who though missing a vowel in his last name was on the Yanks in 1959 and 1960.

The homer was Roger's one-hundredth home run of his career. He's normally a pull hitter, but this time he hit it to the left side of the center-field flagpole and into the street.

Rog is now the thirty-ninth active player to reach the century mark in career home runs. The round-tripper came on his 1,937th official time at bat—giving him a frequency mark of a homer every 19.4 at-bats.

When it comes to homers, Rog does best on foreign ground, as it was his sixty-third career homer not hit in his team's home ballpark.

As a member of the Cleveland Indians, he hit fifteen of twenty-three homers on the road. Then, while playing for the Kansas City Athletics, nineteen of his thirty-five round-trippers were away from his home ballpark.

In 1960, Rog blasted twenty-six of thirty-nine homers on the road, and this season his first three homers (Detroit, Minnesota, and now Los Angeles) were far from Yankee Stadium's so-called right-field porch.

Another significant note is that Rog hit the first home run in the new American League ballparks, Wrigley Field in Los Angeles and Metropolitan Stadium in Minneapolis.

Even though the Los Angeles game wasn't on a school night, I had trouble staying up past midnight. I missed it. Yanks lost 5–3.

***

I read about the Freedom Riders, who were traveling from Washington, D.C., to New Orleans to commemorate the seventh anniversary of the Supreme Court's *Brown v. Board of Education* decision. Segregation in the nation's public schools was ruled unconstitutional.

As a result of reading more than the sports pages, I was getting a broader education, but am still light years from being a brainiac.

May 8

Before the Yanks played a game in Kansas City, they made a trade with the Angels on May 8. They sent Lee Thomas, Ryne Duren, and Johnny James to the Halos for Bob Cerv and Tex Clevenger. Is this the trade that will turn things around for the club? I seriously doubt it.

***

Dating back to 1954, my baseball season ritual has included buying baseball cards.

I love everything about baseball cards: the feel, the design, the way they smell, and sometimes even the pink slab of bubble gum inserted in every five-cent pack.

Card Counter—As a result of my uncanny ability to know which pack of cards held a Roger Maris card, I cleaned up. *Topps® trading cards used courtesy of The Topps Company, Inc.*

I love to trade 'em, collect 'em, and flip 'em either for distance, leaners, knock down, match, or topsies.

I was totally convinced that the Topps Bubble Gum Company scientists had figured out what the formula was to attract kids like me to buy the cards. It included colors, design, and how perfectly the cards fit into a kid's hand.

Even though Maris was with the Yankees in 1960, his Topps card showed him capless as he was with the Kansas City Athletics at the time the photographer shot the photo in 1959. I'll bet the photographer said, "Rog, since everyone knows you will be traded to the Yanks this winter, don't wear the

A's cap so we can use your photo for the 1960 set when you are with the Bronx Bombers."

This year's card, with the photo taken in 1960, is No. 2 in the set of 587 cards. It's a close-up of him wearing a Yankee pinstripes jersey and a Yankee cap with his bat resting on his left shoulder, looking to his right. His eyes are green, kinda like mine.

That was the card I wanted, and I wouldn't be satisfied with just one of them.

For most of the kids I grew up with, buying baseball cards to get your favorite player was a matter of luck. The only card I was interested in was the one featuring my favorite player, Roger Maris. I needed more than luck and flipping abilities.

Starting in the late 1950s, the Topps Bubble Gum Company began issuing baseball cards in twelve-card cellophane packs along with their wax packs. Those cellophane packs, I quickly figured out, provided the purchaser with all the information they needed to know about which cards they would get—by seeing the top front and bottom back cards.

When Topps issued their baseball trading cards in ten-cent cellophane packs, I figured there was a formula by which cards were inserted by machines into packs, both for cellophane wrappers and wax wrappers.

My hypothesis in 1961 was that if Maris was the last card on the bottom of a cellophane-wrapped pack, I figured that the machine that puts the packs together would have a Maris card in it—if, and only if—any of the other eleven cards in front of the Maris card appeared on the top of the see-through cellophane pack.

I was right.

There was no more hoping to be lucky trying to win Maris cards by flipping with my pals or by chance to find a Maris card in a wax-wrapped pack. I had cracked the code. I memorized those eleven player cards that preceded the Maris card when he was the last bottom card. That was my guarantee that his card would be in the pack.

I never told any of my friends. So when it came to getting a Maris baseball card, there was no gambling involved. To some degree, I was using the same illegal gambling principle that card sharks use in blackjack. It was a form of card counting, but for baseball cards.

The other baseball card set issued that caught my eye was from Post cereal. The cards were issued on the back of cereal boxes. No guessing which Post cereal box had a Maris card, because they were not hidden in every box—they were **free**, printed on the box! All I had to do was look on the back of every cereal box on the shelf of every supermarket every day...and sometimes afternoons.

May 6

In the sixth inning of the May 6 game against Kansas City, Maris got hit in the wrist by a pitch from Bud Daley but stayed in the game. Rog ended up going 1-for-4 as the Yanks win 9–4.

May 9

At Hebrew school, one of the so-called mavens of my class talks about the Orioles first baseman who hit two grand slams on May 9. He tells me that the player is definitely not Jewish because his name is Jim Gentile. *Oy gevalt*, I know better. I tell him that it's pronounced Gen-*teel*, not Gen-*tile*.

***

On May 9, Newton N. Minow of the Federal Communications Commission was quoted in newspapers as saying that TV is a "vast wasteland." Obviously, this little fish-minded guy never watched *Bonanza, Candid Camera, The Many Loves of Dobie Gillis, The Rifleman, The Twilight Zone,* or even *Car 54, Where Are You?*

To quote New York City police officer Gunther Toody, lead character of *Car 54,* "Ooh, ooh."

***

As a result of my growing affection for everything baseball, in 1956 I uncovered—with assistance from a "Phillies Presents Baseball Lingo" booklet—baseball's insiders-only secret language that's used primarily by players, coaches, and managers.

I learned that the term for curve ball used by baseball insiders was "Uncle Charley." I also learned that when Yankees broadcaster Red Barber talked about being "In the catbird seat," it referred to a player being in an advantageous game situation. I learned that getting caught in a "run-down" between bases was known as a "pickle."

And if a player had "a cup of coffee," it really wasn't about drinking coffee. Rather, it was a reference to a player who reached the big leagues only long enough to have just "a cup of coffee" before being sent back to the minors.

It seemed like every day I learned something new about baseball's rich communications, which provided me with a great amount of insight about the game.

May 11

My mom thinks I need to have things other than baseball, rock 'n' roll, and Superman comic books in my life. She wants me to be a more well-rounded individual with "culture."

So on May 11 she took my sister and me to see *The Miracle Worker* in Manhattan at The Playhouse on 137 West 48th Street. The play starred Patty Duke as Helen Keller and Suzanne Pleshette as her teacher. If it's not baseball-related, I can't remember diddly squat. So when I watched the play, I was amused that Duke didn't have any lines throughout the play. That's it. I could definitely be an actor if I don't have to remember lines.

***

On May 11 I was baffled by what I learned had happened to a baseball player named Franklin Delano Roosevelt Wieand, better known by his nickname "Ted." In my entire twelve young years of life, I couldn't begin to comprehend what Ted had experienced.

I knew that Wieand began his professional baseball career in 1952, pitching for the St. Louis Cardinals' minor league affiliate, Allentown, Pennsylvania, in the Eastern League.

After bouncing around the minors, he eventually made the majors in 1958, pitching two innings in one game for the Cincinnati Reds and then again in 1960, when he appeared in five games and got dinged for a loss while pitching a total of 4.1 innings.

The scouting report on Ted was that he had a fastball and good control. The right-handed pitcher had been one of five young players in March of 1961 hoping to make the Yankees during spring training in a relief role. The others were Bill Short, Johnny James, John Bronstad, and Roland Sheldon.

Wieand made the Yanks out of spring training, but the term true baseball insiders use is, "Ted went north with the club."

To start the season, Wieand, the lanky six-foot, two-inch, 195-pound pitcher who hailed from Slatington, Pennsylvania, was now one of twenty-eight players on the 1961 New York Yankees roster.

As a member of the Yankees, Ted enjoyed the attention paid by Yankee fans for the start of the season, which began when Mayor Robert F. Wagner of New York City proclaimed that April 10 would be known as "New York Yankee Day."

Although Ted was not part of the Yanks last season on that day, he would have participated in a traditional big New York City parade to honor the 1960 American League champ Yankees, but it was cancelled due to bad weather.

Nonetheless, Ted did make it to the 1961 Welcome Home dinner at a swanky Manhattan hotel.

With red, white, and blue bunting draped throughout the ballpark, Ted was on the field at Yankee Stadium for opening day, April 11. The opponent was the new Minnesota Twins.

You could find Ted's name listed among the team in the scoring section of the slick, twenty-page, fifteen-cent, official Yankee program and scorecard for sale from vendors throughout the big ballpark.

It's there on the Yankees' box score page, to the right of the Old Spice ad, below the L&M cigarettes ad, sandwiched between No. 20 DeMaestri, infielder, and No. 22 Stafford, pitcher.

Ted was on hand when, in a pregame on-field ceremony, *New York Daily News* sportswriter Dick Young presented Roger Maris with the American League's Most Valuable Player award for 1960.

With the hope that he would be a contributor to the 1961 American League pennant race, Ted witnessed the Yanks' 1960 pennant being raised in center field before the game.

Along with his Yankee teammates, Ted toed the first-base line for the 1:30 p.m. opening day pregame ceremony, standing shoulder to shoulder with the likes of Yogi, The Mick, Moose, Bobby, Clete, Tony, Ellie, Yo-Yo, and Roger Maris.

Now as a member of the 1961 Yanks, Ted dealt on a daily basis with Yankee Stadium's legendary clubhouse attendants, "Big Pete" Sheehy and "Little Pete" Previte. It was Big Pete who issued Ted his Yankee pinstripes with No. 21 on the back of his jersey and his name stitched into the collar.

As is the custom in baseball locker rooms, Ted had the responsibility to autograph at least a dozen team baseballs before the game. The process was always the same. A box of a dozen Spalding American League baseballs was placed on the picnic table in the middle of the locker room.

Under the top cover of the box each player's uniform number was listed. Once Ted was done signing all the baseballs, he would cross out his No. 21, indicating he had completed his portion of signing.

Occasionally, Ted sought treatment from Yankee trainers Gus Mauch and Joe Soares. But Ted made sure to minimize his treatment because he didn't want to get the reputation of being a "jaker"—a player who complains incessantly about a real or imagined ailment.

And Ted was on a first-name basis with two of the luckiest stiffs in the world, Frankie Perdenti, the Yankee batboy, and ball boy Fred Bengis.

While anticipating his first appearance pitching in long relief for the Yanks, Ted shared the responsibility of throwing batting practice to the Yankee players with Spud Murray, the right-hander who wore uniform No. 55. It was Murray who was hired by the Yanks for the sole purpose of throwing "fat" strikes to the squad before the game started.

I read where every player taking batting practice wanted fast balls "down the middle" so they could practice their swings. The only exception being Yogi, who requested nothing but Uncle Charleys—curve balls.

On April 12, the *Daily News'* "Diamond Dust" column reported that while Ted was tossing pregame pitches to Elston Howard, the Yankee catcher hit a come-backer that almost drilled a hole in him.

Although he didn't get into the game, Ted traveled by bus with the team to West Point for the April 14 exhibition game played on Doubleday Field against the cadets.

Ted was present for the first twenty-three games of the Yankee 1961 season. He wore the pinstripes when the club hosted the Minnesota Twins. He was there at The Stadium when the Kansas City Athletics, the Cleveland Indians, and the expansion Los Angeles Angels visited the Bronx.

He wore the Yankees' road gray flannels when the team traveled to Baltimore's Memorial Stadium, Detroit's Tiger Stadium (renamed from Briggs Stadium the previous season), Washington's Griffith Stadium, Minnesota's Metropolitan Stadium, Los Angeles' Wrigley Field and Kansas City's Municipal Stadium.

During that period, the Yankees' record was 14–8, which also included the game on April 22 in Baltimore that the umps called at 11:30 p.m.—with the score tied 5–5 after seven innings—after two rain delays.

The game would have to be played over again in its entirety. Had it been ruled a suspended game by waiting until the 11:59 p.m. curfew for an official halt, it would have been resumed from point of cessation prior to another game. Instead, it will become part of a twi-night doubleheader scheduled for Monday, July 17.

Ted was probably collecting a skosh over a minimum major-league salary while watching games from the bullpen. He saw Whitey Ford record his first four wins during that period. He was a spectator when Luis Arroyo recorded his first five saves. He witnessed Roger Maris connecting for his first three home runs in 1961. He also watched the first nine of Mickey Mantle's round-trippers that season.

But, alas, the rule in baseball was that the roster needed to be shaved from twenty-eight to twenty-five players by midnight, May 11. Yankees' general manager Roy Hamey needed to cut three players.

Ted was one of the casualties. His contract was sold to Richmond of the International League. Ted had been a 1961 Yankee for but a mere thirty days, a total of only 720 hours. How much actual 1961 New York Yankee game-action time did Ted experience? Sadly, none.

Why would the Yanks cut a player who never threw a pitch in a game? Had he played in just one game for the Yanks, Ted would have joined the list of players with one big-league game for one team in each league to their credit.

Understandably, you won't find a line in the official record books that notes that Ted played for the 1961 Yankees because, well, he never really played. He was on the roster but didn't get into a game.

After being told by manager Ralph Houk that Ted was cut from the team, Bruce Henry, the Yanks' traveling secretary, handed him his ticket to the Richmond club. But Henry did so with the hope that Ted would be back soon. His ticket was a round-trip.

Ted was never called back to the Yanks. Not even for a cup of coffee.

***

Jimmy Powers' May 11 *Daily News* column noted that while Ruth hit his sixty homers in 154 games, the schedule now calls for 162 games. Powers writes: "If Ruth's mark is to be shattered in 1961, let it be done within 154 games."

May 12

I was appalled to read that on May 12 in Rock Hill, South Carolina, three Freedom Riders were viciously attacked as they attempted to enter a whites-only bus-station waiting area. The victims were John Lewis, a Negro seminary student and member of the Student Nonviolent Coordinating Committee; white Freedom Rider and World War II veteran Albert Bigelow; and Genevieve Hughes, an employee of Congress of Racial Equality.

Is there so much hate in the world that at a certain age we all pick someone to hate? Where's the fun in being a grown-up? Are most people mean-spirited and trying to cause harm to others?

***

I counted on baseball being my safe place. Yankee Stadium, my haven. Or so I thought.

It was May 12, with the Detroit Tigers playing the Yanks in a night game at The Stadium. Without warning, my haven takes a beating. With the Tigers coming to bat in the ninth inning and the score tied, Rocky Colavito suddenly bolts from the playing field to the box seats behind the third-base visitors' dugout to protect his father who was being harassed by a drunken fan.

The fracas delays the game for more than five minutes while the fan is eventually ushered out of the ballpark in the custody of a sober friend. Rocky is thrown out of the game by senior ump Ed Hurley, who cited section 3.09 of the rule book, which states that a player in uniform cannot enter the stands to mingle or fraternize with fans.

Once play resumes, the Tigers take the lead 4–3 as a result of "Yankee Killer" Frank Strong Lary's homer in the ninth and hold on to win the game, while the Yanks fall further behind the first-place Tigers by three-and-a-half games.

Lary and Tigers and beers, oh my.

***

I began collecting baseball player autographs while I was in summer camp miles from a ballpark. Away from home for two months every summer, I learned as a nine-year-old kid there was no question that mail call was almost as important as getting a Dixie cup of ice cream after dinner.

With my bunkmates gathered 'round, our counselor handed me an envelope addressed in my father's horrendous handwriting. My father rarely sent me letters, so I was a bit puzzled as to why now. It had a St. Louis postmark, dated July 27, 1957, and I couldn't believe it made it through the post office because even I had trouble reading his scribbled writing.

I tore open the envelope. Inside was a piece of stationery folded in three places. In the upper-left corner of the letter was a printed shield with a horse. Underneath were the words in large type: THE CHASE. In the upper-right corner, in my dad's scrawl: Thurs. nite 7/25/57.

Oddly, the letter itself was written in script by two different handwritings, both of which were clearly legible.

"Hi Andy, I met your Dad tonight and he tells me you are a Dodger fan. Sorry we lost tonight but will do better."

The second part of the letter, in a different handwriting:

"Our very best wishes to your team and we hope you win the championship. Good luck."

"Duke Snider and Rube Walker"

I looked with amazement, thrilled that this was a letter from two big-league Brooklyn Dodgers. I proudly (and boastfully) showed it to everyone in my bunk.

A few days later, my father called me at camp, which was a big deal. Getting a telephone call from a parent was rare, but if it did happen, it was usually during dinner time. That's when an announcement was made in the large dining room for everyone to hear. Half curious, half nervous, I got on the phone, a two-piece vintage wall phone with a crank. It had one piece to talk into and another to listen.

My father explained that during his business travels in St. Louis, he went to see the Cardinals play the Dodgers at Busch Stadium and stayed at the same hotel as the Dodgers. He ran into Duke and Rube after the game in the lobby and told them what a "giant" fan I was of the Dodgers and that I was on a baseball team vying to win a championship in Pennsylvania.

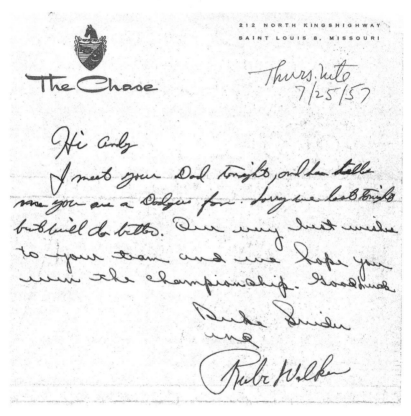

The Chase—This letter written by Duke Snider and Rube Walker in 1957 was the result of a chance meeting with my dad and his thoughtful effort on my behalf.

My dad was sneaky smart. To begin with, since he was a lifelong Giants fan, he had to describe me as a "giant" fan of the Dodgers.

My dad sort of told the truth that I liked the Dodgers, because at nine years old one of the first baseball player's names that stuck with me was Gil Hodges. I was fascinated with the rhyme of Hodges and Dodgers.

And yes, I was playing baseball, at least three times a week, but at a camp in the Pocono Mountains. However, to my knowledge, we weren't vying for a championship.

I asked my dad how Snider did in the game, and the best he remembered was that the "Duke of Flatbush" got a couple of hits. "Did anyone hit a homer?"

"Nope, no homers," he answered.

These were my first autographs of big-league ballplayers. I now had a collection of autographs—two. I framed the letter and hung it in my room as if it was my high-school diploma, which hopefully would happen nine years in the future.

That letter ignited the baseball-autograph-hound-through-the-mail in me.

On a regular basis over the next four years, I would write players requesting their autograph and sending them one of their baseball cards or a picture of them that I ripped from a page in *Sport* magazine. I would always include a self-addressed, stamped envelope and eagerly look forward to a response.

Four years later, the baseball gods provided me with the opportunity to get my first in-person major-league ballplayer's autograph.

My father said he was taking me to see the Yanks play the Tigers at Yankee Stadium on Saturday, May 13, 1961.

It was early in the season, and Detroit was playing at a .700 pace, which I figured they couldn't possibly keep up. The Yanks were in third place behind Baltimore, and I kept reminding myself that it was still very early in the season.

I kept tabs on Roger Maris: He was struggling at the plate with a .217 batting average and had clubbed only three homers.

Was Maris done? Was he a one-year wonder in 1960? Did I pick the wrong guy to be my favorite baseball player?

We arrived after the Yankee Stadium gates opened but before the game. As we walked around to enter The Stadium, my father lightly touched my shoulder to stop me and said, "Hold on, Andrew." I thought maybe he'd changed his mind about going to the game.

He then asked, without pointing, "Do you see that man in the gray suit over there?"

"Yeah."

"That's Jim Hegan. Why don't you catch up to him and get his autograph?"

I knew Hegan was the Yanks bullpen coach and ran up to him with pencil and paper and asked for his autograph. He obliged and then quickly walked into the special entrance for players only. I ran back and showed my dad the signed piece of paper. "Wasn't he once a player?" I asked.

My father told me Hegan was a catcher for the Indians in the 1940s and

'50s. He then explained that he caught one of the best pitching staffs in baseball that included Bob Feller. Hegan called a good game and knew the hitters' weak spots, my dad said. He was on the 1948 and 1954 pennant-winning Cleveland teams and caught every World Series game for the Tribe.

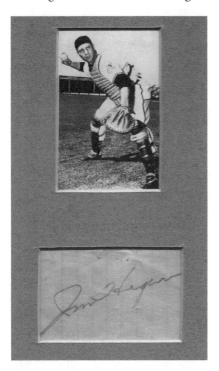

I was impressed with Hegan's record as a player. But, more importantly, I was impressed with my father's knowledge of baseball.

May 13

Film actor Gary Cooper died May 13 at the age of 60. It was Cooper who played Lou Gehrig in the 1942 movie *Pride of the Yankees*. That flick is my all-time favorite baseball movie. I watch it every time it shows up on Channel 9's "Million Dollar Movie" TV show. The fact that Babe Ruth plays himself in the movie is very cool.

I've seen the movie a lot. Yet every time it gets to the last scene I choke up when "The Iron Horse" walks down those dugout steps. Since I know Gehrig is dying, I always think that those are the steps to heaven.

Sign Here—Former player and current Yankee coach Jim Hegan was my first in-person baseball autograph.

***

With the Tigers still in town on May 13, the price of tickets for women is reduced. That will attract more gals, which, in turn, will attract more guys. So it's Ladies Day at Yankee Stadium.

I've always heard that when pitchers throw at a batter and knock him down because he's "digging in," there are some players who dust themselves off and take revenge.

That just might have been the situation with Rocky Colavito, who was ejected in yesterday's game after going into the stands when a fan bothered his dad.

I'm not saying it was that incident that got Colavito's juices going, but "The Rock" went four for five. He socked two homers and a pair of singles today to lead Detroit in a 8–3 win over the Yanks, proving, "Don't knock the Rock."

Bell Ringer—Roger hit his 6th homer of the 1961 season off Gary Bell at Cleveland Municipal Stadium on May 20. Cleveland won the game 4–3. *Photo courtesy of Cleveland State University.*

May 14

Found a note in a May 14 newspaper that I almost overlooked about the Detroit Tigers' second baseman Steve Boros. Detroit infield coach Don Heffner noticed that Boros was bobbling too many balls in spring training and thought his glove was too small and stiff. He got him to switch to a Roger Maris Spalding model, and Boros showed improvement right away.

I wonder how many S&H Green Stamps Boros got when he bought the glove?

May 17

With the Yanks down by five runs against the Senators in the sixth inning at Yankee Stadium on May 17, Rog surprised the Washington infield by dragging a bunt between the pitcher, Pete Burnside, and the first baseman, Dale Long, for a single.

Then in the eighth he connected for his fourth home run of the season off Pete Burnside, but he's still only batting .218. The Yanks lost 8–7.

Maris's slump is now putting me in a slump.

***

Every ballpark has unique aspects that give it a personality all its own. The most distinguishing characteristics that make Yankee Stadium Yankee Stadium include the teal-color paint used in the stands, the façade—which I'm told the correct name used by architects is a *frieze* but I'm still calling it a façade—and the monuments in center field honoring Ruth and Gehrig and other legends.

My own favorite Yankee Stadium feature would be the right-field concrete wall. It's painted teal and is forty inches tall. That wall begins at the 296-foot mark down the right-field line. It quickly shoots out to 344 feet and then the bullpen separates the expensive wooden box seats from the cheap bleacher plank seats.

The Yankee Stadium right-field seat section has its own nickname: the "right-field porch." Almost on a daily basis it provided spectacular views of circus catches (or attempts) as outfielders time their jumps to snag a would-be homer headed for the seats.

Such was the case on May 21 when in the first inning of the first game of a doubleheader against the Orioles with Joe DiMaggio in attendance, Rog connected to a pitch thrown by Chuck Estrada, sending a high fly toward the fence marked 344 FT. in right field.

Baltimore right fielder Earl Robinson drifts back to the wall and attempts to catch the ball before it reaches the seats. He doesn't make the catch and winds up tumbling into the stands. The *Daily News* runs a three-panel action shot of his attempt.

The ball sailing over Robinson's head was Roger's fourth homer in four games. He now has seven for the season.

Yanks won 4–2. Maris's batting average is .252.

There are a lot of things I love about Yankee Stadium, but that forty-inch-tall right-field, teal-colored concrete wall is No. 1 on my list. I'm head over heels about it, which explains why my parents allowed me to repaint my bedroom walls in the color teal and paste on the wall near the ceiling large black numbers and letters, 296 FT. in one corner and 344 FT. in the other corner.

May 22

The assignment for Mr. Goodrich's English class on May 22 was to give a speech on any topic we chose. The topic I selected was Hurricane Diane, which had drenched the Pennsylvania area where I attended Camp Kiowa in August 1955. I was seven years old at the time and vividly recalled the storm's terror.

My classmates were very nervous about getting up in front of the class. Not me. Wanting to do well, I looked forward to speaking to a captive audience.

It was apparent to me that I didn't get the least bit nervous when I had to speak in public. Much to my mother's chagrin, she believed that there aren't many steady jobs out there that paid big bucks for such a talent come the time when I would need a job.

Holding my 5″ × 7″ index card filled with my handwritten notes, I imagined my own musical intro, similar to the theme songs of Jackie Gleason or Bob Hope, as I confidently walked to the front of the classroom.

My approach was to recount my experience as if it was a scary horror story told 'round a crackling campfire. Without saying a word, I scanned my fellow students' faces. Everyone was intently staring at me, so I began.

I informed the class that they were about to hear of a harrowing adventure I had experienced six years before. To make it even more dramatic, I provided a subtext headlined, "An adventure when people lost their lives," making sure to emphasize the word "lives" in a soft whisper.

I began my tale with the basics of who, what, where, and when: "It was mid-August of 1955. I was attending Camp Kiowa in the Pocono Mountains of Pennsylvania when a heavy rain fell."

My speech was filled with specifics of howling wind, loud thunder, and torrential rain that was of biblical magnitude. Even though I wanted to, I made sure not to ad-lib any comedy bits.

For me, making that speech was surprisingly difficult because I avoided relying on my usual doses of "Andy humor." Laughs put me at ease when I speak in front of a group, but I decided this was serious stuff.

"Not far from the bunk I lived in with six other campers, a bolt of frightening lightning hit an empty bunk, and it burst into flames." This was all true. For some reason, I didn't include that we were all scared shitless. But we were.

My audience was mesmerized, and it was readily apparent that this wasn't a typical seventh-grade speech given by a typical seventh grader. I was killing it.

In conclusion, I explained that many campers attending Camp Davis, a mere fifty miles from my camp, tragically died as a result of the storm's fury.

On my notes I had written my closing remark. That after the storm I saw the biggest and most beautiful rainbow ever. But I decided at the last moment not to mention it because it was too much of a change from acknowledging those unfortunate campers who had perished.

I thanked everyone, then closed my eyes while slowly bowing my head. I returned to my seat holding my notecard with both hands on my chest as if it was a prayer book. There was no applause but I thought I did a good job of delivering my speech.

Oh heavens, this might have been a preview of my laugh-less Bar Mitzvah performance to come in September.

***

On Monday, May 22, with two down in the first inning, Maris trotted into the bench and complained he couldn't see, according to a newspaper account. Yankee trainer Gus Mauch bathed Maris's eyes in the locker room, delaying the game about five minutes. Maris went back and completed the inning, but he couldn't bat as he was still having problems seeing.

The problem came about as a result of Maris seeing...poor choice of words...*having* an appointment with an eye doctor earlier in the day.

Get this, the doctor's name is Payne. Seriously. Dr. B. F. Payne found Roger's vision to be perfectly normal, but recommended a particular bathing solution if he wanted to use it.

Dr. Payne explained: "There is positively nothing wrong with Maris's vision. He could pass an eye test to become a jet pilot." He then explained that Maris misunderstood when to use the bathing solution and used it just before the start of the game. It was intended for just before bedtime and the doctor noted that Rog was probably allergic to the solution.

Having a doctor whose last name is Payne should have been a tip-off that something was going wrong.

After the game, Maris was asked about his eyes. His reply: "The front office made an appointment a week ago, when I wasn't hitting. I almost didn't keep it today but they had gone to the trouble..." and he shrugged.

He noted that by ten p.m. that night he could have played because that's when his vision cleared up.

May 25

The day after Maris hit his eighth homer of the season, I couldn't believe a May 25 newspaper article about President Kennedy's proposal that the United States commit itself to landing a man on the Moon and returning him safely to Earth before this decade is out.

It would have made more sense if *The Twilight Zone*'s TV host Rod Serling had been quoted rather than JFK. *Doo-doo-DOO-doo, Doo-doo-DOO-doo, Doo-doo-DOO-doo.*

Shooting rockets into space with a man aboard is one thing, but what the president is proposing is pure science fiction. Cue the announcer, "You're moving into a land of both shadow and substance, of things and ideas. You've just crossed over into...the Twilight Zone." Music—*Bahdump dum.*

***

Beginning in 1959 when *The Twilight Zone* first came on the tube, I couldn't skip a single episode for fear of hearing my friends at school tease me, "Oh, man, did you miss it." Then add, "It was the best one ever."

Each episode was scary because, unlike the horror movies *The Crawling Eye, The Blob,* or *Frankenstein, The Twilight Zone* stories were all too real. They were the take-me-to-your-leader kind of television show.

The first *Twilight Zone* episode was about a man who wanders around a small town without any people. Moments before the show ends, we find out that the man was hallucinating because he had been locked in an isolation box for over 400 hours to simulate what would happen if he traveled in a rocket ship to the Moon.

Tonight's ten p.m. *Twilight Zone* episode on CBS is titled, "Will the Real Martian Please Stand Up," which sounds like the tagline ending of the *To Tell The Truth* TV show.

It begins as two state troopers investigate a report about a UFO crashed in a pond. They locate footprints from the crash site leading to a small road-side diner in the middle of the woods.

Once inside the diner, the troopers determine that there's one extra customer who cannot be accounted for and therefore must be an alien posing as human.

That's what sets my mind spinning as I try to figure out which customer in the diner is not from our planet.

After a couple years of watching *The Twilight Zone*, I'm trained to immediately start to try to guess the ending. The show frequently provides clues to figure it out. However, the shows I like the best are those that I can't guess the ending.

As a result, now I immediately try to figure out the "whodunit" ending of everything I watch on TV or at the movies.

The obvious customer who isn't from Earth is probably not the old man who has an unusual human face with big bug eyes that dart around when he talks.

To determine his worldly origin the trooper tests him with a question: "Who won the World Series race last year?"

Using the word "race" is inappropriate and makes me think that the trooper may be from outer space…just kidding.

But the bug-eyed customer answers in a snappy know-it-all manner, "Pittsburgh Pirates won it—took four out of seven from the Yankees."

Well, that took me by surprise as I didn't need to be reminded about last year's heartbreaker World Series. This is, after all, 1961. But there it is on *The Twilight Zone*.

I anticipated that the old man would add that even though the Yanks lost the Series, they outscored the Pittsburgh Buccos 55–27, and out-hit 'em 91–60. In other words, when the Yankees beat 'em it was by a wide margin: thirteen runs, ten runs, and twelve runs. But when Pittsburgh won, it was a squeaker with never more than a three-run difference.

But he didn't. Instead, the bug-eyed customer chirps back at the trooper sarcastically, "Didn't think us Martians would know nothin' about the great American pastime, did ya? Huh? Huh?"

Turns out the Martian is a normal-looking older businessman who explains in the last scene that he came to Earth to colonize it as he nonchalantly reveals he has three arms.

But as so often happens on *The Twilight Zone*, that wasn't the real ending. The diner's waiter tells the Martian that he beat him to the punch as he is a Venusian looking to do the same thing—colonize the Earth. He then takes off his hat to reveal a third eye in the middle of his forehead.

May 28

Today, May 28, the American League set a major-league record with twenty-seven homers hit on one day. This record-setting accomplishment included Roger Maris's ninth homer of the season against the Chicago White Sox as the Yanks won by a score of 5–3.

Lost among the record-setting accomplishments was the fact that the pitcher who threw the pitch that Maris hit for a home run has the longest name in baseball this season: Calvin Coolidge Julius Caesar Tuskahoma McLish.

The right-hander's nickname is "Bus." Go figure.

***

In the early stages of the 1961 baseball season, one of the Yankees WNBC radio sponsors, Flying A Getty Oil, conducted a "Batboy for a Day" contest.

The winner would get to be batboy for the Wednesday, June 7, game when the Yanks played the Minnesota Twins at Yankee Stadium, starting at two p.m.

This was exactly what I'd been hoping for. It was made for me. It was ideal, a dream come true. I'd be on the field wearing Yankee pinstripes. I'd pal around with Rog and the guys. Maybe take a couple of swings in the cage. Shag some fly balls in right field. I can't lose.

Then I started to calculate the odds of me winning the contest.

If New York had twelve million people, I figured there must be around four million kids and half of them would enter the contest. At least. Therefore, I calculated it was a two-million-to-one shot.

My plan to grab the judges' attention was to use the same creative approach I had used the year before when I entered Cross County Shopping Center's Father's Day contest, sponsored by Gimbels department store.

For that contest, the request for submissions was simple: "In 100 words or less, describe your dad."

Not using any words, on an 8″ × 10″ piece of paper I drew a bag that was tied at the top to keep it closed. On the front of the bag, I drew a large dollar sign.

Naturally, I won.

Now all I had to do was be as clever as that—again. Unfortunately, I never sat down to write, "Why I want to be batboy for a day for the NY Yankees." You can't win if you don't enter.

It was my mom who always encouraged me to always try. Her philosophy was: "If you don't try, you'll never know," adding, "What's the worst that could happen? You don't win, and isn't that where you started from?"

My mom explained that the same rule applied if you wanted something, anything. "You never know unless you ask, and at the very least the answer could be no," she'd say.

Smart lady.

However, when I figured what the chances of winning were, it was overwhelming. I was defeated before I started. I promised myself I'd never make that mistake again. My mom was right. She was always right.

Around the end of May, I read the Yanks' radio station received twelve thousand entries. So I guess I'd miscalculated what the odds would be. The article then mentioned that out of those entries the judges picked ten from which another set of judges would determine the winner.

The winner was fifteen-year-old Theo Cornelius from Port Chester.

Lucky stiff.

Except when the judges asked for Theo's measurements for a Yankee uniform, they found out that Theo was a girl and disqualified her.

So the contest winner became a loser. Life is unfair, especially if you are a girl.

JUNE 1961

"I was hooked on Rog. He was my guy."

June 1

Oh, how I love reading—in big, black, bold letters—the June 1 *Daily News* headline on the back page: MICK, ROG HR, YANKS WIN.

The game story written by Joe Trimble had a line that made me want to sing "Take Me Out to the Ball Game": "Roger Maris and Mickey Mantle strummed their home run refrain again this evening to help pile up an early advantage."

The Yanks are three-and-a-half out of first, and Rog has fourteen round-trippers to Mick's twelve. In the last twelve games, Rog has batted .330 with nineteen RBIs.

I couldn't help but notice that under the back-page bold Yankee headline were two photos of a mob scene storming the Dominican Republic consulate in Manhattan. This related to the assassination of the country's's longtime, ruthless dictator, Rafael Trujillo.

Man, I feel like so many things are happening in the world that I am not aware of and should be. I'm not tuned into world events, but neither are the kids at school because not one of them talked about the assassination. Maybe I'm hanging out with the dumb crowd.

June 2

Roger's wife, Pat, joined him for the Chicago series June 2–4. Rog hit a homer in each game. Those were home run Nos. 13, 14, and 15. That is the residual power of love working its magic. Thank you, Pat.

June 5

The Yanks beat the Chicago White Sox and this was the June 5 *Daily News* back-page headline: MARIS HRs, YANKS WIN, 10-1.

June 6

Maris received his 1960 Gold Glove award for fielding excellence in a Yankee Stadium pregame ceremony at home plate on June 6. The *Daily News* story incorrectly referred to the award as "Gold*en*" Glove, which baffles me, and I am now convinced that just because it's printed in a newspaper does not mean it's correct.

Yanks beat the Twins 7–2 as Ford gets win No. 8. Rog hits homer No. 16, but now the Yanks are in third place (three games back) as Cleveland and Detroit are tied for first.

I wish I could ask someone why the Gold Glove award was presented so late in the season. Shouldn't this award be part of the hardware Maris collected on opening day?

***

At 7 p.m. tonight, June 6, President Kennedy was on TV from the White House reporting to the American people about his recent European trip. I knew that we were going to talk about this in class, so I tuned in. I was intrigued that he was on ABC, CBS, and NBC at the exact same time.

JFK began talking about visiting Paris, Vienna, and London. He spoke about General Charles de Gaulle of France, so I switched TV stations without missing a word JFK said, just to see if anything was different on each station. It wasn't. I must have switched stations at least a dozen times. But for only a second or two.

Then the president talked about his meeting with Mr. Khrushchev. I'm not very good at understanding speeches. I heard words. A lot of words that concerned me. Words like peace, war, cease-fire, world Communism, nuclear test ban, nuclear weapons, Germany, Berlin, peace treaty, war, wars of liberation, missiles, and that war could and should be avoided, if possible.

As a result of meeting with Khrushchev, JFK said dangerous misjudgment should be less likely. I'm troubled when I hear the words "should be."

***

As the school year was finally drawing to a close, I asked Mr. Clements if he and The Sherwoods would play at my Bar Mitzvah reception in September. He agrees, which means, "It's pony time, boogety, boogety, boogety, boogety, shoo."

My relationship with Mr. Clements is different from those with my other teachers. We're kinda buddies, but not really.

Before the last day of school Mr. Clements wished me a fun summer and said he would be in touch with my parents about his band playing at my Bar Mitzvah reception.

He surprised me by handing me an envelope with a note inside:

Andy,

Please know I consider having had you as a student was a major highlight of my inaugural year teaching at Highlands Junior High School. I want you to know I shall never forget the special homeroom group you were a part of.

I have no doubts you will be a success in life because of your upbeat personality, energy, sense of humor and drive. You light up a room.

I sincerely hope you plan to pursue your dream of playing baseball, and if that doesn't work out, being involved with baseball, hopefully with your beloved Yankees. By the way, I'll bet you are over the moon concerning Roger Maris who is off to a great start of the 1961 season.

I look forward to providing the music at your Bar Mitzvah reception after summer vacation.

May your journey in life be filled with good health, success, joy and love. It is my fervent prayer the Fates will somehow, someway allow our paths to cross again.

Fondly, Mr. Clements

Well, I guess I kinda fooled him. Maybe that's what I'm good at, fooling people to think that I'm better than I really am. Is that an adult job?

Probably not.

June 11

It was Sunday, June 11. As I watched the Yankee game on TV, I couldn't help but pay close attention to Roger Maris.

In the first game of the Yankee doubleheader with the Los Angeles Angels, the Yankees held a 1–0 lead in the top of the seventh. That's when the Angels' center fielder, Ken Hunt, hit a towering fly ball off Ralph Terry that was headed for the right-field stands of Yankee Stadium.

Roger raced to the right-field cement wall, near to where it meets the bullpen wire fence. He perfectly timed his leap to snag the ball before it reached the box seats. The momentum of his leap lifted him onto the forty-inch wall.

For a brief moment, Maris put both arms up to control his balance, but teetered backwards toward the front row of $3.50 seats in Section 33 that had just been vacated by two nicely dressed older women.

Once Rog fell in the stands backwards, all that could be seen was the incongruous sight of his spikes as if they were reaching for the sky. For a moment, Maris was out of sight behind the wall. An instant later, he righted himself, popping up as he held his glove high above his head with the baseball clearly in his grasp.

The second-base umpire, Al Smith, at first motioned it was a homer, but changed his decision once he realized Maris caught the ball before it landed in the stands.

The ump signaled out! *Incredible.*

Hunt kept circling the bases not realizing he was a goner.

Had Maris not made the catch, the game would have been tied. Worse, Rog could have been seriously hurt.

When the inning ended the Yankee Stadium crowd gave him an ovation as he trotted to the dugout.

In the top of the ninth with one out, Rog did it again. This time Angel Ted Kluszewski hammered one that was about to land in the Yankee bullpen for a homer when Rog timed his jump perfectly and, with his left arm fully extended, caught the ball before it flew over the fence. This time he stayed on the field as "Klu" just stopped on the base path, hands on his hips in frustration. The Yanks won 2–1.

In the second game, Rog blasted two homers to help lead the Yanks to a 5–1 victory and a doubleheader sweep. He now had twenty home runs for the season, and it was only June 11.

Great catches from other Yanks were sprinkled all over the diamond throughout the second game. Out of frustration, Angels manager Bill Rigney began throwing a white towel out of the dugout indicating that he surrendered after each stunning defensive play, which made me laugh.

I was hooked on Rog. He was my guy, and I didn't have to share him with anyone. Everyone else on earth was a Mantle fan.

***

Way Out—This was the game that convinced me that I had picked the right guy in Maris for my favorite player. Not only did Rog hit two home runs (19 and 20), but he made two fantabulous catches to rob Angel players of homers. One was a shot to the Yankees' bullpen by Ted Kluszewski, while the other was Ken Hunt's towering fly ball headed for the right-field seats which is where Rog ended upside down. *Original art by Russ Opdahl.*

The *New York Post*'s June 12 back page has two headlines: "Sonny Liston Arrested for Posing as Cop" and "Yankees Beat Angels 'In So Many Ways…'"

Jerry Mitchell wrote about Maris's catch of Ken Hunt's towering drive headed for the right-field seats, "Maris got up on his toenails, stretched like a rubber band, gloved the ball and held on to it as he tumbled over the concrete barrier."

The article was accompanied by three photos of Rog teetering on the wall, falling into the stands, then showing his glove over his head with the ball.

There was also a photo of Maris, Berra, and Mantle all smiles in the Yankee locker room as they each hit home runs. Maris is the only one with his hand up in the photo. He is either giving the okay sign or the three-ring sign for Ballantine beer.

June 12

During the June 12 Yankee radio broadcast against the Angels at Yankee Stadium, Mel Allen did a commercial after 7 1/2 innings that, at first, really shook me up.

"I wish the game was over. Not that I don't like the game. I'd just love to have a bottle of Ballantine. I can't have one until the game is over. And I'm thirsty.

"MMMMM...

"I can just taste the tall, cool bottle right now of Ballantine, the most popular beer from the Canadian border to the Florida Keys.

"So popular, in fact, that more than 5 million glasses of Ballantine Beer are enjoyed every day. That's because it's got pleasure. Pleasure is the purpose of the crisp refresher.

"Your first swallow and each one to follow is light and refreshing. Teamed up with its lightness is a stunning mellow lager flavor unmatched in beer today.

"Hope you'll try the crisp refresher, if you haven't already. Enjoy it. How 'bout right now?

"If you're at your favorite tavern, just ask the man for Ballantine, America's finest since 1840."

You had me going there for a minute, Mel.

No Yankee homers, but they still beat LA, 3-1.

June 14

Obviously, the toughest job for the Yankees this season was not pinch-hitting with the game on the line, or catching both ends of a doubleheader, or pitching in relief with the Yanks trailing by six runs.

No, it's being the Yankee players' representative, the guy who deals with the business end of baseball. Bob Turley began the season holding the job, then it was Bobby Richardson, who resigned because it was too time-consuming (plus he was struggling at the plate). Art Ditmar took on the responsibility, but only for a few days as he was traded today, along with Deron Johnson, to the Athletics for Bud Daley.

Whitey Ford is the fourth player to hold the job, as he was elected by the team today, June 14.

***

Ray Keyes reported in the June 14 *Sporting News* that Mickey McConnell, director of training for Little League Baseball, and former baseball general manager Branch Rickey picked an all-star Major League team of former Little Leaguers. Maris was selected. The only other Yankee chosen was The Moose—Bill Skowron.

June 15

Thank the Lord. It's June 15 and finally school is out!

The very second I completed seventh grade at Highlands Junior High School, the summer of 1961 began. I felt the summer belonged to me.

Starting when I was two years old, my parents would take my sister and me out of the city every summer. At first we went to a bungalow colony known as Ben-Ann Cottages, located in the Catskill Mountains of upstate New York.

When I turned three I began attending Camp Kiowa, a sleepaway camp in the Pocono Mountains of Northeastern Pennsylvania, for July and August. Year after year that was my summer routine.

As a result of being accidentally burned in a fire last August, this would be the first time since I was two years old that I would be at home for the summer months.

I continued to diligently follow Roger Maris and the Yankees, but as a twelve-year-old boy, there were other things going on in my world, such as music and, as always, girls, which were becoming a more significant part of my life.

Songs made me happy, think, smile, reminisce, create, and feel good like never before. Songs were inspirational. They made me feel like dancing as long as the song had a good beat and, as they would say on *American Bandstand*, "I rate it at least an eighty-eight, Dick."

Music was the sound of everything in my life. I felt that my favorite songs were written for me and me only. As a result of my love for music, I experienced financial problems for the first time. Let me explain.

In addition to my weekly allowance of two dollars, I also earned money by returning soda bottles from our house to the supermarket, along with those I found in the neighborhood.

The money I spent went to baseball cards and *Superman* comics. But now I felt compelled to also buy certain records. As a result, I had less money for cards and comics.

Records were not cheap. In fact, they cost almost ten times the price of a comic and twenty times the cost of a pack of cards. Such was my dilemma.

Plus, unlike the candy store where I bought my comics and baseball cards, the record store was not close to my house. It was almost a mile by bike. A whole mile!

The first record I ever bought was "I Like It Like That" by Chris Kenner. I couldn't get it out of my head. I loved when it came on the radio. It changed my life. Then I had to buy "Tossin' and Turnin'" by Bobby Lewis. I knew all the words and sang along.

Then there was "Stand By Me" by Ben E. King, "Cupid" by Sam Cooke, and "Hurt" by Timi Yuro. I really liked "Hurt," especially the way the record started with the high voice and no music background.

I was hooked. Music was an addiction—I couldn't get enough of it. Every week there was a new record playing on the radio that I had to buy. Dammit!

Then there was "Quarter to Three" by Gary "U.S." Bonds. But it had little to do with the great beat it had. I was fascinated at how the record began. Get this: The guy was saying dirty words. A couple of my buddies figured this out and told me. But to hear it, you had to listen real closely and know what you were listening for.

Once the needle was placed on the 45 rpm record, you heard hand-clapping and a bunch of guys cheering and counting: "A one, a two, a one, two, three, four. Go, go, open your legs, baby, go, go, open your legs now, baby…"

Incredible, right? I must have listened to it a million times, and it was always there as plain as day. All you had to do was listen.

So my music mania started with that first record I bought, appropriately titled "I Like It Like That." I liked it very much.

June 16

For an Associated Press news feature, Maris wrote an article titled, "Maris Recalls When White Suggested He Pull for Homers," which was published in newspapers around the country on June 16.

The "White" he cited was Jo Jo White, who was his minor league manager when the nineteen-year-old Roger played for Keokuk in 1954.

The article ends with Rog expressing his admiration for Ted Williams: "I've always idolized Ted Williams. He has been a favorite with our whole family. I always looked up to him, and last year I got up a little nerve to talk to him. But I've always tried not to ask him too many questions."

Do I really think Rog wrote it? No, I'm not a kid. I know how these things happen. I think Rog spoke to a reporter who wrote it for him. But I liked it.

Yoo-Hoo, Over Here—Rog wore his Yogi Berra Yoo-Hoo T-shirt under his Yankee jersey. After the game, he would remove his jersey so that all the sportswriters and photographers couldn't help but notice the free advertising for "The Drink of Champions."

June 17

To help promote the Yoo-Hoo soft drink, Yogi Berra distributed T-shirts to players and photographers on June 17.

According to my classmate Gary Baker, Yogi Berra has a financial stake in Yoo-Hoo. Bake knows a lot about a lot.

The design on the white T-shirt is a colorful bottle cap emblazoned on the chest with a portrait of a handsome-looking Yogi in the center.

Wait just a New York second, maybe it's not really Yogi—this guy is too good-looking.

June 18

Sadly, I read a short article that reported Eddie Gaedel died at thirty-six on June 18 in Chicago. Gaedel, who stood three feet, seven inches, appeared for only one at-bat in the majors as a pinch-hitter for the St. Louis Browns on August 19, 1951.

The idea of having Gaedel bat was hatched by Bill Veeck, the Browns owner at the time. Always the showman with the fans' best interests at heart, Veeck was now owner of the Chicago White Sox. He brought the shortest major league player ever back to work for him along with six other "midgets" as vendors in Comiskey Park's box seats at the beginning of the season. His reasoning? "So they won't block the fans' view."

The article noted that there was speculation that Gaedel's death was not from natural causes but as a result of getting beat up by thugs.

What's with this horrible human trend of violence that is ignited by hate around the world?

***

In Jimmy Powers' June 18 *Daily News* "Powerhouse" column, Davey Jones, an outfielder who played from 1901 to 1918, complimented Rog for his spectacular June 11 catch of Ken Hunt's towering drive. "No one in all baseball history ever made a better catch...not even Tris Speaker."

June 20

Even though I'm a freshman at Highlands Junior High School, I bought a 1961 Highlander Yearbook when it became available on June 20. The ninth graders who are graduating have individual portrait photos, while the rest of us are grouped together by class in small photos so you have to really look hard to see who's who.

I decided to ask certain people to sign my yearbook. I had a page for the guys, a different page for the girls and had teachers sign their photos.

All the guys signed "To Pot" while wishing me good luck. Thankfully, none of the girls who signed my yearbook mentioned my nickname. Almost all the girls wrote corny poems such as, "If all the girls were across the sea, what a good swimmer Andy would be."

Mr. Clements drew a silly picture of me next to his signature.

Then there was Miss Menaugh, who wrote, "Best of luck in years to come—and may you someday learn to keep your mouth shut." It's so obvious that Miss Menaugh has a crush on me.

***

The first national publication to feature Maris in 1961 was *Look* magazine. Their June 20 edition had Doris Day on the cover. A four-page spread inside was titled: "Roger Maris: Has he the stuff for stardom?"

The exclusive photo layout was shot by photographer Frank Bauman. The article showed Maris—wearing only a pair of dark, tight-fitting shorts with low-cut tennis sneakers—in his batting stance and swing. With the photos' black background, the lighting illuminated his muscular physique.

The captions were as brief as his tight-fitting shorts. The only other verbiage had to do with the description of how Maris lined up his knuckles.

Seeing Maris out of uniform and just wearing shorts was a bit creepy for me.

June 21

In the June 21 *Daily News* story about yesterday's tilt against the A's, it noted that it was Ralph Houk Night in Kansas City. The Yanks won 6–2 and Joe Trimble wrote: "Here tonight, the red-necked slugger [Maris] blasted his 26th homer."

The term "red-necked" was used instead of the clubhouse term "red ass," or R.A., because the word "ass" is not appropriate for newspapers.

This is another injustice toward Roger because the term "red neck" is also a derogatory term applied to lower-class white Americans largely from the rural South who are crass and unsophisticated. "Red ass" describes an individual who appears to be or is pissed off at someone or something. Those are two distinct and different meanings. Period. It's an injustice of reporting because it misleads readers.

June 22

Kansas City Athletics owner Charley Finley lost the "battle of the bulbs" to the Yanks last night, June 22. Confused? So am I. It seems that the Yanks refused to have fluorescent lights blurring their vision in the visitors' dugout. The Yanks removed them after American League President Joe Cronin told Yankee manager Houk that they didn't have to submit to the annoying glare.

This is a perfect example of putting the visiting team in a situation that would provide the home team an advantage and possible victory.

I've noticed other tactics: the way the infield grass is cut; the soggy dirt around first base so runners who want to steal second base can't get a good lead off first; the tilt of the third base line, which makes a bunted ball roll foul or fair; the lack of heat in the visitor bullpen; or in this case, the glaring fluorescent lights in the visitor dugout.

June 24

On June 24 at Metropolitan Stadium in Minnesota, with the Yanks leading the Twins 8–3, Rog was hit by a Don Lee pitch in the top of the sixth inning. That loaded the bases, but the Yanks didn't score. However, they won 10–7 and are now two games out of first place trailing the Tigers.

June 26

Talk about a baseball player being focused. Get this: The Yanks are in Los Angeles playing the Angels at Wrigley Field on June 26. Yankee catcher Elston Howard was so upset by umpire Joe Linsalata's call when a run scored on what Howard thought was a foul tip in the fourth inning that he forgot to wear his chest protector and caught the fifth inning without it.

June Bloom—Beginning May 17, 1961, Maris hit 23 homers over the next 36 days. Along the way to 61, Roger hit his 21st homer off Jim Perry at Cleveland Municipal Stadium on June 13. The Indians beat the Yanks that day by a score of 7–2. *Photo courtesy of Cleveland State University.*

June 28

With only a third of the season completed, the June 28 *Sporting News* ran a drawing of Mantle and Maris with Gehrig and Ruth behind them. The headline: "Dial M for Murder and Mayhem." It ran with an article about the current-day Yanks shooting to break the old-time Yanks' team home run record.

The article pointed out that the one-two punch of home runs the M&M Boys are aiming for is one-hundred-and-seven set by Gehrig and Ruth in 1927. The paper further explains so far this season that Rog has twenty-seven homers and Mick twenty-four.

So if you follow the sportswriter's thought process and multiply their current total by three, that equals eighty-one homers at season's end for Rog and seventy-two for Mickey. Add them together and the season total for the pair is one-hundred-fifty-three homers.

Come on. This type of calculation is so ridiculous. It would be as silly as a player hitting a homer in the first game of the season, then projecting he would hit one-hundred-sixty-two for the season.

Why is crap like this printed in newspapers?

JULY 1961

"I was in a secret sex club, which my friends and I named 'The 9½ Club.'"

July 1

The Yanks were down to their last at-bats in the bottom of the ninth, trailing the Washington Senators 6–5 on July 1.

Tony Kubek led off with a single. Rog then won the game with a home run, No. 28, against right-hander Dave Sisler at Yankee Stadium.

After Maris circled the bases, Mantle was at the plate to shake his hand as he had done many times before. Rog passed by Mantle without accepting the congratulatory shake, and said to Mick, "What the hell are you waiting for? Don't you know the game's over?"

July 2

I read a newspaper story about writer Ernest Hemingway dying while cleaning his gun in Ketchum, Idaho, on July 2. I heard my parents whisper to each other that it wasn't accidental, but a suicide.

The only thing I know about Hemingway is that he idolized Joe DiMaggio, so he's okay in my book.

***

Another "Diamond Dust" note caught my attention about assistant Yankee batboy Fred Bengis getting hit on July 1 by a line drive in pregame fielding practice. He was sent home and missed the July 2 game. Realizing that I was not talented enough to be a player, I thought this was my opportunity to write a letter requesting an interview for the entry-level position of Yankee ball boy and then move up to batboy. Ball boys are the guys who sit along the foul lines during games.

As my mother would often tell me, "It doesn't hurt to ask."

So I composed a letter and mailed it in. Here's what I wrote:

To whom it may concern,

My name is Andy Strasberg, and I grew up in the shadows of Yankee Stadium at 2180 Bronx Park East.

Currently I live in White Plains, New York, and will turn 13 years old on July 17.

I would like to interview for the job of ball boy as I am a big Yankee fan.

Sincerely yours,
Andy Strasberg

I did receive a response:

Dear Mr. Strasberg,

Thank you for your recent letter requesting an interview to become a Yankee ball boy.

Applicants must be at least 18 years old to apply for the position of ball boy.

Sincerely,
Bill Ackman
Special Services

I had known what the age requirement was for the job, but sent the letter anyway because I had a plan. As a result of the response, I now had the name of someone to contact at the Yankees.

My plan is to send the same letter requesting an interview for the ball boy job every year, so that by the time I turn eighteen, Mr. Ackman will know who Andy Strasberg is and the job I am after.

***

Loved the back-page headline of the July 2 *Daily News*: MARIS HOMER

NIPS NATS, 7–6. There was a photo of Maris crossing the plate and grabbing the hands of Mantle and Kubek.

The photo caption reads: "Going like 60. He started the game 27–25 over Mantle but Mick hit two, so Rog had to get hunk, incidentally shelling the Nats, 7–6." Yet the last line of the caption read: "It's still the house that Ruth built, however."

I have two questions, but no one to ask. What does "hunk" mean? And why bring up Ruth's name? It's a long season, and Maris is only at the twenty-eight-homer mark.

July 3

On July 3 Mick and Rog are quoted about calling homers "tonks."

Maris explained, "You know when you hit a ball good, the sound it makes is 'tonk.' Damned if I know how to spell it. It's just 'tonk.'"

Well, guess what? I'm using "tonk" every chance I get and spelling it the way it sounds, thank you very much.

***

It was reported in the July 2 papers that Maris and Mantle were the only two repeaters from 1960 named to the American League starting lineups for the All-Star Game on July 11 at San Francisco and on July 31 at Boston.

A total of 293 votes were cast for each position by major league players, coaches, and managers.

Each leader for every position won by a substantial margin. The closest voting was for third base, where Brooks Robinson received 173 votes to Harmon Killebrew's 105.

Maris had 233 votes, the Detroit Tigers' Al Kaline had 58, and Al Smith of the White Sox had 2.

Nothing against Al Smith, but can someone tell me why he received two votes? Did he owe someone money or was it a joke? Smith is hitting .276 with eighteen homers. It doesn't add up.

July 4

A crowd of 74,246 attended the Yankee-Tiger doubleheader at The Stadium on July 4. It was the largest crowd in fourteen years. The Bronx Bombers won the first game 6–4, which put them in first place, but only for three hours and forty-nine minutes, after losing 4–3 (in which Maris hit his thirty-first homer) in the nightcap.

***

One of Joe Trimble's *Daily News* game notes caught my attention: "You can tell that Maris is becoming as great as Mantle. A segment of the stadium clientele is starting to boo him."

***

In the seventh inning of the first game, four anti-Castroites leaped out of the left-field corner of Yankee Stadium onto the field, bearing a long banner denouncing "Reds." I'm absolutely positive that the reference was not to the Cincinnati ball club known as the Reds.

You don't mess with Yankee Stadium cops. They rushed in, corralled the trespassers quickly, and dragged them off through the bullpen.

As if that wasn't enough craziness, three more young men immediately showed up in the same spot with a painted streamer. Once again, The Stadium's cops grabbed them and escorted them off the field. Then, from near the Yankee dugout, one more group popped up with a sign reading "Cuba yes, Russia no" and were promptly ejected.

It was evident that the left-field cops were fielding the position better than Colavito, who had made two errors earlier in the game.

***

I was just a few days away from entering teenager-hood and noticed, coincidentally, my growing and intense interest in girls with each passing day.

I had always liked girls; not only the way they looked, but when I could get close enough, the way they smelled.

I can't explain it, but soon enough, that simply wasn't enough anymore. I wanted to kiss them and touch them. Admittedly, I had a lot of questions about girls.

Fortunately for me, the summer of 1961 provided me with the opportunity to learn intimate details about girls, because I was in a secret sex club, which my friends and I named "The 9½ Club."

We took the name from what we heard was going on in a low-income area in White Plains known as "the projects."

Rumor had it that youthful couples who lived in the projects would ride the elevator, purposely stopping it between the ninth floor and the roof. They would then "make out." None of the girls went all the way, but I heard some of them would take off their bras.

Our sex club consisted of two other guys, who were taller than me by at least six inches, and three girls. Believe it or not, one was a redhead, another was a brunette, and my favorite had chestnut light-brown hair and thick, dark-brown eyebrows. Most every summer night after dinner, we'd ride our bikes and meet at Parker Stadium on the high school football field.

At one end of the field stood a gigantic metal scoreboard that was two stories high. Since it was the summer, it was an empty shell and easy for the six of us to crawl inside and comfortably sit on the second level, our feet dangling, while not being spotted from the outside. The six of us would sit around talking about sex.

Nobody got too dressed up. We all wore shorts and sneakers. The girls always wore light-colored blouses that were not very fancy, while the guys wore white T-shirts.

Ever curious, we'd ask sexual questions of each other, using clinical terms for private parts like *penis*—never slang words like *dick*. Our hope was that somebody, usually the girls in our group, had answers about sex stuff before it got so dark that we all had to go home.

Since I already knew about girls' breasts, those were no mystery to me or the other guys. Basically, as girls get older, their breasts become larger. So understandably, none of the guys in our 9½ club were interested in talking about breasts. Well, we were interested in talking about them, but had no questions since we knew what we knew but, more importantly, what happens to us when we talk about them.

The girls were a bit more forthright with questions—they wanted to know why and how boys get erections.

There was a moment of silence.

"Simple," I offered. "Sometimes it happens when we think about things."

"Like what?" I was asked by the brunette.

"You know...." I answered.

"No, I don't, which is the reason I'm asking."

Trying to provide insight, I offered, "Well, sometimes if we think about girls in a certain way."

"What way?"

Embarrassed, I reiterated, "You know...."

"No, we don't," the redhead said emphatically.

With the hope that we could move on to the next question, I answered the question by blurting out, "Their breasts."

"Why?"

Instinctively, I answered honestly, "Damned if I know, but it happens."

"Any other times?"

The two other guys looked at me. This questioning was not going away, and although somewhat uncomfortable with this specific subject, I became the self-appointed spokesman for the guys, so I provided, "Yeah, it also happens from friction."

"Friction?" the redhead asked.

"It happens sometimes when a penis rubs up against something else."

"Like your underwear?"

Oh, my dear god, will this ever end, I thought.

"Yes, exactly," another guy offered.

In a hardly audible voice the chestnut-haired girl spoke: "Can you get an erection when you aren't thinking about breasts or from friction?"

The three of us guys immediately offered the same answer knowingly: "Absolutely."

It was obvious that the six of us felt varying degrees of comfort talking about sex. However, with limited knowledge, I don't think any of us guys really knew what we were talking about.

Which was the reason us guys didn't ask questions about the vagina, which is still a mystery to me. The only fact I knew about vaginas was that girls don't have a penis and they sit down to pee.

Nonetheless, I felt like every night I learned a lot about sex from the girls.

Now, in case you're wondering, none of the club members were boyfriend/girlfriend, if you know what I mean. At least I don't think anyone was boyfriend/girlfriend. I, for one, didn't have a girlfriend.

Early on, we decided to make this a clandestine club. We were sworn to secrecy, so I'm not going to reveal the identities of the others, cross my heart and hope to die. But, trust me, it was an education and the girls were really cute.

July 5

In the July 5 edition of *The Sporting News* there was a note that the Yankees front office share of the gate receipts was a check for $42,000 after playing the Tigers in Detroit in the middle of June. It was the largest check ever made out to a visiting team for one series.

***

Til Ferdenzi of the *New York Journal-American* quoted Maris responding to a reporter who said, "I'll bet you lie awake at night thinking how you're going to break Babe Ruth's record."

Roger's response: "I hope you believe me when I say I never give Babe Ruth a thought. Not now or ever. I do not think about the record. I'm just surprised I'm able to hit this many. Thankful, too."

July 6

I found out for an upcoming movie, *That Touch of Mink*, starring Doris Day and Cary Grant, that Universal Pictures has a film crew taking long shots of the Yankees-Red Sox game on July 6. It's not a baseball movie, but includes a couple of baseball scenes.

***

The back-page photos of the July 6 New York *Daily News* show Yanks pitcher Roland Sheldon, who pitched nine innings and got the win over the Indians yesterday by a score of six to zip. Rog is also in the photo holding his next-door locker mate Elston Howard's jersey with his number 32. That number represents Maris's thirty-second homer of the season.

There's also a great photo of a kid who appears to be my age stretching to catch Maris's homer with his glove ten rows back. The caption said he missed it. Tough noogies, kiddo.

July 8

Yanks are in first place by half a game after beating Boston at The Stadium. Dick Young's July 8 "Diamond Dust" column noted: It was Family Day for the players. The tally: seventeen wives and thirty-eight kids. Young added that most of the wives were dolls.

July 9

With Rog hitting his thirty-third homer on July 9 and one game past the midway point of the 162-game schedule, Dick Young's last line in his game story for the July 10 *Daily News* was, "Soon, they'll start taking the boy seriously."

July 10

On July 10, a week before my thirteenth birthday, I read that the Yankees, along with a few other teams, are taking advantage of the fact that baseball games are not being played in their ballparks the day before the All-Star Game. So they are holding tryouts for qualified players ranging in ages seventeen to twenty-three.

I can't begin to imagine what it would be like to have a catch at Yankee Stadium or take a few cuts in, as Mel Allen calls it, "The Big Ballpark."

***

Until I read an Associated Press sidebar on July 10, I was unaware that Clete Boyer, the Yanks' acrobatic third baseman, traded his uniform No. 34 for No. 6 on June 16. However, No. 6 may not be his lucky number as he made three errors in the first two games with the new number.

Baseball player uniform numbers fascinate me, as do lucky numbers. The Yanks gave Hank Bauer's uniform No. 9 to Maris when he joined the team in 1960.

For the past few years, all my buddies seemed to share the lucky number of seven, so naturally I needed a different number. A number that I could own, one that would bring me luck and happiness.

What are the chances that I would find my lucky number as a result of attending Hebrew school? I learned that the Day of Atonement (Yom Kippur) is the only one of God's annual feast days of worship that requires believers to fast for one day. Considered by many Jews to be the holiest day of the year, it begins at sunset on day nine of the seventh Hebrew month. The day is devoted to praying for any sins committed.

I'm told that nine also represents the biblical term "The Fruit of the Holy Spirit," which are Faithfulness, Gentleness, Goodness, Kindness, Patience, Self-control, Peace, Love, and Joy.

And the date of my upcoming Bar Mitzvah is the ninth day of the ninth month.

That's it. I got it! Nine is mine and Roger's.

July 12

In the July 12 issue of *The Sporting News*, there was a double-page Louisville Slugger bat ad for the All-Star Game with facsimile autographs of those players who use their bats on pages 28 and 29. Among the player photos and autographs was a headshot of Maris and his signature.

I stared at his signature and began daydreaming about someday getting his autograph. For me, the best souvenirs are the ones that are not for sale in a store.

You're going to think I'm cuckoo, but here's my reasoning, as I slowly raise my right hand with my index finger pointing at my temple doing slow, small, clockwise circles. When it comes to autographs, I'd rather have a photo of me with the person I met.

Seeing a photograph is more meaningful than an autograph, which to me is essentially a written receipt of having met someone.

But I may be talking out of my ass because I have never met a big-league baseball player. Getting Jim Hegan's autograph on May 13 doesn't count because he's a Yankee coach.

Meeting Roger Maris would be so cool. I can't imagine it.

The ultimate "not for sale" souvenir would be one of Roger's bats, which I know would happen once I can leap tall buildings in a single bound, bend steel with my bare hands, see with X-ray vision, and fly like Superman.

And the ultimate, *ultimate* souvenir would be catching one of Roger's home runs. Since I have never even come close to catching a foul ball at a game, I have calculated that my chances of snagging a Maris homer would be approximately, absolutely, positively one hundred percent never going to happen in a million infinity eons.

***

I'm aware that my fascination with signatures may be extreme. Any time I get a chance to practice signing my name, as if a fan asked me for my autograph, I do it. That means writing my name about a dozen times on a white blue-lined sheet of paper.

Cursive writing is not something that comes naturally to me. I'm a printer. But I'm sure that nobody wants a printed autograph. It has to flow.

Mickey Mantle's *M*s are distinctive and the circle dot over the *i* in Maris is so cool.

There's not a lot of letters in "Strasberg" to make it look cool. But God knows, I've tried about 10,000 times. I've tried a big *A*, a big *S*, and a small *g* with a tail that loops around underlining my entire name.

I'll keep practicing, but I think I need to change my name to something like Marty Morris.

July 13

July 12, the day after the All-Star Game was played in San Francisco's

Candlestick Park, the *Daily News* had a back-page photo of both Rog and Mick chasing Roberto Clemente's drive to the outfield fence that went for a triple in the second inning.

Clemente scored off a Bill White sac fly, and the National League won the contest by a score of 5–4.

Joe Reichler of the Associated Press wrote that Rog spoke frankly about his dislike for the wind and weather at Candlestick Park: "If I had to play here all the time I'd quit." Rocky Colavito agreed with Rog, explaining that if he were traded to the Giants he'd be the longest holdout in history.

July 15

Yanks win 9–8 over the White Sox on July 15 and are tied for first place with the Tigers.

This game tickled me because Ralph Houk started three catchers. Behind the plate was Johnny Blanchard, in left field was Yogi Berra and playing first base was Elston Howard.

Rog had a great game. He hit his thirty-fifth homer, led off the sixth inning with a triple and doubled home the tying run in the ninth inning. He ended up a single away from hitting for the cycle. In the field he threw out two runners, one of 'em at home.

Here's how Rog cut down the runner at home: In the eighth inning, Luis Aparicio was the lead-off batter who as a result of a walk, steal, and wild pitch was at third base.

Nellie Fox hit a fly to short right that Rog caught and threw a strike to catcher John Blanchard, stopping the fleet-footed Luis from tagging up and and trying to score. The throw was a beauty.

Then Jim Landis flied out to Rog in medium-right center, and this time Little Looey dashed to the plate. Rog threw another strike, and, bam, Blanchard caught it on a fly and tagged out Aparicio for a double-play. Inning over.

Maris is more than just a slugger. He's a fly chaser with a strong and accurate arm.

July 17

Today, July 17, was a significant and memorable date in my entire life for four reasons:

No. 1—I finally became a teenager, as it was my thirteenth birthday.

No. 2—On this date baseball great Ty Cobb died at seventy-four years old. Rest in peace, Georgia Peach.

No. 3—Roger Maris clouted his thirty-sixth homer—then lost it in the rain!

How could this be? The Yanks played a doubleheader in Baltimore today, winning the first game 5–0. In the second game, Maris hit his thirty-sixth homer off Orioles right-hander Hal "Skinny" Brown. The *Daily News* described it as a "prodigious blast."

Just three outs away from counting as an official game after four innings (and the Yanks ahead 4–1), the second game was halted because of rain. After waiting over an hour, the umpire crew of Charlie Berry, Joe Linsalata, Frank Umont, and Bob Stewart called the game off.

What would have been Maris's thirty-sixth homer was washed out!

After the game, Roger was quoted about the lost home run: "You can't fight City Hall." At the time I wondered if that homer would be of significance in the home run derby.

No. 4—Baseball's Commissioner Ford Frick committed a grave injustice. At a press conference, he made the following ruling regarding the single-season home run record:

Any player who may hit more than sixty home runs during his club's first 154 games would be recognized as having established a new record. However, if the player does not hit more than sixty until after this club has played 154 games, there would have to be some distinctive mark on the record books to show that Babe Ruth's record was set under a 154-game schedule and the total of more than sixty was compiled while a 162-game schedule was in effect.

Daily News sportswriter Dick Young suggested that Frick consider using an asterisk should a new record be set. It was reported that Frick liked Young's suggestion about an asterisk next to the player's name.

Hold the phone. Record-keeping is supposed to be free of value judgments. A record is a record. Interpretations of records, or how they should be kept, should be settled before or after the season—but not during the season. Frick's ruling upset me.

I found it curious that there was no mention of Babe Ruth breaking the then home run mark in 1919 when he hit twenty-nine homers. That topped Ned Williamson's record of twenty-seven homers set in 1884 playing for the Chicago White Stockings.

In 1884, the schedule was 112 games, compared to the expanded 140 games in the 1919 season that Ruth played. So using Frick's reasoning, Babe didn't eclipse the previous home run record with his 112th game of the season, as he then only had twenty-three homers. He broke Williamson's record in game 134.

Did I mention that Frick's ruling pissed me off?

One more item to make my point, as I can't let go of this. Williamson played in Chicago's Lakefront Park. According to my baseball history books, the distance down the left-field foul line was 180 feet. Down the right-field line was 196 feet.

The rule in 1881 was that any ball hit over the fence was a ground-rule double. But the following season the rule changed, so the same poke clearing the fence was considered a home run.

Williamson's single-season home run record would stand until 1919 when the Babe hit twenty-nine over the fence.

Sounds unfair to me.

Furthermore, and finally, it's not the number of games a player plays but the number of plate appearances that matter. It is possible for a player to be inserted into the lineup late in the game as a defensive replacement and never get a plate appearance.

Therefore, a player could possibly play in 154 games or 162 games and never step into the batter's box.

Even though I'm thirteen years old today, no one listens to me. Okay, I'm done bellyaching.

For those who think that I forgot that today was the twentieth anniversary of DiMaggio's fifty-six hitting streak being stopped in Cleveland, well, I didn't.

***

Admittedly, everyone in my life knew that growing up I was a momma's boy. But it wasn't exactly or totally my fault.

I was a victim of my mother cuddling me, coddling me, humoring me, overly protecting me, and spoiling me at every opportunity so that I would be a happy boy growing up.

What made me happy? Baseball!

Therefore, my mom would go out of her way to incorporate baseball in my everyday life. She would buy me presents such as baseball cards, baseball magazines, baseball books (fiction such as a Chip Hilton sports story, *Payoff Pitch* by Clair Bee, and nonfiction *Lucky To Be a Yankee* by Joe DiMaggio), baseball equipment, baseball souvenirs—and provide a limited amount of money for whatever baseball thing I wanted.

I'm confident you see the pattern.

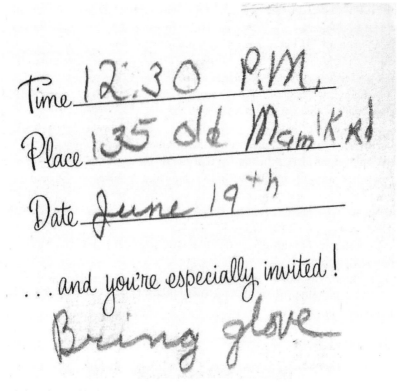

Here's the Catch—My traditional July birthday party—a game of baseball with my friends—had to be celebrated in June each year before they all went on vacation. Remember…you gotta bring your glove.

It was my mother who realized that in order for me to have a birthday party that included playing a baseball game, it needed to be scheduled at least four weeks before my actual July 17 birthday while everyone was still in school and not on vacation.

She did so every June starting when I was seven. It became known as "Andy's Baseball Birthday Party" and the invitations noted that each invitee needed to bring their glove.

It was also on my pretend birthday that my mom would go out of her way to find a baseball-themed birthday card for me. On a few occasions, she'd make one by drawing a baseball scene and printing "Happy Birthday, Andy."

And, yes, it was my mother who helped me decorate my bedroom in a baseball motif that included hanging baseball photos and pennants and painting outfield numbers on the wall, which I thought was perfectly normal. Luckily, she agreed.

My mom was indeed my best friend. When I was nine, I had a bad case of the flu that resulted in a high temperature of 102 degrees. My mom was so concerned about my well-being that for several nights she slept on the floor next to my bed. As if that wasn't dedicated enough, on one of those nights, around three a.m., while I was hallucinating from the high temperature, I woke her up and begged her to play baseball with me.

Right now, right here in my bedroom.

So our make-believe, previously unscheduled baseball game took place under the lights in my bedroom. My mom pitched imaginary baseballs while I swung an imaginary bat.

I announced my at-bat as if I was Yankee Stadium public address announcer Bob Sheppard, complete with the reverberation.

"The next hitter, *hitter, hitter*, is Andy Strasberg, *berg, berg.*"

With each swing, I mouthed what I thought replicated the sound of the bat connecting with the pitched ball from my five-foot, two-inch, sneaky-fast right-handed mom.

That sound was immediately followed by me exhaling to mimic the roar of my thousands of approving fans, cheering me on as I circled my bedroom with my arms up, making sure to touch each imaginary base before I was tucked back in bed and placed my head on a baseball-themed pillow case.

No, I wasn't wearing baseball pajamas, but only because my mother said she couldn't find any in my size.

Eventually, of course, my baseball obsession became my mom's great concern. In the early stages, I'm sure she figured it was nothing more than a little-boy thing. Then she must've hoped it was similar to losing baby teeth…my infatuation would eventually loosen its roots and one day just fall out of my life.

It didn't. My obsession with baseball became more intense, more involved, more—much more—of my life.

For the last couple of years my mother would often voice her concern to anyone who would listen: "If Andrew only knew his schoolwork as well as he knows baseball…because baseball is not going to help him later on in life when he's looking for a job."

However, I was getting too old for a birthday party. Frankly, the parties should have stopped last year or the year before when I turned eleven.

I decided to start a new birthday tradition. One that would actually take place on the date of my birth, July 17. I would call a friend to play catch.

Having a catch with at least one friend is a variation on my original birthday party theme. However, since it was raining on my actual birthday this year, I met my friend Gary Baker in the multi-level parking garage of the Alexander's department store in White Plains.

We tossed the ball around trying to throw hard enough that when the ball hit the other guy's glove, it would make a "smack-*pop*" leather-on-leather sound that echoed off the garage's cement walls.

I'm going to try my best to keep having a catch every year on my birthday as long as I can find someone to play with, hoping I never get too old to play.

July 18

With the Yankees playing the Senators in Washington's Griffith Stadium on July 18, the team scheduled their second annual "Roll Call Night" with a delegation of members of Congress, their families and friends numbering approximately 1,500 as guests.

Before the game, there was a home run hitting contest with three players from each team partnered with an elected official, who each had an at-bat to hit homers.

Maris was paired with thirty-five-year-old Republican Representative Charles E. Goodell of Jamestown, New York. Rog managed to hit one homer of the five pitches he saw.

Fifty-six-year-old Republican Representative Edwin Dooley of Mamaroneck, New York, was partnered with Mickey Mantle, who won the contest by hitting three of five pitches out of the park. One of Mantle's pregame shots hit the last row of the left-field bleachers.

According to newspaper reports, none of the lawmakers reached the fence.

During the contest, when Mantle was batting, there came a steady booing from the Yankee bench. Turns out the boo-er was Whitey Ford, who explained after the contest that he wanted Mick to feel at home. He was referring to the fact that Yankee Stadium fans boo Mantle every time he doesn't homer.

Mantle was awarded a $100 bond for winning and earned a season pass to the remaining Senators home games for his partner Dooley.

Yanks won the game by a score of 5–3, putting them in first place as Mick hit two homers and is now tied with Rog at thirty-five each.

***

The Associated Press ran a story about Willie Mays being broke. Say hey, I'm not a math wizard, but how does a guy make $85,000 a year playing baseball—and approximately $15,000 more for appearances and endorsing products—and wind up broke?

This all came about as Mrs. Mays sued Willie for separation maintenance the day before the All-Star Game on July 11. A San Francisco judge granted Mrs. Mays a $250 weekly allowance. Mrs. Mays said that when Willie is in San Francisco he will stay in the same house—but in a bedroom on the opposite side from hers.

Obviously it's a big house, so I'm sure they'll be safe at home.

July 19

In the July 19 *New York Daily News*, Mantle and Maris were now being compared to Damon and Pythias. I had to look that one up and found that the reference is to the Greek legends who were celebrated friends.

July 20

In the July 20 edition of the *Daily News*, Jimmy Powers wrote about a fan, Wally Wallace from the U.S. Soldiers Home in Washington, D.C. Powers devised a system that rates hitters, which piqued my interest.

Under his system, he assigns 1.6 points for a home run; 1.4 for a triple; 1.25 for a double; and .75 for a single.

With that as a measuring stick, at the All-Star break he came up with Maris trailing only Cash, Killebrew, Mantle, Howard, and Gentile. Maris sits in sixth place in Wallace's calculation rather than fortieth place under the standard batting-average system.

***

Home run hitting contests are popping up all over the place. The Tigers had Rocky Colavito and Norm Cash take their hacks against the Orioles' Jim Gentile and Gus Triandos in a pregame contest on July 20 in Detroit.

Each player was given eight fair balls. Each player knocked three over the fence, so a playoff round took place in which each player was allowed three swings. Triandos connected twice and won the hundred bucks prize money, Cash came in second place, while Gentile and Colavito tied for third place.

I read that Gus didn't play in the game that Baltimore won 4–2, yet there was no reason given for him not playing, which I find curious and frustrating.

***

Project Mercury astronaut Virgil "Gus" Grissom's sixteen-minute suborbital flight aboard Liberty Bell 7 on July 21 made him the second American to travel more than one hundred miles in space.

The flight had a combination of good news, bad news. While Grissom returned safely to Earth, his capsule sank to the bottom of the Atlantic Ocean three hundred miles southeast of Cape Canaveral, Florida, as a result of the escape hatch being blown off.

I am a big believer in the synchronicity of events. A little more than a week earlier, the movie *Voyage to the Bottom of the Sea* was released in theaters across America.

Coincidence? Maybe…but then again, maybe not.

July 22

Dick Young in his July 22 *Daily News* column "Young Ideas" congratulates Frick for his ruling that, for purposes of challenging Ruth's record, the count will stop at 154 games.

Hey, Dick, nothing like picking your spots. Why not also make a ruling about the pennant being decided at 154 games? Young's a brown-noser.

***

As if the added eight games and two All-Star Games plus an exhibition game with the cadets at West Point wasn't enough during the 1961 Yankee season, management scheduled an exhibition game against the San Francisco Giants at Yankee Stadium on July 24.

San Francisco won 4–1 in front of 47,346 fans.

This would be the first time the Giants—or as my dad called them, the "Jints"—played in New York since they left for San Francisco after the 1957 season.

The game was delayed for twenty-two minutes because of rain that muddied the field, which canceled batting practice and a home run contest featuring Willie Mays and Orlando Cepeda vs. Maris and Mantle.

Minor league pitcher Al Downing, according to the newspaper, threw 141 pitches in seven innings. Mick hit a home run in his first at-bat. That homer, according to the wire service, traveled 420 feet. Mays, who was the major draw, drove in the winning runs with a single.

The game was a benefit for sandlot baseball in the metropolitan area, but some of the money raised will also buy equipment for kids in the Triple Cities, the home of the Class A Yankee farm team, the Binghamton Triplets.

July 23

There are times during a Yankee broadcast when I'm not smart enough to understand what Mel Allen is talking about.

For example, Mel was doing the radio play-by-play on July 23 against the Red Sox from Fenway when he said, "I've been getting my Proverbs before my Wise Sayings here."

Then he said: "I must be in the subjective mood today. It's a terrible thing for a fella to come to work with a dangling participle. Especially when the clubhouse doctor is in the clubhouse."

I gotta start paying more attention in English class.

The Yanks lost to the Red Sox, 5-4.

July 24

An American passenger plane was hijacked from Miami on July 24 and forced to fly to Havana, Cuba.

July 25

Los Angeles Times sports columnist Jim Murray began his July 25 column by stating, "Ford Frick isn't the worst commissioner of baseball in history but he's in the photo." You got to love Murray.

***

July 25 was Roger's most productive single-day home run performance. In a doubleheader against the White Sox at Yankee Stadium, he hit two homers in each game, bringing his total to forty while the Yankees won both games.

The back page of the July 26 *Daily News* had a bold, all-caps headline, a beauty: **MARIS HITS 4 HRS.** The sub-headline: **Yanks Thrash Chisox, 5-1, 12-0.**

Honestly, it wasn't until this day that I actually thought that Rog had a solid chance to challenge Babe Ruth's single-season home run record set in 1927.

The Yanks are now leading the American League by a half-game. Dick Young wrote that with forty homers, Maris is running away from Babe Ruth's ghost like a scared kid in a graveyard. Rog was now twenty-five games ahead of Ruth's game pace when he hit sixty.

I loved the line Young wrote: "The people roared; my, how they roared. Seeing a man hit his 40th homer, and realizing it is still July, is a mighty thrill." Maybe I was too harsh in calling Young a brown-noser.

"Diamond Dust" noted that "The M-boys" have banged back-to-back homers for the fourth time this season.

July 26

Talk about what have you done for me lately….On July 26, right after Rog blasted four homers in a doubleheader, the Yankee fans booed him for not running out a slow roller to first base in the first inning. After the game, Maris explained that he thought the ball was foul and when he realized it wasn't, it was too late, as White Sox first baseman Roy Sievers scooped it up and tossed it to pitcher Ray Herbert for the out.

***

Back-up backstop Yankee Johnny Blanchard hit two homers on July 26 in his first two at bats against the White Sox at Yankee Stadium as New York won 5–2.

The last games Blanchard played in were this past Friday and Saturday at Boston's Fenway Park, where he homered as a ninth-inning pinch hitter in both games, thus becoming only the seventh major leaguer to hit four homers in four consecutive at bats.

Crash. Boom. Bang. Pow. Wow.

July 27

The *Chicago Sun-Times* ran a story on July 27 that claimed Yankee players favor Mickey Mantle as having a better chance than Rog to break Ruth's record. In an informal clubhouse poll, Mantle was a four-to-one favorite among the players.

The story says one reason Mantle is given such a big edge over Maris is that he is the better competitor and a more experienced hitter.

I don't believe the story. Yankee teammates may think that, but would never tell a reporter.

***

Two months before my thirteenth birthday on July 17, my parents had asked me what I wanted for a gift.

Easy.

Since I was at the mercy of my parents' adult chaperone edict, I knew that the only way I could attend a game at Yankee Stadium was if my dad took me. I decided we should see the Old Timers game on the afternoon of July 29. Watching the legends who played before I was born and then seeing the current Yankees was my idea of double-delight heaven.

We knew The Stadium would be packed, so we ordered our tickets through the mail. A week or so later, we received two tickets behind the plate. Well, they were behind home plate…but in the Upper Deck in Section 1.

The location was fourteen rows up in the Upper Stand Reserved section. I had sat there a couple times before. From that distant vantage point I could see the entire field from foul pole to foul pole, even though the players looked like teeny, tiny specks.

Only a couple of days before, my dad really surprised me. On the spur of the moment, he decided to take me to see the Yankees play the Chicago White Sox in a night game at Yankee Stadium on July 27.

Although he didn't say it, I'm sure he took me to what would be the first of two Yankee games in a span of three days because he was also paying close attention to the home run race between the M&M Boys and got caught up in the excitement.

On that day, Mick's homer total was at thirty-nine as a result of hitting one out the day before. Rog had forty homers because he had smashed four in a doubleheader against the Pale Hose a couple of days earlier. Interestingly, those were the same home run totals when Mantle and Maris finished the 1960 season ranked first and second in the American League. But it was the other way around—Mick had forty and Rog thirty-nine.

With more than two months left in the schedule, those homer totals for last year were going, going, gone, for sure.

This would be the third game of the 1961 season I attended.

Down by the River—The corner of River Ave. and 157th St. is where the excitement for me begins. *Photo by Don McNeish.*

My dad parked in a lot close to 167th Street, about seven blocks from the ballpark. As we walked down River Avenue toward Yankee Stadium, every time the Elevated 4, D, and B trains—each thundering about thirty feet overhead—went by in either direction, I cupped my hands over my ears and flapped them to create the *wa-wa* muffled sound of the train wheels running on the tracks above. For me, that was very much a "kid thing," dating back to growing up in the Bronx just four miles from where we were.

We passed row after row of street vendors hawking peanuts and baseball souvenirs. But since this was the first of two games this week, I didn't want to seem greedy and insist that my dad buy me something. That rare dose of self-restraint became more difficult when we passed Manny's Baseball Land, which offered at least a thousand things for sale that I wanted. I blurted out, "Dad, let me just look around."

"Not today, son," he said as he kept walking. I didn't put up an argument and felt bad that I had asked.

It was unusual for my dad and me to arrive more than fifteen minutes before the game. But here we were: about to walk into Yankee Stadium almost an hour before the first pitch.

That meant we would watch batting practice, a rare treat. I might have been the only fan who enjoyed watching carrot-topped right-hander Spud Murray of Media, Pennsylvania, throw BP for the Yanks.

There were no lines around any of the six Yankee Stadium ticket booths that resembled small beach-bungalow cabanas on the corner of River

Avenue and 157th Street. My dad approached a booth and asked the ticket seller for the two best he had near third base. I listened and watched closely, knowing that someday soon I would be on my own to buy tickets. I wanted to see how such an important business transaction was done.

The ticket seller quickly pulled two tickets out of his stack of tickets and demanded payment: "Seven bucks."

My dad gave him a ten-dollar bill. In return, he was given two purple-colored Yankee tickets along with three one-dollar bills. He handed one of the tickets to me and we passed through Gate 6 and into Yankee Stadium.

Through The Stadium's catacombs we went, up the short-angled ramp of a dark tunnel. Following a sudden burst of sunlight, we came upon a gorgeous sight—a freshly manicured baseball field in front of the right-field stands and the immense and expansive ballpark of 60,000 seats. *Whoa!*

The transitional experience of walking through the dark tunnel under the stands always intensifies my sense of sight, sound, smell—along with an expansive grin.

Even though the summer sun was still illuminating this part of baseball's universe, the lights were already on, which always made the green, green grass look even greener, if that's possible.

The air was filled with the sweet sounds of leather baseballs getting knocked by wooden bats. Which reminds me: I never could understand how a ball made of twine covered in leather that's hit by a bat made of ash wood could make such a distinctive sound.

The closest I could come to replicating that sound is sucking my tongue in the roof of my mouth and then letting my tongue smack the bottom of my mouth with the short echo sound created by my cheeks. Try it. See what I mean?

Since there was not much for early-bird fans like us to cheer about, the other sound I heard throughout The Stadium was idle fan chatter accompanied by organ music, further enhanced by the aromatic alchemy of cigar smoke and spilled beer.

We briskly walked to Section 18, past third base along the left-field line. A few thousand fans scurried around The Stadium. Most, like me, simply couldn't sit still. My father sat down in pipe-railed Box 286B, Seat 1. Eager to roam, I told my dad that I was going to walk around the majestic stadium as the White Sox took batting practice.

Batting practice produces a sound of bat meeting ball that has a distinct rhythmic cadence. The pace is set by the pitcher throwing to hitters, which reminds me of the tempo of a blacksmith hammering a horseshoe. Maybe ten to fifteen seconds between pitches. *Knock…*fifteen seconds. *Knock…*fifteen seconds. *Knock…*fifteen seconds.

This is my haven, a joyous atmosphere. I'm comfortable and happy. I love being here.

I drifted out to the left-field stands, just past the left-field foul pole into home run territory. Even though right-hander Ralph Terry was on the mound that day for the Yanks, I knew that most of the White Sox hitters in the starting lineup were right-handed.

Batting-practice baseballs would occasionally be belted into the seats. This would set off a mad scramble of fans if a ball wasn't caught on the fly. Like in a pinball machine, balls would ricochet off the concrete floor, wooden seats, and metal handrails that enclosed a group of seats and occasionally bounced up against one of the infamous view-obstructing columns that supported the upper deck.

Since attending my first game in 1957, regardless of where I sat, I wanted to catch a ball hit into the stands. I figured out mathematically that the chances of that happening depended on the number of fans and my seat location, plus my ability to successfully catch a ball.

I figured that for most games there were probably twenty or so balls that were fouled off into the stands during a game and maybe a couple of homers. I computed that number with the attendance and where I was sitting and quickly figured that I had a rat's chance in hell to get a souvenir baseball. At least during an actual game.

During batting practice, however, the odds against grabbing a ball come tumbling down. But here's the caveat: With the batting cage around home plate, it was impossible for a batter to foul off a pitch and have it reach the stands. Yet, with the pitcher grooving them to hitters, a bunch of balls were screaming off bats, landing in the outfield stands with some regularity.

These were known as "BP homers." Many of the batters who hit them were known as one o'clock hitters an hour before the game, meaning they'd hit lots of 'em during batting practice because of the slower, easier-to-hit pitches, but not so much during games.

Left-handed-hitting second-baseman Nellie Fox stepped into the cage to take his cuts. In addition to being a solid defensive player, Fox was notorious among us kids because he always had a big wad of tobacco that puffed out one of his cheeks.

Nellie, known as the "Mighty Mite," began his baseball career in the bigs in 1947—a year before I was born—with the Athletics when they played in Philadelphia.

Fox hardly ever struck out and was more of a "Punch 'n' Judy" hitter. He would choke up on his thick-handled bat and spray the ball around the field rather than try to hit homers. Nellie never swatted more than six homers in any season and perfected the "butcher-boy chop," which is when a batter turns to bunt and then swings the bat, replicating the appearance of a butcher cleaving a piece of meat.

Fox swung at the first BP pitch he saw, and rather than pull the ball he punched a long fly toward left field down the line. With no fielders to catch it, the ball landed on the warning track, taking a high bounce that headed toward me.

My heart began to race as I watched the ball illuminated by The Stadium's lights as it arched against the Bronx blue sky. My legs went wobbly as I tried to steady myself in anticipation of fans pushing me out of the way. I had trouble controlling my elbows, arms, and hands to prepare for the catch.

Somehow, the ball landed in my bare hands. Jesus H. Christ....I got it!

This was truly amazing. Overcome with glee, I ran back to where my dad was sitting and showed him my prized American League baseball.

"Did you catch it on a fly?" he asked.

"Yeah, but it was a ground-rule BP double. I caught it on the high bounce," I said, trying to make the catch more exciting and difficult than it was.

My dad appeared proud as his large fingers wrapped around the ball, holding it as if he was going to throw a cross-seams fastball, and then switching to a curveball grip.

Throughout the game, I kept looking at the ball and smelling it. I love the cowhide leather aroma of a new glove, and now I was falling in love with the horsehide leather smell of a big-league baseball.

In the fourth inning, my joyful Yankee Stadium experience is interrupted by a Bob Sheppard public-address announcement that reminds me the world is a scary place.

"All men of Battery B, Third Battalion, report immediately to their base," he said, referring to the Nike missile installation in Brooklyn. I think about the bomb shelters I've been hearing about.

The Yankees beat the White Sox 4–3. Rog got a couple of hits but no homers. Mick got only one hit, so the home run race of Mantle and Maris was still stuck at forty and thirty-nine.

Hit by a Fox—I still can't believe my incredible good fortune of catching a batting practice ground-rule double hit by Nellie Fox during batting practice at Yankee Stadium. My heart raced as the ball bounced off the left-field warning track and into my trembling, bare hands. I got it!

As we drove home that night, I couldn't stop from staring at my authentic Yankee Stadium BP baseball hit by Nellie Fox.

As carefully as I could that night when we arrived home, I used a pen to inscribe 7/27/61 on the ball. I placed my prized baseball and game ticket in a special plastic trophy ball-holder that was a replica of a baseball infield diamond. I thought this appropriate due to the significant intrinsic value it possessed among my treasured worldly belongings.

July 29

Two days later, July 29, the morning of the Old Timers game, threatening clouds turned into a steady light rain as my dad and I headed back to Yankee Stadium. Because we were hardy New Yorkers, we knew a little bit of rain can't hurtcha.

My dad turned off the Major Deegan Expressway at the Yankee Stadium exit. The traffic was heavier than what we had experienced a couple of days earlier because of the scheduled pregame festivities and the ongoing home run derby between the M&M Boys.

My dad tried to park in the same lot as two days before. But by the time we arrived there was a sign out front—FULL—because about twice as many fans were going to this game.

We knew that BP would be canceled for the active players as a result of the lengthy introductions and the scheduled two-inning game for retired players.

I once again looked forward to the joyful experience of walking into The Stadium, which was now decorated in the upper deck with draped Yankee American League and World Series pennants dating back to 1921.

Before we reached our seats, I knew we were too far from the field to ever think that a foul ball could reach us, which was fine with me now that I owned a big-league baseball. But I did think about it. Our seats were behind the plate in the upper deck.

Now it was obvious the Old Timers game would not happen. The tarp covered the infield.

There would, however, be the formal on-field introductions by Mel Allen. This has always been my favorite part of any Old Timers game.

Mel began by informing the fans that because of the inclement weather, the Old Timers game was cancelled. He announced: "But let's say hello to them right now," which got the crowd to applaud.

The Old Timers' teams were composed of former Giants and Dodgers versus former Yankees, and included familiar names such as Gil McDougald, Leo Durocher, Wally Pipp, Waite Hoyt, Dizzy Dean, Max Carey, Bill Terry, Phil Rizzuto, Allie Reynolds, Irish Muesel, Tommy Henrich, Bobby Thomson, Frankie Frisch, Charlie Keller, Lefty Gomez, Jackie Robinson, Dixie Walker, Pee Wee Reese, Frank Crosetti, Zach Wheat, Joe Dugan, Johnny Sain, Tommy Holmes, Allie Reynolds, Jerry Coleman, and, of course, Joe D.

I've always felt, since I was ten years old, that I could do as good a job as the legendary Mel Allen—if only I was given the opportunity. I watched as "The Voice of The Yankees" began to announce the attending players.

Honestly, it's not difficult to extol the virtues of each old-timer along with mentioning their nickname. My God, I've done it a thousand times in my bedroom holding a hairbrush.

"Ladies and gentlemen, he was the American League batting champ in 1939 and 1940. He won the American League MVP in 1939, 1941, and 1947.

"He hit in fifty-six consecutive games in 1941. He covered the immense centerfield in this ballpark and every American League park with grace and dignity beginning in 1936 and through the 1951 season. He played on thirteen All-Star teams, ten pennant winners and nine world championship teams.

"He was elected to baseball's Hall of Fame in 1955 and his uniform No. 5 has forever been retired by the New York Yankees. Ladies and gentlemen, here he is, the Yankee Clipper...Joe DiMaggio."

Then I'd make the sound of the cheering crowd by opening my mouth, lips protruding, and exhaling in a slow, deep noise.

Once the game between the Yanks and Orioles began, I was disappointed that Maris didn't play. He had a pulled leg muscle.

Nonetheless, the highlight between the Birds and Bombers was Roger's replacement, Yogi Berra, who hit a line-drive homer in the eighth inning. The final score was 5–4 as Whitey Ford notched his nineteenth victory. But more importantly, the win kept the Yanks in first place over the Tigers in the American League pennant race.

The home run race barometer didn't move that day, but Mick was still twenty games ahead of Ruth's 1927 pace to reach sixty homers with Rog twenty-one games ahead of The Babe.

As we headed out after the game walking down the ramp to the street, my dad reminded me that the game was a birthday present. He had another special surprise as part of my gift: "Are you hungry?" he asked. "I'm going to take you for a steak where the players go for dinner."

"We're going," he said with delight, "to Paul Daube's Famous Steak House."

As we walked, my dad explained that for the last thirty years ballplayers had been going there, dating back to Babe Ruth.

We passed the Jerome Cafeteria across the street from The Stadium and turned up 161st Street, walking the three blocks to the restaurant on Courtlandt Avenue. As we got closer, I spotted above the restaurant's awning an arrow-shaped sign that proclaimed "The Dutchman"—which didn't make sense to me. I'm thinking, if this was a pizzeria, would the arrow sign read "The Italian"?

We walked inside to the very small restaurant that had just a few tables covered with white tablecloths. Strangely, the floor was covered in wood shavings, which, according to my dad, was a long-standing tradition. That also didn't make sense to me. This is a restaurant, not a woodworking factory. What do wood shavings have to do with steaks?

The smell of steaks cooking and cigars being smoked filled the restaurant and was delicious. I was trying to imagine where The Babe would sit. We sat off in a corner as my father kept an eye on the door waiting to see which players would be walking in.

I ordered a medium T-Bone steak smothered with onions and French-fried potatoes, which I thought was very "baseballistic."

After twenty-five minutes, three men walked in, including a tall, thin man around fifty years old, wearing a tie and jacket. My father leaned over and in a soft voice identified the slender, well-dressed man. "That's Paul Richards. He's the Orioles' manager and was a catcher in the bigs in the nineteen-thirties and -forties."

I instantly recalled that Richards was featured in a 1957 razor promotion offering a free flip-book—Gillette Finger-Tip Movies—revealing secret baseball signs. I acquired three of these flip-books through savvy swapping of Zorro comics and baseball card dupes.

Once they sat down, I asked my dad if I could get Richards' autograph. But he was one step ahead of me, pulling out a slip of paper and pen from his jacket that he passed on to me.

I approached Richards and handed the pen and paper to him without mentioning that I was at the game that his team just lost and asked if I could have his autograph. He didn't say a word and quickly signed the paper and handed it back to me. "Thank you," I said and headed back to our table.

After dinner, while my dad was sipping his black coffee, he asked our waiter for a menu to take with us. Seeing that, I was puzzled. I didn't think this was a takeout joint like the Chinese restaurant near our home.

After my dad paid the bill, the waiter handed him a Paul Daube's Famous Steak House menu. When we were walking back to the car, my father handed the menu to me and said, "Here's a keepsake from your first big league steak and one of the best restaurants you'll ever go to."

That, I understood.

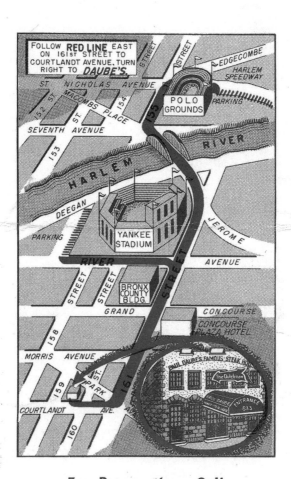

For Reservations Call
MO 9-8282

A Steak Out—After attending the July 29, 1961, Yankee game, my dad surprised me with dinner at Paul Daube's Famous Steak House. I could eat a medium T-bone steak every day from this joint.

You would think that baseball scriveners would be the most intelligent and objective when it came to anything to do with baseball. Most of all when voting players on to an All-Star team. Think again. Either some writers don't take it seriously or are incapable of making informed decisions.

When *The Sporting News* came out with the writers' All-Star Game selection, Maris was chosen to play right field for the American League by fourteen writers. Okay, that makes sense. Coming in second place was Al Kaline, who was named on two ballots. I kinda understand that selection.

But here's where it gets ridiculous. Doug Brown of the *Baltimore Evening Sun* was the only scribe who selected Willie Tasby over Maris. Huh? *Willie Tasby?* Come on, you've got to be kidding me. Tasby's only game playing right field this season was on June 9.

Then there's *Cincinnati Post and Times-Star* baseball writer Earl Lawson, who had Maris creatively selected to play left field.

I wonder if the newspaper ink used in Baltimore and Cincinnati was a bad batch that affected those writers' common sense.

***

Although I was a natural right-handed swinger, I am attempting to make the switch to become a left-handed swinger like Roger. Realizing it would take work, I began practicing in the basement.

I place a Styrofoam ball approximately the size of a baseball on the end of an empty toilet-paper roll that I taped to a milk carton, which sits on a small kitchen step stool. The ball is in my strike-zone height. The whole shebang cost me zero.

As I begin to concentrate on moving my feet, hands, and hips toward the ball that isn't moving—while holding a plastic bat near my left shoulder—I take a stride with my right foot toward the imaginary pitcher throwing to me.

Trying to mimic Maris, I take a slight upper-cut swing. Sometimes, I swing over the ball, missing it completely, which produces a swish-of-air sound.

More than I'd like, my uncoordinated left-handed swing is under the ball, and my plastic bat smashes the cardboard toilet-paper roll. The Styrofoam ball drops to the floor.

Step, swing, roll my wrists, hit the ball, ending my follow-through while holding the plastic bat with my right hand, à la Maris. Then I pick up the ball and repeat.

To speed things up I need to call Ray Simons, who I guarantee would be more than willing to replace the ball on my makeshift batting tee after each swing.

Ray is my best friend. He is my favorite person. What qualities are necessary to be my favorite person? That we laugh a lot and talk about stuff. Important stuff like girls, baseball, school, and stuff like that.

July 31

The second All-Star Game was held in Boston's Fenway Park on July 31.

Rog came in second with 233 votes compared to Norm Cash who had 235 votes. Mickey had 230 votes.

Rog pinch hit in the fourth inning for Johnny Romano and popped out to second base. The game resulted in a 5–5 tie, called because of rain.

So, historically, it's a "kissing your sister" game.

***

I found it most interesting that *Sports Illustrated* weighed in on the home run derby with an article by Walter Bingham in their July 31 issue.

It starts off with an ominous line that tickles me—yet at the same time troubles me—when it alludes to the many players since 1927 who hoped to reach Ruth's sixty-homer mark: "Seriously attacked it, but for every June challenge there has been a September reckoning."

Bingham states that the relationship between Mantle and Maris is "outwardly cordial," implying that they don't get along. He then notes that both players are brooders and inclined to sulk. This is the first mention I've seen of their friendship not being genuine.

He acutely analyzes Frick's announcement about the 154-game schedule by providing a possible scenario of Maris hitting his sixty-first homer in game No. 154 while Mantle only has fifty-nine. Eight games later, Maris doesn't hit another homer while Mantle hits three more, making Maris the home run champ in the mind of Frick, but Mantle the single-season home run champ. Bingham brings up a good point.

His other point I found interesting is this: In 1927 a ball that bounced into the stands was counted as a home run. The *Sports Illustrated* writer explained that historians have confirmed that Ruth didn't have any bounce homers but—and that's a big *but*—Maris has already bounced two balls into the stands, which would have been homers in 1927.

AUGUST 1961

"The Hebrew Hammer."

August 1

The day after the All-Star Game, it was reported in a number of August 1 newspapers that Roger Maris, owner of the most important leg injury since Ann Pennington twisted an ankle, was asked how it felt.

"So-so," he replied with a dour face. "When I started to bear down running a couple times yesterday (at the All-Star Game in Boston's Fenway Park), I could feel the muscle giving, so I let up and took it easy."

Not having any idea who Ann Pennington was, I asked my mom. She quickly responded that I should ask my father. I was smart enough to drop the subject right then and there because since it's a girl and the subject is legs, Pennington must be a touchy, "hands off" subject.

Once again I learned that any time one parent tells me to ask the other parent, I figure nothing good is going to come out of me following up to get an answer.

***

The *Daily News* ran a story that Negro baseball players throughout the league will ask the team owners for a one-roof policy in Florida so that every member of a ball club can stay at the same hotel. This is the policy that the Yankees began in spring training this year.

***

It was also announced today that Ralph Houk was suspended for five days, which equals seven games, and fined $250 for his July 30 outburst and brush with ump Ed Hurley over a third-strike call on Clete Boyer in a game with the Orioles. Yankees coach Frankie Crosetti will handle game strategy like he did for a June game in Detroit when Houk was sidelined for the same offense.

***

Parties are divided into two categories—kids parties that are filled with giggles and usually happen during the day, or those early evening parties that my cool friends and I call "make out" parties. When Johnny Mathis' *Greatest Hits* album is played, the lights are dimmed or shut off and it's kissy-face time.

Unfortunately, since I don't have a girlfriend, that's my cue to move to the middle of the room and do my Johnny Mathis impression while holding an invisible microphone and mouthing the words to "Chances Are."

When do I know when to stop? When I hear, "Sit down, will ya Pot."

August 2

In the second game of an August 2 doubleheader against Kansas City at The Stadium, Rog was hit on his right leg by Art Ditmar in the third inning. After the inning was over, Maris came out of the game and was replaced by Hector Lopez.

Now I'm getting concerned about the "Maris Injury Jinx."

Two years ago, while with the Athletics, Rog was stricken with appendicitis. Last season, Rog hurt his ribs trying to break up a double play. Both times his plate productivity was greatly diminished.

Fingers crossed that he's okay.

***

As I read through the August 2 *Daily News*, I was stopped in my tracks by another scary headline on the front page: N.Y. AIR UNITS TOLD: BE READY. Underneath was a smaller head: Guard and Reserves Alerted.

This was done as a precaution if the Berlin crisis worsens. The Cold War is getting warmer.

Below that scary story was a photo of sixty-two-year-old Del Webb, co-owner of the Yanks, and his forty-year-old new bride, Toni Ince.

The Yanks are in first place over Detroit by two-and-a-half games.

***

Meanwhile, in *The Sporting News*, the same Del Webb was quoted by Braven Dyer of the *Los Angeles Times* as selecting Mantle to top Ruth's mark. According to Dyer, Webb said, "It stands to reason that I would pick Mantle over Maris." He backed up his comment by explaining, "Mickey hits right and left. Maris has trouble hitting left-hand pitching."

For crying out loud, why the hell is Webb shooting off his mouth like that? This infuriates me. Isn't he supposed to do the parent thing and have no favorites?

***

In the first game of an August 2 doubleheader at Yankee Stadium, with the bases full of Yanks in the bottom of the ninth and the score tied at five, Bob Cerv hit a dribbler to third base. Rog was on third base and dashed for home plate. The August 3 *Daily News* back page printed five multiple stop-action photos by photographer Frank Hurley of Maris sliding into home plate as Joe "Piggy" Pignatano, the Kansas City Athletics catcher, couldn't hold on to the ball.

The newspaper photo captures home plate ump Joe Paparella with his right arm up signaling "out" as Maris slides into home plate and the baseball bounces away.

Paparella must have changed his call to "safe" after seeing either the ball squirt away from Pignatano or the *Daily News* photos.

***

Sid Gray of the *New York Post* has written a series of articles titled "A Man Named Maris." I enjoyed reading them because there were a lot of new tidbits.

Like the time Rog was playing outfield for the 1954 Keokuk Kernels in Iowa and ran through a fence to make a catch and held on to the ball.

Or when on August 23, 1959, the Kansas City Athletics held a Roger Maris appreciation ceremony between games of a doubleheader. How did Rog show his appreciation? In the first game he came up in the bottom of the ninth with two outs and KC trailing the Washington Senators by a score of 7–3 with bases loaded. He struck out.

Details on

ROGER MARIS
Appreciation Day

Sunday, August 23

With Appreciation—On August 23, 1959, Kansas City showed its appreciation for the Athletics' right fielder, Roger Maris, with a ceremony between games of a doubleheader at Municipal Stadium. With two outs in the bottom of the 9th, the bases loaded, and the A's trailing the Senators 7–3, Rog came to the plate and could tie it up with one swing. Unfortunately, he struck out to end the game.

I also read that the Athletics—before trading Rog to the Yankees—almost traded him to the Pirates for Don Hoak, Bill Virdon, and a pitcher.

But the prize surprise was uncovering that the four-room apartment Roger shares with Bob Cerv and Mickey Mantle is located on Seventh Avenue in Jamaica, Queens.

Oh, if I could only drive, have a car—and a driver's license—I'd find that apartment.

August 3

Another plane hijacking attempt on August 3, this time in El Paso, Texas. Is hijacking becoming an epidemic?

August 4

An unidentified baseball writer, who for good reason was not identified, refers to Maris as the "Fargo Flailer" in an August 4 article.

Puh-*leeze*. Give. Me. A. Break. *Fargo Flailer*. I don't think this is going to catch on or be a challenge to the Babe's Sultan of Swat moniker.

***

The August 4 edition of the Passaic *Herald-News* has an entry form for baseball fans to predict the number of homers Mick and Rog will hit this season.

The fan who guesses correctly wins a $100 U.S. Savings Bond. Second prize is a $50 bond and third is a $25 bond. On the chance that there is more than one winner, the tiebreaker is the fan who comes closest to predicting the total paid attendance when Mantle hits his last homer of 1961. The deadline for entries is midnight, August 9.

What is the fascination with guessing games? Is it a chance to win something or just the fun of playing? I get it. I get it. The newspaper is not interested in Maris and Mantle. It's a get-rich-quick scheme for those people who enter the contest, but the bigger payoff is that the newspapers get more sales from people wanting to read their paper or subscribe.

I'm done with guessing contests.

August 5

In the August 5 game at Yankee Stadium, Maris squeeze-bunts against the Twins for the first run with two outs in the third. The Yanks win 2–1. It is noted that Rog averages a homer every 9.6 at-bats, compared to Mantle at 8.6 and Ruth at 9.

***

Did you know that five million glasses of Ballantine beer are enjoyed every day? It's true. Mel Allen told me that during every Yankee radio broadcast.

***

Babe Ruth's adopted daughter, Dorothy, who lives in Wallingford, Connecticut, was quoted in an August 5 Associated Press story about Mantle and Maris's assault on her father's home run record. "I would not mind if the record was broken because it is good for baseball." She added, "I think the Babe would like to see it broken too."

August 6

I had to laugh when time was called in the third inning of the first game of the doubleheader at Yankee Stadium against the Twins on August 6. The delay was caused when the chest protector worn by plate ump Ed Runge deflated and needed to be pumped up with air.

Rog had eight at-bats in the game that went fifteen innings, but only managed a single. Mick had four knocks that included two bombs and now has forty-two homers. Yanks won the first game 7–6, then took the second game 3–2.

***

Sportswriter and cartoonist Murray Olderman of the Newspaper Enterprise Association began his August 6 "Between You 'n' Me" column by quoting a sarcastic Mickey Mantle before a game. "Got a new idea," said Mantle, waving a bat and sidling along Maris, "for a picture…Let's pose me and Roger together—for a change," with a wink.

August 7

A surprise bunt by Maris drove in a run to tie the Angels in the bottom of the third at The Stadium on August 7. After the game, reporters asked Houk, who was back managing the club after his suspension, about the Maris bunt. He said it was Maris's own idea.

On the other side of the ball, with one out, Rog dropped a fly ball off the bat of Billy Moran in the ninth. Two batters later and the game was over, as the Yanks won 4–1.

It may be too late in the season, but with Maris bunting more often he may have decided to change direction and—rather than hit homers—go after the record for most bunt singles in a season. Just kidding.

August 8

August 8 is the only Ladies Night on the Yankees' schedule, and the Angels are in town.

It's eighty degrees. I'm listening to the game in my bedroom with the lights out and a sheet over my head. The game is tied 4–4 going into the bottom of the tenth inning.

With Tony Kubek on second base after a lead-off double, Maris's sudden-death single wins it for the Yanks against the Angels. The Yanks are now in first place by three games.

**

A Keene Shot—The 1961 Los Angeles Angels' batboy, Scott Keene, brought his camera with him on a 17-game road trip that began at Fenway Park on August 2 and concluded in Washington, DC, on August 17. Yankee Stadium was part of the team's itinerary. Keene snapped this photo just as Rog turned around. In the background is a young Howard Cosell explaining something to a Yankee player hidden behind Rog.

Joe Trimble wrote in his August 8 *Daily News* column "Quips 'N' Quotes":

Unlike Commissioner Frick, I have no reverence for Ruth or his records. Now that Frick has tried to throw a protective cloak over the Babe's 60-homer mark, I hope both Maris and Mantle smash 61 or more.

I'd like to see them do it in 140 games but if it takes 162, or 163 counting the tie the Yanks played, then it will still be a record as far as I'm concerned. And the day that one of the M-squad does it, I hope I'm there to lead the cheering.

Instead of demeaning the records of today's players by putting an asterisk (for apprentice allowance, maybe) on their records, Frick ought to put a prize for the ball. He should offer $1,000 to the fan who gets it, then have the ball bronzed and mounted at Cooperstown. If it happens to be an inside-the-park home run, then let him give the money to charity.

As a fan, Frick is entitled to his opinion. As commissioner, he has no right to tamper with any records. The record is for a season, not a specified number of games.

Well, that appears to be sound and logical reasoning.

August 9

In the August 9 *Sporting News*, the front-page story details the paper polling sportswriters across the nation for their views on the 154- vs. 162-game schedule as it pertains to the home run record.

They were also asked if the Frick rule should be confined to Ruth's home run record or to others' records, such as Lou Gehrig's 184 RBIs or Bob Feller's 348 strikeouts?

Thirty-seven reporters supported Frick's decision and eighteen were opposed.

I thought for sure that Jimmy Powers of the *Daily News*, who is fifty-eight years old and ten years older than my dad, was going to side with Frick. Boy, was I surprised.

Powers' quote was well thought-out and articulate. He wrote:

I feel that the 154-game restriction is ridiculous. There have been so many changes through the years, playing habits, the physical layout of the parks, encroachments on space in so many ways that the record book would be full of asterisks if we tried to reduce everything to a certain era and 'freeze' it.

As a member of the Baseball Writers Association of America class of '26, I took a back seat to no one in pitching typographical rose petals at the Big Bam. But all that is past. Life does not consist of wallowing in the past or peering anxiously at the future. We should appreciate life as it is now, whether it offers little or much. Life is now, this day, this hour and it is probably the only experience of the kind one is to have. Mantle, Maris et al are the players who are in the parks now. Let us sit back and enjoy them.

Also printed in this edition of *The Sporting News* were the results of their survey at the All-Star Game in Boston where seventeen players from the two circuits were asked about Frick's edict. The vote was twelve to five in favor of the Frick decision.

***

The Sporting News printed players' comments in the August 9 issue as to how they felt about Frick's ruling:

Stan Musial: *It is a good rule. Baseball records were based on 154-game schedules.*

Man, is he wrong. Stanley, check out the number of games Ned Williamson's single-season home run record was set in 1884 compared to when Ruth broke it in 1919.

Dick Donovan: *I think it's a fair way to make the record for 154 games.*

Warren Spahn: *It should be the way the commissioner ruled.*

Roy Sievers: *Why shouldn't it count if one of the players breaks it in a 162-game schedule? I'd like to see it done without restrictions.*

Ernie Banks: *I don't like the ruling.*

Al Kaline: *Whoever hits 61 homers is entitled to the record, no matter how many games it takes.*

Jim Gentile: *If it's going to be done, it should be done in 154 games.*

Dick Stuart: *I do think it should count if it's made in the regular schedule.*
Yogi Berra: *I can't comment on the subject.*
Whitey Ford: *I'm all for the commissioner's decision.*

***

After the August 9 day game at Yankee Stadium against the Angels, Maris, Luis Arroyo, and Bob Cerv made an 8:30 p.m. appearance at Bat-A-Way, located at Surf Avenue and West Sixth Street in Brooklyn's Coney Island. The *Daily News* reported that Arroyo hit a longer drive than Rog in the batting cage.

It's not that I have anything against Brooklyn…well, that's not exactly true, because growing up in the Bronx my parents impressed upon me that Brooklyn is a million miles away. I was told that people from the Bronx don't go to Brooklyn, and people from Brooklyn don't go to the Bronx.

***

According to a United Press International story, Maris and Mantle get the green light to go for homers, not for batting average. Who gave them permission is not mentioned, but I gotta believe it was Houk. "The funny thing about it," Maris said, "is that I'm not doing a thing differently since I got the okay."

August 10

The August 10 *Daily News* back page has a picture of the mayor of Fargo, North Dakota, Hershel Lashkowitz, with a street sign "Maris Avenue." It should be "Maris Line Drive."

There's a lot of bandwagon traffic on Maris Avenue, if you get what I'm driving at.

***

With baseballs landing on the other side of outfield fences at what seems to be an alarming rate, one of the theories is that balls are "livelier" this season compared to previous seasons.

Jimmy Powers of the *Daily News* points out in his August 10 column that, unlike golf, major league baseball does not employ an independent firm to test baseballs to see if they are manufactured consistently.

Powers quote American League President Joe Cronin as telling him: "Manufacturers of the American League baseball inform us no changes have been made in the making of the baseball."

***

The Associated Press reported that Roger's boyhood parish, Cathedral of St. Mary in Fargo, North Dakota, was rooting for the Yanks right fielder. Msgr. L. J. Arrell requested divine intercession, first asking his flock to say a prayer "for the sick of the parish and the boys in the service," then adding, "and for those who don't think it's too silly, for Roger Maris."

***

An August 10 Associated Press story written by James Marlow details how JFK has approved a plan by which Vice President Lyndon Johnson would assume presidential responsibilities should Kennedy be unable to fulfill them.

I know what that means. If Russia drops a bomb on the White House and JFK is injured or killed, Johnson will take over. That thought and this news story petrify me because I get the sense this is inevitable. I think I'm going to puke.

***

My mother was never short in offering me advice. She seemed to always have a saying that summed up the point she was making.

That's what I thought about when I read the August 10 Associated Press report in which the Federal Trade Commission issued a warning that if an individual doesn't actually use a product, he should not endorse it. This all came about as a result of Mickey Mantle endorsing Ponca City milk, a product he doesn't drink.

I could hear my mom say, "Mickey, honey, there's no use in crying over spilled milk."

August 11

People who wouldn't know the infield fly rule from a ground-rule double, or first base from the keystone bag, are now reading the sports section—maybe for the first time ever—and getting interviewed about the home run record.

An August 11 *New York Times* survey of fans in the city revealed that thirty-nine out of fifty want to see Ruth's record broken. I wish I had a dime for every fan that uttered, "Records are made to be broken."

***

The Yanks were in Washington, D.C., on August 11, playing the Senators at Griffith Stadium, when in the fifth inning Rog faced Pete Burnside and hit a pop foul that should have been caught. But second baseman Chuck Cottier and first baseman Bud Zipel got their signals crossed, and the ball dropped between them. Maris hit the next pitch out of the park for home run No. 42.

This one kinda makes up for that July 17 homer that was washed out.

August 12

For the umpteen millionth time, I heard the most-overused saying in baseball during the Yankees' August 12 radio broadcast from D.C.

Mel Allen began by stating the obvious, "The Senators are in the throes of a losing streak and the Yankees in the height of a winning streak. Percentage-wise, they both have to come to an end. Today or tomorrow."

Wait for it. Here it is: Allen finished with, "That's baseball."

That makes the umpteen millionth and one.

Meanwhile, Mickey Vernon, the Washington Senators' manager, borrowed a page from Lou Boudreau's infield shift playbook when Rog came to the plate in Griffith Stadium.

Get this, Danny O'Connell, the third baseman, moved over to where the shortstop would normally play.

Bob Johnson, the shortstop, was positioned where the second baseman would be.

Second baseman Chuck Cottier was playing short right field.

Bud Zipfel, the first baseman, was deep at first base.

Chuck Hinton, the left fielder, was almost in center field.

But too bad, Mr. Vernon, all of your position jockeying didn't work.

Rog hit a Dick Donovan pitch for a high, towering home run over all of them for his 43rd homer, which tied up the game at 1-1.

Unfortunately, the final score was 5-1. The Yanks lost.

August 13

Mick and Rog, both sore and weary, skip batting practice prior to the doubleheader against the Senators in Washington on August 13.

This is the point in the baseball season that players call the "dog days of summer," for god knows why. I'm guessing it has to do with the fact that dogs have been involved with baseball almost from the beginning.

They were team mascots and good-luck charms in the 1880s. That ball-park staple—the hot dog—was first sold at ball games by Harry M. Stevens, probably the day after teams started providing mustard and needed something to put it on.

Here's my lousy impression of a stadium hawker: "Hey, getcha hot dawgs here," or, "Who wants a red hot?"

I'm pretty sure my introduction to baseball came as a result of a dog story from the *Dick and Jane* books when they played ball with their dog, Spot.

"Look," said Dick.

"Look at Spot."

"Spot wants to play ball."

Perhaps these are the mid-summer "dog days" of the season because baseball is riddled with dog-related terms: Getting the collar, throw him a bone, being dog tired, players barking at umps, our shortstop dogged it and, as a result, he's in the manager's doghouse, and my puppies are hurting.

It wouldn't surprise me to read game accounts that noted pitchers who weren't on a short leash had managed to strike out nine batters in a game. You score that K9.

Doggone it, Mickey Mantle's father, Mutt Mantle, must have been a dog lover, don't-cha think?

I always howl when my cousin Tony proves to me that his dog, Sandy, knows baseball because not only does he eat dog food from Red Heart, the same company that in 1954 produced baseball cards, but when Sandy is asked who holds the home run record for a single season he barks, "Rooff."

That's one smart puppy.

***

Making news on August 13, East Germany placed a barbed-wire curtain across the East-West Berlin border. Because school is out, I can't eavesdrop on the smart kids' conversations to find out what the hell is going on over there. I have to keep reading newspaper accounts.

***

The August 13 *Daily News* column, "TV Alley Tells Me..." is about the goings-on behind the TV screen. It is written by Charley Channel, which I'm sure is a phony-baloney name. Channel used Roger Maris's name to compliment the president of CBS-TV, stating that "Jim Aubrey is considered the Roger Maris of the internationally famous Westhampton Mallet Club."

Now I've heard everything. There's a club of adults who hammer square pegs into round holes?

***

The night of August 13, at 9:35 p.m., a twenty-five-minute CBS radio show titled "The Battle of the Batters" had former big leaguers Rogers Hornsby, Waite Hoyt, Hank Greenberg, and Charley Berry discussing Mantle and Maris going after Ruth's home run record. I missed it.

August 14

On page 1 of the August 14 issue of the *New York Times* was a lengthy story by Howard M. Tuckner, headlined: "Is the 1961 ball livelier than the Ruthian variety?"

By the third paragraph I lost interest. The scientific tests show that maybe it is, and maybe it isn't. *Ugh.* Very unscientific. Uninformed writers are now filling newspaper space with baseball articles that have no insightful conclusions.

Here's how the test was conducted: Balls were shot out of a Remington Arms Ram cannon in Central Park. One ball used was from 1927, one from 1936, and one plucked from a current batch at Yankee Stadium.

The testers were Foster D. Snell, Inc., consulting chemists and engineers at 29 West Fifteenth Street.

Edwin L. Parker, president of A. G. Spalding & Bros. had a say in the article, explaining that their American League baseballs' coefficient of restitution (I looked it up—that term indicates the rebounding quality of the ball off a surface) has not changed in the past thirty-five years.

Well, that was a waste of ink.

***

In an August 14 story written for Hearst Headline Services, Bob Considine, who penned the book *The Babe Ruth Story*, quoted Maris making ref-

erence to Mantle's uniform number: "If anybody breaks it, it will be No. 7."
Also included in the story is a quote from Mantle: "I hope Maris hits 80 this
year," then added, "...and I hit 81."

Considine's credibility drifted out the window for me when he incorrectly noted that Maris is in his third year with the Yankees. How difficult
would it be to check and realize that it's Roger's second season with the
team?

I was amused to learn that Bill Ackmann, head of the Yankee organiza-
tion's special services department, is the ghostwriter for Mantle's fan mail.
In contrast, Considine mentions that Maris personally responds to letters.
Considine pointed out one such letter that Rog wrote to a delinquent South-
ern boy—who was identified as Vernon—touched the youth's family, who
sent Roger a detailed thank-you note.

Considine covers all the bases when he quotes Babe's widow, Claire: "I
hope the Babe's record is never broken."

The story also included the players' business manager, Frank Scott, who
realizes their earning potential: "I figure whoever breaks it can come up
with at least fifty good $10,000 deals over the next two, three years."

That equals "half a mil," if my math is correct.

***

JFK asks Congress on August 14 for $73.2 million for stockpiling food
and medical supplies as part of the nation's expanding civil defense program.

I walked into our kitchen and looked on the shelves where we store
canned food. There's maybe three days' worth of food. Without question, I
am certain that a nuclear attack from Russia is going to happen.

***

I spent a quarter on the August 14 issue of *Newsweek* because there was a
drawing of a batter that appeared to be Mantle swinging a bat on the cover.
"HOME RUN YEAR TARGET 60" appeared in bold black block letters.

Dick Schaap wrote the article. He provided a couple of interesting tidbits
about Maris that were new to me:

Mantle, Maris, and Cerv pay a combined rent of $251 a month for their
four-room apartment in Queens.

Maris buys $100 suits from Simpsons of New York.

While growing up, Maris was paid $1 an hour for laying railroad ties.

I honestly have no idea why I'm collecting these pieces of what many consider useless information.

***

August 14 is a hot Monday summer afternoon. With Mantle and Maris tied at forty-five homers each, a contingent of New York baseball writers played their annual baseball game at Bear Mountain State Park, which is about fifty miles north of Yankee Stadium.

One of the two teams is comprised of writers who will cover the Mets, the newly formed National League team, in 1962. The other is made up of Yankee scribes. Both team rosters shared certain similarities. The players were not very talented, overweight, and slow-reacting. These guys make their living writing about the game, not playing it.

Dick Young displayed his baseball savvy by managing the Mets team and by not playing.

There was, according to newspaper accounts, a lot of huffing and puffing, pulled muscles, a stable of charley horses, sore shoulders, and a bruised sternum.

Shortstop Murray Olderman of the Newspaper Enterprise Association won the Edward McKeever Trophy, named after the former Brooklyn Dodger owner. It's the game's Most Valuable Player award.

The most noteworthy play of the game was turned in by Yankee broadcaster Mel Allen who played center field. While going after a towering fly ball hit by *Daily News* cartoonist Bill Gallo, Mel fell flat on his face, which resulted in the artist being able to touch 'em all.

I'm guessing that the sportswriters were reminded that baseball is a lot harder than it looks.

Taking turns umpiring the bases were Ralph Houk, Yogi Berra, Ralph Terry, George Weiss, and Roy Hamey.

Final score was 9–6, the Mets writers beating the Yankees writers.

***

The names Mantle and Maris are now showing up in non-sports *Daily News* columns such as "Around the Dials" by Matt Messina, "What's On?" by Ben Gross, "On the Town" by Charles McHarry, "Dream Street" by Robert Sylvester, "Hollywood" by Hedda Hopper, "News Around the Dials" by George Maksian, "Little Old New York" by Ed Sullivan, "The Inquiring Photographer" by Jimmy Jemail, and "Voice of the People" by readers.

✳✳✳

Theater-goers in the northeastern states are being treated to the baseball-themed musical *Damn Yankees* starring Julie Newmar, who plays Lola.

The play is obviously about the Yankees of the 1950s but also includes the devil, greedy temptations, a sexy girl (Lola), and an old guy who wants to play for the Washington Senators.

The play opened August 7 and ran through August 12 at Storrowton Music Fair in West Springfield, Massachusetts.

It's a Piece a Cake—At 3 years old, I began attending sleepaway camp for two summer months. It was at camp that I celebrated my 4th birthday with a cake. Not only did I need help in cutting the cake, I also needed help in making my bed, getting dressed, and tying my shoelaces in the morning.

Then the play moves on to Westbury Music Circus in New York's Long Island, where the curtain goes up August 15 for a week's run, followed by the Meadowbrook Dinner Theatre in Cedar Grove, New Jersey, from September 12 through September 17.

Truth be told, I love musicals. My appreciation came about as a result of attending summer camp. Kids would put on shows for the enjoyment of counselors and other campers.

My first role I played was Nana the Dog in the camp production of *Peter Pan*. Of course, I was a natural for the role, having years of experience crawling around on all fours, simply because, at four years old, it wasn't that long ago when I had learned to walk. Crawl on all fours? No problem! That's how I used to get around.

In addition to my gifted acting, Nana and I were the same size, so the costume was a perfect fit.

What a thrill it was for me to make my acting debut in this historic tale, brought to life on Camp Kiowa's recreation hall stage in front of 120 campers. Truth be told, in my heart, at the tender age of four, what I really wanted to do was direct—my true calling.

It should also be noted that Nana's dialogue was not merely that of a common stage dog that would simply bark, *"bow wow"* or *"ruff ruff."* Not at all. I'm proud to state that I memorized my lines—*"woof! woof!"*—right away. I was, as they say in theater parlance, a "natural."

There were, however, a number of things that transpired in the play that puzzled the inner me. I was always led to believe that Peter was a boy. However, in our production, that role was given to a girl. Odd.

To make matters more confusing, everyone, including boys, was required to wear facial makeup...eye shadow, rouge, and lipstick. Theater people, go figure.

And I still don't understand why this show was called a play. At four, with all my years on this earth, the word "play" meant having a catch, coloring, stacking blocks or rolling Silly Putty...fun stuff like that.

Moments after the show was over, everybody in the cast wrote their names on the backstage wall near the ceiling. I was asked to participate in this age-old Camp Kiowa tradition. However, I declined, not out of modesty but because at four years old I didn't know how to write.

In that same summer, one experience left me somewhat unclear as to its purpose. Our bunk—comprising six guys, all of whom were older, with the exception of my buddy Artie Rasher—was planning a raid on the girls' bunks in the middle of the night.

Shower Shot—One weekend every summer, the fathers of Kiowa campers would play the counselors in a softball game. My dad was always the hit of the game because he played without a shirt and in his boxer drawers. As my dad would say, he could "hit the piss out of the ball," sometimes landing over 300 feet away, near the bunkhouse where boy campers took showers.

Here's how that escapade unfolded: I am sound asleep when a bunkmate wakes me up and says, "Get your robe on, put on your moccasins, and grab your flashlight. We're going over to the girls' campus." I am in a sleepy fog but I can see the light from the other guys' flashlights cutting through the bunk's darkness.

I hear someone ask what time it was and the answer: 12:30 in the morning. I follow my bunkmates' instructions, and we sneak out of the bunk, making sure the screen door does not loudly slam shut, as it did all the time.

I should have worn sneakers because my moccasins are immediately soaked from the middle-of-the-night dampness of the grass. I try to keep up with everyone as we make our way over to the girls' side of camp. We cut through the woods so no one would see us.

We get to the girls' bunk and slowly step in. Our flashlights are aimed on the floor. Then, when we're inside standing in the middle of the sleeping girls' beds, one of my bunkmates yells, "Raid!" We all shined the lights on the girls as they're startled out of their sleep.

I have no idea what we are doing, why we are doing it, or what to expect. Some of the girls scream, "Oh, my God, it's boys!" And that's it.

We leave, running back to our cabin, giggling like...little boys.

Summer is full of life's mysteries when you are four, but that was nine years ago. My life is all about baseball now.

August 16

The August 16 *Journal-American* began a series describing how New Yorkers could do if Manhattan was attacked. The headline: "IF WAR COMES TO N.Y. WHAT WOULD YOU DO?"

A guy who attends Hebrew school with me said exactly what I was thinking: "That's scary shit, man."

As if we weren't frightened enough, the Civil Defense sirens were tested throughout the five boroughs today at eleven a.m. Of the city's 733 air raid warning sirens, eleven failed to work. In Queens, six were silent; in Staten Island, three, and in Manhattan and Brooklyn, one each. Bronx sirens had no trouble at all, which meant that Yankee fans had the best chance of surviving an attack.

***

It's Very Claire Now—At 26 years old, the attractive Claire Hodgson, a model and part-time Broadway actress, married Babe Ruth in 1929. At the time of the 1961 M&M home run derby, she was considered the First Lady of Baseball, and the obvious proxy for the Bambino, who passed away in 1948. *Photo courtesy of the Stevens family.*

Three hours later on August 16, it's Babe Ruth Day at Yankee Stadium as the Yankees play the White Sox. Babe's widow, Mrs. Claire Ruth, is in attendance. Rog hit the first pitch he saw for his forty-seventh homer and then the third pitch in his second at-bat for another home run, No. 48.

With the score 4–4 going into the bottom of the ninth inning, Yankee Bob Cerv pinch hits for pitcher Ralph Terry with the bases loaded. Warren Hacker replaces Turk Lown on the mound and faces Cerv, who gets hit by a pitch that ends the game. Yanks win 5–4 and are still in first place by three games.

***

The Senate was in full debate on foreign aid later that August day when it was interrupted for an important announcement from Senator Milton R. Young (R., N.D.). He proudly announced that, "Roger Maris, a North Dakota farm-raised boy, hit two more home runs today." He then added, "We expect him to break the record by quite a few." He then sat down beaming, according to the news report.

***

The Associated Press ran an August 16 story about Rog with the headline: "Maris Angry About Foul; Missed 47th." It seems the White Sox nipped the Yanks 2–1 behind the four-hit pitching of Juan Pizarro on August 15. In the sixth inning, Maris's drive went foul by no more than four inches—according to Rog.

The article described Maris's swing as he "pole-axed a curve." Rog said that at the last second the ball hooked foul. "That makes it about five or six near-misses I've had this year—that I know of," he complained.

Frustrated Rog kept talking. "They say those things even up. That's a lot of hogwash. They never do. All I know is they owe me about four because I got two homers this year on drives that hit the foul pole."

***

With all that was going on today, August 16, there was one "Yankee Fan" who was not interested in the Maris-Mantle home run chase.

It was a three-year-old brown gelding named "Yankee Fan," who won the six-furlong race at Rockingham Park and paid $7.60, $3.80, and $2.80 across the board at the Salem, New Hampshire, race track.

August 17

Newspapers across the country ran an Associated Press story on August 17 quoting Rog as saying, "I want the dough, not the record." This quote made me realize that baseball is not just adults playing a game. It's a business. Team owners are hoping to make money; radio and TV stations that carry the games are hoping to make money; and so are the players. So I propose that Rog earns a salary next season that equates to a thousand bucks for every homer he hits this season. Sounds fair to me.

**

Arthur Daley's column, "Sports of the Times," in the August 17 edition of *The New York Times*, is exactly what I was searching for. Daley wrote about the casual conversations around the batting cage. He titled it "Overheard at the Stadium."

He quoted both of the M-boys. Mickey wanted to know why photographers take the same photos day after day of Rog and him before the game. He guessed that something must happen to the negatives that made them unprintable. After posing, Mick politely but sarcastically asked the photogs if they wouldn't mind if he took batting practice.

Daley went on to note that White Sox left-handed pitcher Frank Baumann complimented Rog after seeing one of his shaving commercials on TV.

Two infielders, Clete Boyer and Billy Goodman, talked about the time Jimmy Piersall was at bat and hit a grounder that went through Clete's legs and it was scored as a hit, implying that Piersall intimidates official scorers.

Rog might have had the best line in the article as conveyed by Daley when he saw White Sox catcher Bob Roselli walking toward him at the batting cage. Rog announced that Roselli resembled a brewery truck slowly lumbering along.

**

In the sixth inning of the August 17 game with runners on first and second and no outs, White Sox manager Al Lopez moved his shortstop some ten feet on the other side of second base when Maris came to bat. Rog pulled the ball on the ground to the first baseman who got the force out at second base, while the runner on second moved to third. Mantle pushed the run home on a fielder's choice. The Yanks won 5–3 and now lead the American League by four games over Detroit.

**

Luis Arroyo received an anonymous letter on August 17, postmarked from Jersey City. It read: "I don't like Puerto Ricans. The next time you go to the mound in Yankee Stadium I'm going to shoot you through the head."

This is baseball. It's a game to be enjoyed. It's upsetting to read that people get so worked up they have to threaten the lives of others. The letter is now in the hands of authorities and precautions are being taken to protect Arroyo.

August 18

I think my parents have subscribed to *Life* magazine since before I was born. Along with public school's *Weekly Reader*, *Life* has to be one of the world's most recognized publications. To many readers, it is the nation's foremost authority on cultural trends and the state of the American experience.

The August 18 cover has a color portrait of Maris and Mantle shoulder to shoulder in front of an out-of-focus black-and-white photo of Babe Ruth. The title: "Will Yank Sluggers Smash 60 Homers? The Real Odds."

***

I'm noticing stuff in newspapers about music now. Saw an ad in the August 18 *Daily News* proclaiming that Paul Anka's recent three-day appearance at Freedomland broke all attendance records. That had to be as a result of puppy love for Anka or his song "Puppy Love."

August 20

According to the August 20 "Diamond Dust" notes in the *Daily News*, Mudcat Grant of the Indians used unorthodox methods to stop Maris by feeding him nothing but breaking balls in an August 18 game. Cleveland won 5–1. I gotta ask: If it worked, what's unorthodox about that? It doesn't appear that sportswriters read what they write to see if it makes sense.

***

There's a whole lotta shakin' going on as rock 'n' roll concerts are scheduled all over the Tri-State area this summer. One of these days I have to attend one of those boss concerts. Murray the K and his Swinging Soiree are at Palisades Amusement Park. The groups playing are The Shirelles, The Belmonts, Jordan and The Fascinations, Bruce Bruno, The Halos, and Tina Robbins. Clay Cole's Record Wagon is also appearing at Palisades, starring Tommy Hunt, Cathy Jean, and Brian Hyland.

Palisades' admission is only thirty cents, and every Wednesday and Saturday a thousand bags of assorted Bonomo Turkish Taffy are given away free.

And there's always the opportunity to swim in the world's largest outdoor saltwater pool.

Splash. *Wheeeeeeee!*

***

Maris was asked on August 18 by Frank Eck, the Associated Press sports editor, if the bat he's using this season compares to the bat he used in 1960. Rog explained that last season he used a bat with a thicker handle. This season, on occasion, he's using a Bob Cerv model that is one inch longer and two ounces heavier than his thirty-three ounce, thirty-five-inch bat.

***

My dad's friend Mel Goetz sent me an entry form for another Mantle-Maris guess-how-many-home-runs contest. This one was from the August 19 *Express & News* of San Antonio. Winner gets fifty bucks. The contest runs until September 15 and the earliest postmark that comes the closest wins.

I could use the money, but I'm not playing.

***

Roger Maris is hitting home runs on what seems like a daily basis, and I'm enjoying every minute of it. A lot of players are belting homers this season, but none, thankfully, at the same pace as Rog.

For me, what makes Maris's homers distinctive from those of other players is the smoothness of his ever-so-slight, uppercut swing from the left side of the plate. Rog completes his swing after he connects by holding his Louisville Slugger with his right hand extended behind him, while his left arm trails across his chest as if to underline his swing for emphasis.

For decades, the traditional follow-through swing for all players was to hold the bat with both hands after taking a cut at a pitch.

After I had spent hours studying photos of Rog's swing, my vivid imagination convinced me his swing resembled that of an ancient Asian saber-fighter.

"Aa! Sou?"

Saber-fighter Swing—After connecting for his 61st homer of the season, Rog completes his swing by holding his Louisville Slugger with his right hand extended behind him, while his left arm trails across his chest as if to underline his swing for emphasis. *Photo courtesy of National Baseball Hall of Fame.*

As a result of media attention, even non-baseball fans know that Maris is a prodigious home run hitter, but they tend to overlook that he's also an incredibly skilled outfielder. After all, playing the outfield is more than just catching a ball in the air. Roger excels in all the components necessary for patrolling American League outfields.

To begin with, Rog gets a jump on the ball as soon as it is hit. Instinctively, he calculates in which direction to move. In for a shoestring catch just before the ball touches the tippy-tip of grass blades. Back for an over-the-shoulder catch of the ball in the webbing of his glove. Or to his right or left, gliding without hesitation.

He possesses God-given quick-burst acceleration to sprint toward the ball to catch it.

Without using a slide rule or logarithm, Rog determines by the sound of the bat meeting the ball how far it will travel, and by the ball's trajectory where it is going…but more importantly, where it will land.

Throwing the ball after catching it in the air or scooping it up off the ground is the beginning of a well-executed outfield play. There are three basic elements involved with a throw from the outfield. Fortunately, Rog is one of the best at each element: accuracy, arm strength, and knowing where to throw the ball.

Hitting a home run can win a game, but so, too, can catching a ball headed for the gap or gunning down a base runner trying to take an extra base.

For me, one of the most dramatic plays is when an outfielder catches a ball headed over the fence, turning what appears to be a sure home run into a harmless out.

When I play fungo home run derby with Bobby Serrano, I derive more enjoyment from pulling a would-be homer back from going over our agreed-upon homer demarcation that could be an actual fence, wall, hill, or—if it's February—a plowed snow bank, rather than hitting a homer myself.

Often it is said that baseball is played on both sides of the ball, offense and defense. In the seventh inning of today's August 19 game against the Indians at Cleveland Municipal Stadium, Rog demonstrated his defensive prowess.

Cleveland's Willie Kirkland hit a Whitey Ford pitch that was headed over the fence in right field and would've tied the game. At the moment the ball was hit, Rog "got on his horse" and went after it.

Once Maris arrived in front of the right-field chain-link fence, he looked up, timed his jump with an extended left arm and glove hand three feet beyond the top of the four-foot fence to snag the baseball for an out.

It would also appear that today was not a great offensive day for Rog, as he went hitless in five at-bats. Yet the box score indicates that he helped the team by grounding out to first base and moving Billy Gardner to third in the top of the tenth inning. Gardner eventually scored on an Elston Howard single that put the Yanks ahead by one run.

The next day, August 20, the newspaper featured a photo of Maris's defensive gem. It was crucial to beating the Indians in ten innings as Whitey Ford notched his twenty-first win of the season.

Love his swing, enamored even more with Rog's catch.

***

The *Pittsburgh Press* begins promoting their Mantle-Maris Home Run Derby contest on August 20 with an article detailing the rules and an entry form to fill out and mail in.

The deadline is August 29 and the prize money is $500. In the event of a tie, the money will be divided up equally to all winners.

The entry form has eight questions to be answered:

Will Mickey Mantle break Babe Ruth's record of 60 home runs in 154 games?
YES or NO

Will Roger Maris break Babe Ruth's record of 60 home runs in 154 games?
YES or NO

*How many home runs will Mickey Mantle hit in 154 games?*_____

How many home runs will Roger Maris hit in 154 games? _____

How many home runs will Mickey Mantle hit in 162 games? _____

How many home runs will Roger Maris hit in 162 games? _____

How many runs batted in will Mickey Mantle have for 162 games? _____

How many runs batted in will Roger Maris have for 162 games? _____

The decision of the judges shall be final.

***

Maris played for the Indianapolis Indians in 1956 and was very popular with the fans, so I was not surprised to see the *Indianapolis News* run a home run contest in their August 20 edition. The first prize was $50, second $25, and third $15. There were also five additional prizes of $3 each.

***

The Yankees were in Cleveland playing a doubleheader against the Indians on August 20.

During the Yankee radio broadcast, Mel Allen outdid himself in calling Roger's 49th homer.

It was the first game when Maris came to bat in the third inning against Jim Perry.

Allen stated, "Now, Roger Maris." Then he added, "And listen to the crowd," which I could hear at home.

I figured Rog had a lot of fans at the game because it was there in 1957 that he began his big-league career with the Tribe.

Earlier, Mantle had homered for his 46th of the season. Allen explained that the Indian fans wanted to beat the Yankees, but they also wanted to see home runs from both Mickey and Rog.

The count went full, 3 and 2, when Rog connected with the payoff pitch.

Mel provided listeners with his classic home run call, "There's a deep drive to right field. It is going, going, it is gone. How about that! Number 49. It's 5 to nothing, New York."

But Mel ain't done. By no means. In his next breath, he added, "Dial M for Murder."

Then, from out of the clear blue sky, Allen quickly added, "Thunder and lightning have struck in Cleveland."

Continuing the theme, he finished with this clever reference, "And Hale's on the bench," acknowledging the Yanks' newly acquired Bob Hale.

That cracked me up.

I thought, "How does he do that?"

Mel's the best. Period.

Final score, 6-0, Yanks win.

It was the fourteenth time the M&M Boys connected in the same game this season.

Twenty-five minutes later, the second game began but not before a young woman leaped onto the field and circled the bases.

I think the Indian fans are eerie but what do you expect when their ballpark's home plate is a sacrifice fly from a lake of the same name.

Phil Rizzuto was back on the mic doing the play-by-play as the game started.

Top of the second. Nobody out. Mantle on first. Berra up. The count went to 2 and 2.

Indians catcher Johnny Romano caught Gary Bell's next pitch, called ball three by plate ump Cal Drummond. Not happy with the call, according to Phil, Romano held his mitt where he caught it to make sure the ump knew it should've been called a strike.

Next pitch, Yogi hit a liner to right center that Jimmy Piersall snagged, a great catch, and then doubled up Mantle, who thought the ball wouldn't be caught and was past second base, halfway to third.

Johnny Blanchard followed Berra in the lineup, but before he can see a pitch a fan fell out of the right-field bleachers and onto the field, albeit in foul territory. The game was delayed as they removed the fan by stretcher to get him checked out.

Scooter said the fan looked okay as he appeared to be talking a little bit.

It wasn't said, but my guess is the fan had one too many beers.

As if that wasn't enough, in the eighth inning, another fan from the right-field stands approached Jimmy Piersall in the outfield, and when the centerfielder wouldn't shake his hand, the fan made a threatening gesture. The result: Piersall attempted to kick him in the ass as the fan ran off.

Cleveland has more than its share of crazies.

***

From the August 20 *Daily News* "The Inquiring Photographer" by Jimmy Jemail: "The News will pay $10 for each question accepted for this column. Today's award goes to Lionel E. Trotman, 466 Quincy Street, Brooklyn."

The Question: Will the home run competition between Mantle and Maris be good or bad in the long run for the Yankees?

Lt. Bernard F. Toner, New York Police: *Good. Mantle is at last showing the potential that baseball men knew he had all along.*

Edward W. Weed of Connecticut: *If Maris and not Mantle breaks Babe Ruth's record, the long range effect will be bad because Mantle is the best all-around player in baseball.*

Caro Austin, manager of Atlantic Beach Club: *Bad. If Mantle or Maris breaks Babe's record, fans won't be talking about them and the Yankees the way people have raved about Ruth and the Yankees over the years.*

Bert Fink of the Bronx: *Good. Mantle and Maris are pros. Baseball is their bread and butter.*

Edward M. Carlough of Livingston, NJ: *It's the best thing to happen to the Yankees in a long time.*

F.K. Clausen of Smithtown, NY: *The rivalry may become bitter because Mantle has the disadvantage of batting behind Maris.*

***

For the first time in twenty-nine years, the Negro American League All-Star Game has moved out of Chicago's Comiskey Park to Yankee Stadium.

Held in conjunction with the sixty-second Grand Lodge Negro Elks Convention, the event included a three-hour parade down Nicholas Avenue past 145th Street in Harlem that, according to a newspaper report, 100,000 turned out to see.

The starting pitchers for the August 20 game were Satchel Paige of the Kansas City Monarchs for the West, and for the East, the Birmingham Black Barons' Pete Gilliam.

It was Paige's first appearance at Yankee Stadium since 1953 when he was with the St. Louis Browns.

Satchel was quoted how he would pitch to Mantle and Maris: "You keep the ball low and away from those boys, and they ain't gonna pull it." Then he added, "Did you ever see Ted Williams pull the ball on me?" Satchel paused briefly, then answered his own question: "You did not."

Fourteen years after Jackie Robinson broke the color barrier in the major leagues, many believed that the Negro leagues were headed for extinction. There are now only four Negro American League clubs operating: the Kansas City Monarchs, Detroit Stars, Birmingham Black Barons, and Raleigh Tigers.

The pregame entertainment had the players in a three-legged race, egg-and-spoon race, circling the bases against time, and catchers throwing into a barrel for accuracy contest.

Someone should give a prize to the fan who correctly guesses Satchel Paige's age as he will be the headliner at Yankee Stadium.

Playing in front of 7,245 fans, Paige pitched a strong three innings for the West over the East.

The final scoree had the West victorious by a score of 7–1, with Paige named the game's Most Valuable Player.

August 21

One of the most overlooked but noteworthy dates in the Yankees' 1961 season was August 21. Here's why:

Taking advantage of the team's off-day in Los Angeles, Mantle, Maris, and Berra went to the Universal Studios movie lot to shoot a cameo as themselves in the romantic comedy *That Touch of Mink*, starring Cary Grant and Doris Day. Delbert Mann was the director.

Their scene was filmed on Sound Stage 37, where the 1925 silent movie *Phantom of the Opera*, starring Lon Chaney, was shot. Today's scene took place in what is supposed to be the Yankee dugout at Yankee Stadium during a game. The movie was scheduled for release in June 1962. The scene lasts less than a minute.

Seated in the dugout, the players are wearing their Yankee uniforms, with Day and Grant in civilian clothes. L to R: Maris, Day, Mantle, Grant, and Berra.

Former American League umpire Art Passarella played the role of the home-plate ump. The scripted dialogue begins after he calls a strike on an unidentified Yankee batter:

Doris Day: *Strike? Hey, ump, shake your head, your eyeballs are stuck. Well, it was a ball. It was this far from the plate.*
Ump: *Little lady, will you let me umpire this game? You've been on my back all night.*
Day: *Mickey, you saw that pitch. It was a ball, wasn't it?*
Mantle: *It looked like it.*
Ump: *You're out of the game, Mantle.*
Day: *What? Roger, how'd that pitch look to you?*
Maris: *It could've missed the corner.*
Ump: *You're out, Maris.*
Day: *Yogi?*
Berra: *It's a perfect strike. The ump was right.*
Ump: *I don't like sarcasm, Berra. You're out of the game, too!*
Day: *You can't do that!*
Ump: *Lady....*
Day: *Where's the manager?*
Grant: *I think he's hiding.*

***

On August 21 my father decided to reward me for all the time and effort I was putting in studying for my Bar Mitzvah. In the early afternoon, he took me to a local amusement park, Playland, in Rye, New York, which was less than ten miles from our house but light-years away in fun.

I love this place.

It has rides; a fun house; shooting galleries; burgers, fries, and pizza; bumper cars; and an old roller coaster that looked like a stiff wind could knock it over. Playland also has a batting cage, where you can hit hard rubber baseballs off Iron Mike pitching machines into the Atlantic Ocean.

It is also the only place where I could buy black-and-white baseball exhibit cards, which were the size of postcards.

It was there, as we walked around, that my father spotted a tall man strolling along the boardwalk with a boy who looked to be around my age. Suddenly we stopped.

"I don't believe it," my dad whispered to me. "What are the chances?"

I had no idea what he was talking about.

He pointed and asked, "Andrew, do you see that man over there with the kid?"

"Uh, huh" I said.

"Do you have any idea who that is?"

"No," I answered.

"That's Hank Greenberg. He was a great home run hitter for the Tigers in the 1930s. He's Jewish, and they called him 'The Hebrew Hammer.'"

Well, now he's got my attention.

"Hank Greenberg," my father continued, "was the last player to challenge Babe Ruth's sixty home run record. In 1938 he hit fifty-eight homers."

I was mesmerized. How is this possible? The Hebrew Hammer here in Playland?

With no further explanation, my father handed me a pen and paper, and we went up to Hank. My father introduced himself and then me. He explained to Greenberg that we were at Playland because I was working on learning my Torah portion for my Bar Mitzvah, and he felt that I had earned a break.

Hank smiled with approval. We shook hands and Hank introduced his son, Steven, to us. I asked for Hank's autograph, and he graciously signed the small slip of paper for me.

Honestly, how was this possible that I would meet one of the greatest home run hitters in baseball in 1961 in the heat of the home run chase? I am certain that there is a God, and he loves baseball just like me.

***

Roger and Pat Maris's new son—who will eventually be named Randy—is born today, August 21.

***

It was splashed all over every newspaper that Senator Milton R. Young of North Dakota told the Senate on August 21 that it is "now apparent that Roger Maris who has hit 49 homers will break Babe Ruth's home run record."

Senator, thanks for your prediction, but I suggest that you stick with shaking hands and kissing babies.

***

Joe Trimble of the *Daily News* has labeled the home run derby as the M&M "Beltathon." How cool is that?

***

In preparation for the anticipated windfall or—quite possibly—avalanche of endorsement opportunities, Roger has incorporated himself in Missouri. In other words, Roger is a business unto himself.

Once again, I have no idea what this means or what its advantages might be. Other than that Rog is going to be making a lot of money through product endorsements, speeches, and personal appearances.

August 22

Dick Young begins his August 22 "Young Ideas" *Daily News* column with, "D-Day for the M&M Boys is September 20. That night in Baltimore, the Yankees will play Game 154."

He quotes Maris on his point that the focus should not be on the number of games, but on the number of at-bats a hitter has.

"If I break it," he says, "then it's OK to say that I should do it in 154 games because I have more at-bats than did Babe Ruth."

What Rog is saying makes sense to me. It's not the number of games but the at-bats. In other words, if you go into a game for defensive purposes in the ninth inning and never get an at-bat, you are still given credit for playing a game.

Young supports Rog's argument. He says that nobody was counting at-bats when two players came close to Babe's sixty homers. The first was Jimmie Foxx when he hit fifty-eight homers in 1932 and had 702 plate appearances in 585 at-bats; the second, Hank Greenberg who, in 1938, had 681 plate appearances in 556 at-bats.

Young also states the baseball commissioner believes that the game is in transition with further expansion coming in the next five or six years. That there will be three major leagues or two leagues with twelve teams split into six-team divisions, and that baseball will return to the 154-game schedule.

***

The Empire State Building sold for $65 million on August 22. The seller: Henry Crown. The buyers: Lawrence A. Wien, Peter L. Malkin, and Harry B. Helmsley. The price, which does not include the land, is the highest ever paid for a single building.

I imagine King Kong has got to be turning over in his grave.

***

Dave Lewis, sports editor of the *Long Beach Independent* newspaper, refers to Mantle and Maris as Murder and Mayhem in his August 22 column, "Once Over Lightly." He points out that fans are divided 75–25 in favor of seeing the homer record broken. Baseball players are split about 50–50.

Old-time players, of course, don't want the record eclipsed, period.

***

On August 22, Associated Press newspapers around the country are quoting former Yankee pitcher Ryne Duren, who was traded to the Angels on May 8, as saying: "I think Maris will understand it when I say I'm pulling for Mantle to break the mark. I hope he smashes the record—but not off me."

***

The Yankees were in Los Angeles beginning August 22 to play a three-game series in Wrigley Field against the Angels. Wrigley has a stated capacity of 20,450, so the Angels had to notice that six days earlier on August 16 the Dodgers played the Reds in the Los Angeles Coliseum and drew 72,140 fans.

There must have been some consideration given to moving those Angel games approximately two miles west from 425 East 42nd Place to 3911 South Figueroa Street. Imagine the number of fans who would have flocked to the colossal Coliseum to see the Bronx Bombers swinging for the out-of-whack fences in a facility that was constructed in 1923, the same year as Yankee Stadium.

The field was originally intended for sporting events such as football and the Olympics, so it had to be refabricated for baseball to accommodate the Dodgers in 1958. The left-field fence screen was 60 feet high and only 201 feet down the line, while the right-field foul line is now 333 feet and 380 feet in the right-field power alley, with a 6-foot-high wire fence.

***

The Rajah hits homer No. 50 on August 22. He is the ninth man to smash that number of home runs in a season. This is the fourteenth time it has been accomplished.

So who was the last player to hit his fiftieth homer in the big leagues before the calendar turned to September? Ruth? Nope. No one. Rog stands alone on this and the number of games is not a factor because the measurement is the number of calendar days.

The first time Ruth reached fifty homers was in 1920 when he clouted fifty-four. In 1921 he hit fifty-nine. In 1927 he hit sixty, and in 1928 he hit fifty-four.

Of the four times Ruth hit fifty or more homers in a season, the earliest occurred on September 3, 1921.

For those who count games, this was the Yanks' 124th game for Rog, and it was the 125th game for Ruth back in 1921. So there.

August 23

More phony-baloney politicians inserted themselves into the American League pennant and home run races. On August 23, New York Governor Nelson Rockefeller responded to a bet Michigan Governor John B. Swainson proposed on July 20 that he would wager a bushel of Michigan apples that the Detroit Tigers would win the American League pennant. Not to be outmaneuvered, Rocky gave Swainson 3–1 odds—in bushels of New York apples—that the Yanks would win the pennant.

Additionally, Rockefeller noted that the Tigers needed a little bolstering, so he sent each member of the Tigers a pound of New York State butter and a dozen eggs.

The New York governor proclaimed that if either Maris or Mantle hit a record sixty-one home runs, he would send Swainson "one of our prize New York dairy calves."

***

Bill McGrotha mentioned in his August 23 *Tallahassee Democrat* "From the Sidelines" column that Ed Sullivan is willing to pay $10,000 for an appearance on his TV show to whomever breaks Ruth's record. The greatest amount paid by Sullivan for an appearance went to Elvis Presley, who according to newspaper reports, was paid $50,000 for three appearances a few years earlier.

***

The *Indianapolis News* noted in the August 23 edition that so far they have received 291 entries to its contest as to which player will break Ruth's record. The newspaper provided a tally showing that Rog leads with 78 entries, while Mickey only has 13.

So I'm guessing that the 291 entries must be a typo…or someone at the paper knows all about the "new math" that schools are teaching kids like me.

***

After nine innings, the Yankees and Angels are tied at six runs each on August 23.

In the tenth inning, Maris hits a triple off the center-field fence 412 feet from home plate—his third triple of the season—driving in Billy Gardner. Ron Moeller comes in to relieve Jim Donohue on the mound and promptly uncorks a wild pitch as Maris scores. The Yanks hold on and win 8–6.

***

Sid Hartman, sportswriter of the *Minneapolis Morning Tribune*, penned a story on August 23 about baseball "bird-dog" scout Frank Fahey. He noted that Fahey's Cleveland Indians scouting report dated August 12, 1950, was the first one he filled out about Roger, who was playing in the regional American Legion tournament in Dickinson, North Dakota.

Fahey, who is currently scouting for the Dodgers, was quoted: "Roger weighed 150 pounds and stood about 5' 8" as a 15 year old." He reports that it was Owen Martinez of the Cubs who a couple of years later brought Rog—who had put on twenty pounds—to Chicago for a tryout in Wrigley Field. That didn't end well because they told Roger he was too small.

Eventually Fahey proudly recalls that Cleveland signed him. Then he talked about Roger's success this season. "Maris hasn't surprised me at all. He had all the tools even as a Legion player."

August 24

The *Kansas City Times* reported on August 24 that in Raytown Missouri, where the Maris family has lived since 1958, the Cosentino Brothers market is following Roger's season by announcing over their public address system every time he hits a homer.

The article also pointed out that Rev. John R. Quinn, Maris's pastor at St. Bernadette Catholic Church, recalled that in 1959 Rog served as chairman of a drive to collect $125,000 toward construction of a new church.

***

I knew it. I saw it coming. On page 5 of the August 24 *Daily News*, there was an ad promoting a home run guessing contest that paid out $1,500 every week starting on Sunday, August 27.

Everyone is looking to make a buck on M&M's assault on the home run record. Speaking of M&Ms, it doesn't take a rocket scientist to figure out that any day now the manufacturer of the popular chocolate candy will somehow take advantage of M&M making headlines around the country.

***

Joe Trimble of the *Daily News* points out on August 24 that unless Mantle gets moving, soon it will be a one-man race against Babe Ruth's ghost, as Maris needs eleven homers in thirty games.

***

The home run race is quickly spreading to sections of newspapers. In the August 24 *Daily News* there's a double-truck, full-page ad for "VIM, the World's Largest TV & Appliance Chain." The ads' headline is "61 Home Run VALUES!" with a line-drawing of a right-handed batter's follow-through swing in the lower right-hand corner.

Items offered in the ad include a 13-cubic-feet, two-door, auto-defrost Frigidaire refrigerator for $214.88, a 23" Admiral consolette TV for $169.95, a deluxe portable sewing machine for $39.95, and a Roto-Broil can opener at $8.88. No down payment, up to three years to pay.

***

With each passing day, as rock 'n' roll becomes more important to me, I can't help but notice announcements for live music shows.

On page 284 of the *Daily News*, there's an ad for Murray the K's Big Boss Holiday Show at the Brooklyn Paramount located at Flatbush and DeKalb, with headliner Jackie Wilson. The show, starting August 25, will run for twelve days. Also on the bill are Jerry Lee Lewis, Etta James, The Chantels, Curtis Lee, The Cleftones, and The Belmonts.

Brooklyn is far away in another universe, plus the cost of tickets is over my head. I'm going to have to be content with just listening to Murray the K's Swinging Soiree on 1010 WINS.

A-a-h bay, woo, a-a-h bay, woo. Kuhwasawasawa!

***

According to a sidebar in the August 24 *Daily News*, bettors aren't panicked by the way Roger Maris and Mickey Mantle are hitting home runs. Oddsmakers quote a 13–10 price that Rog won't beat Babe Ruth's sixty homers in 154 games. The man-to-man price against Mick surpassing the Babe is 2–1. To date, Rog has fifty round-trippers while Mickey has forty-six.

***

I'm starting to read articles comparing baseball in Ruth's time to baseball now. It's impossible! Everything is different. I did, however, enjoy reading a story about Ruth hitting lots of homers off mediocre pitchers. Many argue today that, with two more teams added this season, Maris is facing pitchers who aren't big-league quality.

August 25

Roger's father, fifty-year-old Rudy Maris, is a mechanical supervisor for the Great Northern Railroad. He was quoted in an August 25 Associated Press article as saying, "Roger is a thriller, that's what I think he is. The constant pressure on that guy….Gee, I don't know how he does it."

***

The August 25 *Daily News* was filled with Mantle and Maris items even outside of the sports section.

"The Inquiring Photographer" question was asked along Henry Street in Brooklyn: Are you looking forward to the possibility of a Yankee-Dodger World Series?

Charles D. D'Acoli of Queens said yes. He'd prefer the Yanks play Los Angeles rather than Cincinnati.

Meanwhile, Ed Sullivan's "Little Old New York" column reported that the price for a TV appearance by the M&M duo is now $15,000.

Wait, there's more. Nick Manero, who owns Manero's in Connecticut, my favorite steak restaurant, was also quoted in Sullivan's column: "Remember when MM used to mean Mickey Mouse or Marilyn Monroe instead of Mantle-Maris?"

Plus, there's a photo of Roger's father, Rudy, pointing to the newspaper headline of his son's fiftieth homer. When asked for a prediction of how many homers Roger would hit, Rudy declined but offered that he hoped his son or Mantle would break the record.

August 26

The front page of the August 26 *Daily News* has a photo of Rog with wife Pat looking at their new son, who is still unnamed. The caption reads, "The Pride of a Yankee."

In Dick Young's August 26 "Young Ideas" column, he reprinted a letter from Frank Jaroncyzk, a fan from Uniondale, New Jersey, who has a question:

"Suppose, at the end of 154 games, Maris has 61 homers, then does not hit another. And suppose, at the end of 154 games, Mantle has only 59, but hits 3 more so that at the end of 162 games, he finishes with 61. By your way of thinking, Maris's record will stand ahead of Mantle's. Is this fair? Please use logic not sentiment."

Young's response: "Have you watched a horse race where a nag comes from far back, and barely misses at the wire? He would have won it if the race was 10 yards longer, people say. Same thing here. The race is being run over 154 games, according to Commissioner Frick. If Maris does it he will have broken Ruth's record. If Mantle then passes him, Mick will have established a record for 162 games. That's as logical as I can get."

***

Maris must have signed a deal with Cooper Tires, because since May

1 friends from around the country are sending me newspaper ads with Roger's picture over the headline, "Maris Gets 50% Boost."

The ad also notes that Cooper Lifeliners are built with a new super mileage Turbo-Tread that is 9% wider and 9% deeper than other new car tires.

Hmm, 9%? Coincidence? I don't think so. It's gotta be the work of some smarty-pants copywriter who knows that Maris's uniform number is 9. Okay Mr. Smarty Pants, go to the head of the class.

August 27

The August 27 Sunday *Daily News* back-page double-stacked same-size headlines: "51 FOR MARIS, YANKS WIN," and below, "HOMER CONTEST ON TODAY."

An entry form is printed in the paper with details of the contest rules. I found it interesting that an entrant must predict that Mantle and Maris hit at least one homer in games played September 4 to September 10, inclusive. It further states that if either player fails to hit a homer, the contest will be canceled, and the prize money will be added to the contest of the following week.

What must be a tiebreaker is that every entry must also predict the total number of base hits Mick and Rog hit during that period.

***

In the August 27 *Daily News* "Voice of The People" column, reader Raymond Juan of the Bronx wants to know why rain-shortened games cannot be resumed later in the schedule. He writes a player could hit his sixtieth and sixty-first home run in his first two at-bats, but if the fifth inning isn't completed and called off, those at-bats won't count.

Okay, question asked, yet there's no answer. Why print such a letter? It's a disservice to the reader. I'm guessing that the answer is the same as why does a batter get four balls and only three strikes? "That's baseball."

***

Now that I am scouring every page of a newspaper, I noticed in the August 27 *Daily News* a list of the best-selling records in the country: 1) "Michael" by The Highwaymen, 2) "School Is Out" by Gary (U.S.) Bonds, 3)

"Take Good Care of My Baby" by Bobby Vee, 4) "Hurt" by Timi Yuro, 5) "Last Night" by the Mar-Keys, and 6) "I Like It Like That" by Chris Kenner.

I agree, but not totally. "I Like It Like That" should be No. 1 as I can't get it out of my head. And with school approaching, I also love the lyrics of "School Is Out," which strikes a chord with me because they say something about rooting for the Yankees from the bleachers and not worrying about teachers.

***

I'm probably the only fan who listens for asides from Yankee broadcasters during games.

At one point during the August 27 game against the A's in Kansas City, Phil Rizzuto told his Yankee radio audience that when the Yanks were up, the Athletics' left-handed pitcher Jim Archer was at the edge of the dugout, filming each hitter's at-bat.

Scooter theorized that Archer would study them over the winter so that he might be able to pitch them a little bit better next year.

I can't imagine how cool those movies are.

Then I heard about the shifting of the infield on Rog.

This time, former Yankee Hank Bauer was now the KC pilot, calling the shots. Dick Howser, Bauer's shortstop, was at second base, with Wayne Causey, the third baseman, all alone between third and second in the short-stop's slot.

The A's have three men between first and second.

The reason for all of this, according to Scooter, was that Rog had hit maybe three or four balls to the left of second base all year.

For this game, Rog hit three ground outs to second base, walked, and fooled 'em all with a deep fly to left field.

Later on, Scooter handed the mic to Mel Allen in the eighth inning. With KC's Deron Johnson at the plate, Mel painted a word picture about how the season was going, "Boy, this pennant race is getting to be like a hickory nut. Hard to crack open to start with and once you do, it's hard to get at the goodies."

How does Mel come up with these gems?

In the last of the ninth, with the score 8-4 in favor of New York, nobody out, Jerry Lumpe on second, Mel delivered another beauty.

Joe Nuxhall, batting for Bill Kunkel, hit a line drive down the right-field line that, according to Allen, was foul by just inches.

To further make his point he explained, "I only put it this way, if it had been any less foul, it would have been fair."

Nuxhall eventually flew out to Mantle in deep center field.

For my money, Mel Allen is the Bard of baseball.

It's obvious that I have a limited vocabulary that is a grade above Dick and Jane books. I don't know too many words, so Bard is not a word I use a lot. In fact, this is the first time ever.

Occasionally, when I see or hear a word that tickles me, I try to use it to sound smarter.

Unfortunately, I either don't use use it correctly or mispronounce it, which makes me a Bad Bard Boy.

Yankees won 8-7 and had Monday off before playing the Twins in Minnesota on Tuesday.

August 28

On page 11 of the August 28 *Daily News*, there's a one-third-page ad for a home run contest placed alongside Macy's liquor sale for gin, whiskey, and vodka. So the hidden message is before you make a guess in a home run contest, have a drink or two.

***

My dad's friend Smitty sent me the sports section from the *Standard-Sentinel* of Hazelton, Pennsylvania. I figured that the reason he sent it was there was a photo of a young woman named Mary Alyce Chabalko, who's holding a baseball from the late nineteen-twenties, one from the nineteen-thirties, and a 1961 ball to show that the current ball has a broader stitch. It's obvious that with a broader stitch that the ball gives a pitcher a better grip and thus greater control over the ball's movement.

***

The *Saturday Evening Post* runs an ad in a few August 29 newspapers promoting its article, "Mighty Mr. Maris." The *Post* tempts readers by proclaiming how readers will learn what Maris has to say about his reputation as a hothead, and why he didn't want to join the Yankees in the first place.

***

Jack O'Connor, 51, a prominent baseball executive, died of a heart attack in Daytona, Florida, on August 29. O'Connor first met Maris in Fargo when he was a front-office exec of the Fargo-Moorhead team and Maris was the batboy. While working for the Cleveland Indians O'Connor was instrumental in signing Maris to a professional baseball contract.

August 30

As reported in a variety of newspapers on August 30, an IBM electronic brain predicted that Maris would hit sixty-one homers in 154 games and sixty-four in 162 games.

Excuse me, but computers predicting baseball outcomes is pure science fiction, just like flying cars, Dick Tracy TV-telephone watches, and robot maids. It's a waste of ink.

***

With the Yanks in Minnesota playing the Twins on August 30, the Bombers win 4–0 and now are in first place by two-and-a-half games. Mick hit No. 47, which moved the team within one homer of tying their own American League team record of 193 circuits set last season.

***

The 1961 Yankee payroll for players, coaches, and manager is something like $1,200,000, according to Dan Daniel in *The Sporting News*. I know I'm being critical, but "something like" is a term I don't often see in a newspaper.

August 31

The *Daily News* is now running small boxes describing each at-bat for Mantle and Maris. On August 31, the paper, printed that Rog struck out in the first inning, walked in the fourth, flied to center in the sixth, and singled in the eighth.

***

Daily News sportswriter Joe Trimble's August 31 game story ends with a "Diamond Dust" note that, prior to tomorrow's game, "Maris will be honored by his hometown of Fargo, North Dakota, for his inspiration to the youth of America, his contributions to baseball, and his loyalty and devoted service to his hometown." Not leaving well enough alone, Trimble ends with, "Nice thought, but he hasn't been there in years and says Kansas City is his home."

In the same paper I see a great action photo on the back page of Rog sliding into Billy Martin at second base to successfully break up a double play of Mickey's grounder. No one in the American League breaks up double plays sliding into second base better than my guy Rog.

***

On August 31, I'm puzzled by an Associated Press photo of ten-year-old Curtis Flinck of Grand Rapids, Minnesota, having Maris autograph his right-arm cast while Mantle and Killebrew look on. Who arranges for a kid to meet the players? I'm pretty sure a regular fan doesn't call up and say, "Hey, my kid's arm is broken. Can he meet Mantle, Maris, and Killebrew?" I'll bet the kid's father either is a bigwig, has a ton of dough, or works for the newspaper or the Twins. Color me green with envy.

SEPTEMBER 1961

"Babe Ruth is the silent partner in these $500,000 deals."

September 1

There are not enough days in September for all the crapola that is going on in my life.

Chronologically speaking, it's time to go back to school, which earns a big *whoopity doo* from me.

Then, not long after the first bell rings at Highlands Junior High School, I, along with classmate Danny Lyman, will be at the Jewish Community Center Temple's pulpit reading our Bar Mitzvah Torah portion.

I'm also aware that any day now, the seventh and last "I gotta have" series of Topps baseball cards will arrive at candy stores. Hopefully, the series will include another Roger Maris card.

After the first few series of the Topps 1961 baseball cards came out, I knew I would no longer purchase them at the S. S. Kresge, F. W. Woolworth, or M. H. Lamston five-and-dime stores. They all made the mistake of ordering a huge shipment of baseball cards in the beginning of the season, not realizing that, shortly before the last firecracker went off a week after Independence Day, the first few series were no longer desirable because collectors like me already had these cards in their clutches.

Hey, Mr. Woolworth, get a clue and order each new series of cards as they are issued.

Starting in mid- to late-August, my two places to buy cards were either Raiders candy store or the Westchester County Book & Toy Store.

Starting about four years ago, the telltale sign that a new series of baseball cards arrived at a store was the dozens of baseball card wrappers strewn on the street in front of the store. As easily as I sensed the Good Humor ice cream truck coming down the street, I could spot those wrappers a block away.

When my friends and I entered the store, the clerk behind the counter would see us frantically looking around bug-eyed. He would then point to the cards on the counter, saying, "Over here." How did he know what we wanted?

After purchasing my cards, I'd go outside and pick up those wrappers on the sidewalk with the thought that someday the kids who threw them away will want them, and I'll be the only one who has them to trade.

Once home I'd carefully unwrap the just-purchased cards, making sure I removed the wrappers without tearing them.

Then, three packs in, there it is. Bingo. Not for trade. Hands off.

Card No. 576: Roger Maris All-Star!

You think I'm cuckoo, don't you? Well, check back with me in ten years, and I'll let you know how it went with those baseball card wrappers.

***

The October No. 148 issue of *Superman* comics will show up on newsstands in a few days. This is the issue that will feature Mr. Mxyzptlk.

Unlike baseball cards, I don't have to get every issue of *Superman*. To begin with, I am not a fan of Mr. Mxyzptlk. The premise is silly. I'm supposed to believe he can be banished to his fifth-dimension home for ninety days only if someone can trick him into saying or spelling his own name backwards. My goodness, I'm not a child. In four months I'll be thirteen-and-a-half years old.

***

I'm also counting on the Yanks capturing the 1961 American League pennant mid-month, while my guy Maris at least ties and hopefully breaks baseball deity Ruth's home run record soon after.

Shooting for 60—Both Rog and Mick were chasing the ghost of Ruth. *Courtesy Library of Congress.*

That's a lot of stuff for one kid, even at thirteen, to handle. Think about it—keeping up with school (social studies, algebra, science, and English), Yankee games, my favorite TV shows and news programs, memorizing Hebrew lessons, listening to my favorite 45s, collecting baseball cards and comic books, trying to get the attention of one cute girl. Plus, on top of all that, a guy has got to eat and sleep, too.

Most of all, I'm now having trouble reading all the newspapers that friends and relatives are sending me, not to mention the New York–area newspaper accounts of Roger Maris. Each newspaper is trying to provide unique angles of Maris and Mickey Mantle to attract readers.

New York papers are a boatload. Count 'em—there's *The New York Times, Daily News, New York Mirror, Journal American, World Telegram & Sun, New York Herald-Tribune, New York Post,* Long Island's *Newsday,* plus New Jersey and Connecticut papers. Somebody throw me a life preserver, I'm drowning in printer's ink.

And, as a result of reading more than just the sports sections, I'm acutely aware that the world outside of my universe is in turmoil with tyranny, wars, bombs, prejudices, killings, and hate.

Finally, there's my mother's warning about braces hanging over my head. I know that every day is a day closer to getting them, which means everyone will be calling me "metal mouth."

Is it any wonder that times are good or bad, happy or sad?

September 2

Casey the Computer, an electronic brain at a statistical tabulating office in St. Louis, took a 300-hour cram course on statistics of performances by Maris, Mantle, and Ruth before starting to calculate predictions on June 26.

After Maris hit his fifty-second and fifty-third home runs off the Tiger pitchers Frank Lary and Hank Aguirre today, September 2, Casey computed Maris's chances as fifty-five out of one hundred to break Ruth's record of sixty homers. Mantle is two out of a hundred.

As it relates to 154 games, Casey the Computer predicts that Maris will hit sixty-one homers and Mantle fifty-five.

For the entire 162-game schedule, Casey predicts Maris will reach sixty-four and Mantle fifty-eight, barring injury.

***

Taking advantage of their enormous popularity, Mantle and Maris formed a company. A contract was drawn up by Thomas Miller, a lawyer with offices at 350 Broadway in Manhattan, between newly formed Mantle Maris Enterprises, Inc. (a Delaware corporation) and Biljac Products Co., Inc., to produce personal wear for men and children—underwear, pajamas, robes, sweaters, hosiery, beachwear, sweatshirts, dress shirts, and all categories of shoes and footwear.

***

Baseball writers were looking for any angle when it came to writing about Mantle and Maris. The problem was that there was no way to tell if their writing was accurate.

One writer, Lyall Smith of the *Detroit Free Press*, wrote that after today's game in which Rog hit Nos. 52 and 53, he observed that photographers were asking Rog to pose by holding up five fingers on one hand and three on the other hand. Then, during interviews with reporters, when a clubhouse boy brought Maris a paper cup with crushed ice, his hand was shaking. For clarification, Smith pointed out it was not a tremor, but a shake.

Smith explained that after the interviews he was talking to another writer who observed the same shaking. The unidentified baseball scribe made light of the situation by suggesting Maris might be worried about how he was going to please the photographers by holding up fingers in anticipation of his sixty-first homer.

***

Leonard Koppett's story in *The Saturday Evening Post*, "Mighty Mr. Maris," has much of the normal biographical information, such as Roger and Pat were married October 13, 1956. It also covers Roger's baseball history in the minors and majors before he was traded to the Yankees in the winter of 1959.

However, when I got to the paragraph about Roger and Pat having three kids, I started to lose interest because Pat gave birth to a fourth baby, a boy, a couple of weeks ago. I suspect this article was written and printed long ago.

I did, however, enjoy reading Koppett's last paragraph: "At any rate, it's M-a-r-i-s now, and it's a name you may someday be reading on a plaque in Baseball's Hall of Fame."

September 3

After a three-game series that ended September 3, the Detroit Tigers left Yankee Stadium with an additional three losses to the Yanks and a check for $49,000, the largest take-home slice of the gate from a three-game series in a visitors' ballpark in the Tigers' long history.

***

The September 3 *Daily News* front-page headline read, "Maris: 52, 53." Below that was a smaller headline: "Needs 8 to Top Ruth's Record." The front page had that photo of Rog holding up five fingers with his right hand and three fingers with his left hand.

***

The *Los Angeles Times* sportswriter Gene Earl had an interesting note in his Sunday "Sports Book" column. He wrote about former Yankee first-baseman Babe Dahlgren, who replaced Lou Gehrig in the Bronx Bombers lineup when Gehrig fell ill in May of 1939. He quoted Dahlgren's letter to Yankee General Manager George Weiss two days after trading for Maris in December of 1959. "I want to compliment you on the recent deal you made. I think you won several pennants in obtaining Roger Maris. I honestly feel that as time passes this deal will be considered a master stroke. That boy is capable of slamming 60–70 homers a year and he has the short porch to hit with the ability to pull."

September 4

In the top of the seventh inning during the first game of the September 4 doubleheader against the Senators in the "Big Ballpark," Phil Rizzuto turned over the Yankee radio mic to Mel and introduced him by saying, "Ready to carry you the rest of the game, Mel Allen."

After Mel greeted the radio audience with his signature, "Hello there, everybody," he thanked Phil, then quickly called the first pitch to Bennie Daniels, who hit a fly ball to Yogi in left field.

Allen responded to Phil's introduction, telling his listeners, "I'm really not going to carry you folks the rest of the way. Not physically up to it."

He paused, then added, "In fact, I'd wish you'd carry *me* the rest of the way." I could hear him chuckle to himself. Then he added, "Going mountain climbing."

He finished his thoughts with, "I know it's Labor Day."

I had no idea what Melvin was talking about. No matter. Yanks won 5-3 over Washington.

September 5

The day after Labor Day, junior high school started for me. This time, I was no longer on the bottom of the student pile in seventh grade. I was now an eighth grader, which meant that I had a year's experience of knowing how to act and behave socially in school.

***

According to one source I found, Roger signed a simple one-page agreement sent to him care of Frank Scott at the Biltmore Hotel, Suite 318, Madison Avenue and 43rd Street in Manhattan. The agreement is with RONCOM Productions about appearing on *The Perry Como Kraft Music Hall* TV program in a few weeks.

For the appearance. Maris would receive $7,500 within ten days following completion of the recording of the program.

September 6

The talk going around school concerns the Cold War with Russia. These were scary times. I wanted to talk about Maris and the home run derby;

unfortunately, it wasn't easy to introduce a topic other than the worrisome state of the world.

During lunch, one of the smart kids talked about what happened in August when East Germany began erecting a wall along the border to replace the barbed wire separating East and West Berlin. One kid said it was inhumane, which was the second time I had heard that word. The first time had to do with the crimes that Eichmann was being tried for.

Another kid sitting next to me said that the USSR was performing nuclear tests. He mentioned they had a bomb bigger than the one we dropped on Japan to end World War ll. What would happen if there was a nuclear war and we lost? We would all be Russians.

"I'd rather be dead than red," said a lot of my schoolmates. With each passing day I got more scared but didn't tell anyone. I wondered: Why can't we all just be friends?

Fear of a drastic change of life was now living in my head with the Russian threat. It was like a headache but different because I couldn't take an aspirin to get rid of it.

***

In the bottom of the third inning, as the Yanks were coming to bat against the Senators at Yankee Stadium, a lunatic dressed in a Civil War Union Army uniform wandered out of the right-field stands toward first base before being stopped by stadium security.

I'm starting to think weirdness is contagious among fans attending Yankee games this season.

***

In a game the Yanks won 8–0 at Yankee Stadium, Rog tied the Babe when he hit his fifty-fourth home run against the Senators' right-hander Tom Chaney in the fourth inning.

You're thinking, *whaaat*? Don't get your panties in a wad—I was referring to 1920 when Ruth hit a total of fifty-four homers that season.

By the way, Roger's homer was caught in the Yanks' right-field bullpen by reserve first baseman Bob Hale, who made a hale of a catch.

***

Someone sent Rog a gold-painted bat as a gift, and as he showed it to newsmen he said, "I guess it's for when I go on color TV." He also mentioned that for the last couple of weeks he's been keeping the baseballs he hits for homers that are returned.

An unidentified reporter asked which baseball he would cherish more, No. 60 or 61?

He replied, "If I'm fortunate enough to reach that level, I'll give you the answer then."

***

Another scary sign of the times is that someone mentioned that President Kennedy signed a law making it a federal crime to hijack or attempt to hijack an airplane.

September 7

Maris surprised everyone in the first inning against the Indians on September 7 at Yankee Stadium. With Kubek on third base, and everyone thinking that Rog will swing for the fences, he laid down a bunt. The Tribe was caught flat-footed as Kubek scored and Rog got to first with an infield single. In the third inning, Rog connected with Cleveland's Dick Stigman's second pitch, a curve ball, for his fifty-fifth home run.

In his postgame interview, Houk mentioned that Maris's bunt should prove that he is out to win games, not to break home run records.

Yanks win 7–3 and are now in first place ahead of Detroit by nine games. The Yanks' magic number is fourteen. Any combination of New York victories and Tigers losses totaling fourteen gives the Yanks another American League pennant.

***

San Francisco Chronicle columnist Art Rosenbaum revealed that Mantle and Maris have matzo ball soup at the Stage Delicatessen in Manhattan after every night game. Rosenbaum's insightful reporting suggests that matzo ball soup may be playing a part in their shared home run rampage.

***

It came to light today that what I have been taught throughout my years of school is all wrong. Because today I read a United Press International article by Gary P. Gates titled: "Ain't, Ain't, Ain't, Ain't, Ain't, Ain't—So There!"

According to Gates's article, a*in't* has been added to the forthcoming *Webster's Dictionary*. And get this: The new volume asserts that there are some prepositions you can end a sentence with.

September 8

Everyone is trying to make a buck off Mantle and Maris. American Excursions took out newspaper ads for their package deal of train transportation from Philadelphia to Baltimore for the September 19 doubleheader when the Yanks play the Orioles.

The ad headline: "SEE MARIS-MANTLE, Twi-nite Doubleheader." Cost for train and game reserved-seat ticket: $10.90.

September 9

Little-known but vitally important Spud Murray, the Yanks' thirty-two-year-old, 6' 4", 190-lb. batting practice pitcher was the subject of a *New York Times* article written by Wilbur Bradbury in today's paper.

The opening paragraph was poetic and told the story of Spud's job. "Meredith Warrington (Spud) Murray is a right-handed pitcher in Yankee flannels who accepts singles with indifference, doubles with equanimity, triples with approval and home runs with a smile. Murray is the Yankees' official batting practice pitcher."

Bradbury reveals in the article that at this point in the season (141 games), Spud has given up the combined total of about 280 batting-practice homers to Mantle and Maris.

The breakdown of pitches thrown to players is two rounds of six hits a batter. That works out to 120 pitches, which is the equivalent of a full game in which, like other pitchers, Spud loses perhaps three to four pounds.

The article ends with a Murray quote about Mantle and Maris: "Roger is the type of guy who gets a streak and can hit ten in a row." Murray adds, "They don't pitch to Mantle the way they do to Maris, but he can hit one any time. I'd like to see both of them break Babe Ruth's record."

***

Former big leaguer Rube Oldring died today at the age of seventy-seven.

He began his thirteen-year playing career in 1905 for the New York High-landers, first as an infielder, then as an outfielder.

***

Smitty was the name of my dad's best friend when he was growing up in the Bronx. I never knew or asked what his real name was. We just called him Smitty. On occasion, our family would visit Smitty and his family.

I don't know anything else about Smitty other than a couple of years ago, when I was eleven, he promised that for my Bar Mitzvah he would give me a wall calendar that features a naked picture of Marilyn Monroe.

I've seen it. She's sitting on a red curtain with her left arm behind her head as if she's stretching, and she's as naked as a jaybird!

Guess what? The big day has finally arrived. It's September 9, and my Bar Mitzvah is at 10:30 this morning. I'm hoping Smitty remembers his promise but that he gives it to me when nobody is around.

My Bar Mitzvah is taking place at the White Plains Jewish Community Center Temple. It's actually two Bar Mitzvahs but only one service.

The other kid who is having his Bar Mitzvah is my junior high classmate Danny Lyman. I know him. He's very smart. He's a good guy, but we aren't buddy-buddy.

If you are wondering if I learned anything from all the time I went to Hebrew school, or was I just memorizing everything I would say at the service? It's a combination. But, man, I'm glad that my Bar Mitzvah service will all be over. For me, I struggle with English, so to read and understand Hebrew, well, to put it plainly, I was out of my league.

My Bar Mitzvah day started off with a professional photographer coming to our house to shoot photos of my sister, father, mother, and me getting ready in unnatural set-up poses. Trust me, never in my life have I looked into my parents' bedroom mirror while my dad ties his tie or my mom fixes her hair. But I did this day.

"Okay, Andrew, smile," the photographer urged just before he shot each photo.

The one posed photo I did like was of my sister, Bobbi, and me, along with my parents, Helene and Sidney, walking down the front stairs of our house. It kinda looked like a photo that would be taken of the Kennedys.

I knew that the best photos would be of people who didn't know what the photographer was shooting, such as when our family was the last to arrive at the temple. The photographer got a shot of us walking in while one of our invited guests overtly gestured looking at his watch as if to say, "You're late."

As the service was about to start, while sitting with Danny, Cantor

Smolover, and Rabbi Schwartz on the pulpit, I looked out over the fans...*er*, audience...*uh*, I mean congregation. I can't explain it but I was excited to "perform" in front of people. It felt comfortable for me. I guess at heart I am a ham. A Jewish ham.

When it came time for me to read the Torah (here comes another baseball cliché), I hit it out of the park.

Dressed to the Nines—On our way to my September 9 Bar Mitzvah, the photographer my father hired posed my dad, me, mom, and sister for this President Kennedy family–like photograph.

Once the service was over, there was a reception for attending family and friends. But I had to stay back for more posed photos in the temple and then meet with Rabbi Schwartz in his office.

I had no idea why I was in the Rabbi's office but quickly found out. He began by complimenting me on how well I did in reading from the Torah. He asked if I would be interested to read my Torah portion again for the Rosh Hashanah service.

"How many people usually attend the service?" I asked. The Rabbi said it would be at least four to five times the size of the congregation that attended my Bar Mitzvah—probably around a thousand people.

That was exactly what I was looking for—a larger audience. I said, "Sure, for a thousand people, I'd be happy to do it."

Then he looked at me with a stern expression. "Today, Andrew, you are a man. You are a full-fledged member of the Jewish community with the responsibilities that come with it. These include moral responsibility for one's own actions. You are entrusted to make your own decisions." Then, in a business-like, though friendly, manner, he asked, "Will you be continuing your Hebrew studies?"

Before I answered, with no disrespect, looking beyond the Rabbi, I threw out a question—"How'd the Yankees do today against Cleveland?"—hoping that one of the temple office employees who were staring at the Rabbi and me would answer.

Somebody raised their voice with joy and said, "Yanks won eight to seven. Maris belted No. 56 off of Jim 'Mudcat' Grant in the seventh inning."

With my question answered, I turned my attention back to Rabbi Schwartz and answered, "No, I'm done after the Rosh Hashanah service."

I couldn't risk any more time for religious studies when it was apparent that I was a devout baseball fanatic of theological proportions. I felt that my time during the baseball season was to watch, play, read, and collect everything baseball.

The Rabbi had a blank look. He was speechless. So instinctively, to brighten things up, I said, "Let's go to the reception. I'm hungry."

My Pal Mic—This photo was a setup at my Bar Mitzvah reception. There was a stage, an audience, and a microphone, so I couldn't resist hamming it up. Joining me on stage holding a saxophone is my 7th grade homeroom teacher, Mr. Clements, who along with Duke Diacomo on drums and "Crazy Joe" Renda on the electric piano as The Sherwoods provided the rock 'n' roll music that day.

The reception was in the same building as the temple. It was set up with six large round tables for the adults and a head table in front of the stage for me and others attending who were my age.

Sitting at my table were a couple of relatives, kids who had invited me to their Bar Mitzvah (it's the unspoken obligation that if you invite me to your Bar Mitzvah, I will invite you to mine), my real friend Ray Simon, and a few really cute girls.

During the reception, the photographer, who was starting to bug me for posed photos, wanted a shot of me on stage holding a microphone like Elvis, as if I was singing with The Sherwoods in the background and Mr. Clements holding his saxophone. No one had to tell me to smile, as I was more than okay with that shot.

By the way, the band was fantabulous. Duke Diacomo was on drums, and "Crazy Joe" Renda sat at the electric piano. They played the hits: "Dream Lover," "The Stroll," "The Hully Gully," "It's Pony Time," and, to appease the adults, yes, we did the "Bunny Hop." Hop, hop, hop.

My biggest problem when dancing is if I see dancers who don't have rhythm. They throw me off. I lose a step or two. The other challenge I have is when I see the adults who are trying to clap to the beat, yet no two of them are clapping on the same beat. How is that humanly possible?

The one song that got everyone out of their seats was The Sherwoods' version of the newest dance craze, "The Bristol Stomp." Come on everybody, get on the dance floor and join in. The joint is jumping.

A few minutes later the band played "The Twist." I love to dance so, as I had done at school socials, I grabbed my classmate Linda Blauner, and we became the center of attention, twisting on the dance floor while everyone watched and clapped to the beat.

Before I danced again, my father told me to stop by every table to say hello and thank people for coming. I knew the real reason was for me to pick up some Bar Mitzvah *gelt*, which means gift pens and envelopes with checks.

While making my rounds, I received at least seventy *mazel tov*'s, sixty hand shakes, two dozen hugs and a smattering assortment of overweight old women's wet-cheek kisses that included, "You're such a man now."

Then it was time for more posed pictures, this time with the six invited boys. Then me with the six cute girls. The last posed shot was of me lying on a bench as if I was drunk with a bottle of champagne.

Enough already.

I had to start thinking about my future. Now that I was a man I would try to convince my parents that I could attend Yankee games without a chaperone during the 1962 season.

Oh, I almost forgot….I needed to see Smitty before he leaves. I think he has something for me. *Fershtays?*

Here's a New Twist—When I hear certain songs like "Bristol Stomp" and "The Twist," I just gotta get up and dance, man. Here I am dancing with Linda Blauner. Notice my dirty pants around the knees. It's from kneeling on the floor doing the Twist, which I always include at least once every time I'm on the dance floor.

***

Maria Beale Fletcher of Asheville, North Carolina, is crowned Miss America. It seems to me that every pretty girl gets the best grades in school and, no matter what they wear, they always look boss.

September 10

Dick Hackenberg of the *Chicago Sun-Times* came up with a great idea. He suggested that the White Sox fireworks from its famous exploding scoreboard be shot off not only for hometown players hitting home runs, but when they play the Yankees for either Mantle or Maris blasting one. It didn't happen. My guess is that the Sox thought the idea was a dud.

***

The day after my Bar Mitzvah, September 10, a Sacramento restaurant owner by the name of Sam Gordon made news stating that he would pay $5,000 to the fan who caught the baseball that Maris hit for his sixty-first homer.

I was incredulous. Five grand is a ton of moola.

***

Rosh Hashanah, the Jewish New Year of 5722, begins tonight at sundown. The ten-day holiday of reflection and repentance culminates with Yom Kippur, the holiest day of the Jewish calendar. It means "Day of Atonement" and calls for self-examination and determination to live on a higher moral plane in the future.

I can't wait to use the line with my classmates, "*Oy gevalt*, it will take me weeks to stop writing 5721 on school papers."

***

Maris turns twenty-seven today. He was born September 10, 1934, while Babe Ruth was playing for the Yanks. I looked it up to see what Ruth did that day. No game was scheduled, but Ruth did play the day before and was two-for-three, getting a single and a double.

***

With a little checking into baseball records, I found that on the date Roger was born, the following players hit homers: Hank Greenberg* (Tigers), Mel Ott (Giants), Gus Mancuso (Giants), Hughie Critz (Giants), Al Simmons (White Sox), Cliff Bolton (Washington), and Ralph Winegarner (Cleveland).

*I, not Ford Frick, put the asterisk on Greenberg because he hit two homers in that game, which brought his total to twenty-three for the season.

***

For years I have collected the great color photos of baseball players that appear from time to time in the *Coloroto Magazine*, an extra publication in the Sunday edition of the *Daily News*. Today's September 10 edition has a beautiful color front-page portrait of Maris.

In the profile inside, Maris described how he was virtually kidnapped by the Yankees in one of their periodic raids on Kansas City personnel. The trade was lopsided in the Yankees' favor and never turned out as "good for both teams."

***

It seemed like everyone with the exception of maybe the A&P grocery store ads acknowledged or made reference to Maris and Mantle.

A few *New York Daily News* display ads incorporated the homer theme, such as the photo of WNBC radio's Jim Lucas wearing a Yankee cap with the headline: "Will Jim Lucas Hit 60 Home Runs?"

Now that's a stretch.

***

A story appeared in the *Miami News* that told how Maris, Mantle, and Bob Cerv are sharing a four-room apartment somewhere in Jamaica, Queens. Mickey and Bob have twin beds in the bedroom. Rog sleeps on a green studio couch in the living room. Team members are sworn to secrecy.

When a reporter asked Mantle where he lives in Queens, he quickly answered that he had just moved to Tenafly, New Jersey, and offered to give his new address—all with a straight face. Elston Howard was nearby and overheard the address, which happened to be his. You got to think Ellie wasn't pleased about that.

The article also noted that Maris drives the three players in Mantle's white 1961 Oldsmobile to Yankee Stadium every day.

Maris was asked if he has any hobbies, and he said he liked bowling when he's home in Missouri, but hadn't tried it during the baseball season.

I love these tidbits of information about Maris. Don't ask me why. I just do.

***

Today's *New York Daily News* has "The Inquiring Photographer" by Jimmy Jemail. The question: "How do you compare Maris and Mantle with Babe Ruth?" The answers were from men who saw Ruth play.

F. Tucker of Brooklyn: "Maris is a consistent slugger."

Harry Green of Forest Hills: "Maris is one of the greatest players of all time."

Ed Fuchs of Ozone Park: "Mantle and Maris are minor leaguers compared to Ruth."

***

I must have heard a million times the commercial for Palisades Amusement Park with WABC's DJ Bruce Morrow. There will be twenty acts including Chubby Checker, Dion, Bobby Lewis, Chuck Jackson, The Shirelles, Nino & the Ebbtides, The Jive Five, Timi Yuro, The Earls, and many others. The cost? Only thirty cents admission on Sunday.

***

The editors of *Popular Mechanics* magazine tested and compared baseballs from Ruth's time against current American League baseballs at Armour Research Foundation at the Illinois Institute of Technology in Chicago.

Their findings: Ruth's baseball core was much heavier, more dense, and the ball weighed less than the minimum five ounces as prescribed for today's baseball.

Okay, so there's a difference. Shouldn't the editors have come to a conclusion as to how that difference influenced home runs? Well, they didn't. So what's the purpose? Anybody, anybody, anybody?

I wasted my time reading that and will never get those three minutes back.

***

What a Sunday doubleheader at Yankee Stadium today. The temperature was in the nineties and humid when the first game with the Cleveland Indians started.

In the fifth inning of the first game, the Tribe's Vic Power got hit by a Jim Coates pitch. On his way to first base Power made menacing gestures toward the Yankee pitcher.

It looked like there was going to be fisticuffs (my term, not anyone else's) as Coates kept throwing over to first base with Power just standing on the bag. With each throw over, Power would shout at the Yankee pitcher.

Then, in the seventh inning with two outs, Mantle walked and John Blanchard stepped into the batter's box against pitcher Frank Funk. Watching on TV, I was mortified to see two teenagers run toward Jimmy Piersall in center field.

Piersall has been a target of taunts from fans since his mental breakdown became public through his memoir *Fear Strikes Out* in 1955 and the 1957 movie of his life with the same title.

Those deranged "JD" punks picked the wrong player to mess with. Before the stadium security and players rushed to Piersall's aid, the Cleveland center fielder had decked one with a left and kicked the other one in the ass as the youth was trying to get away.

It wasn't a pretty sight. It was a small riot of sorts. Why do people hate other people? What motivates people to harm other people? What's going on?

This is baseball. I don't understand any of this. Perhaps as I get older it will make sense to me.

Is the world full of hate?

Now that I'm 13, I wonder every day why people hate other people.

Is it because of different religious beliefs, where they are from, skin color, the way they act, or things they say?

What are the origins of hate?

Is it a natural human condition?

I love the Yankees, but I don't hate the Detroit Tigers. I just dislike them immensely.

I certainly don't hate anybody enough to hurt them. Does it mean that as I get older, maybe I will learn to hate and want to harm people?

Almost on a daily basis, I read in the newspapers about a stabbing in Queens, the atrocities of Eichmann, Khrushchev's threats, and Castro's dictatorship.

I'm relatively new to this planet, but it seems like humans have enough challenges with sickness, accidents, and natural disasters such as hurricanes, tornadoes, earthquakes, and who knows what else.

Why can't people live together in peace, harmony, and love?

Perhaps when I'm fourteen or fifteen years old, I will understand. And, hopefully, I will also find out what girls really, truly want.

A Real Kick in the Ass—Indians centerfielder Jimmy Piersall gives his attackers this boot during the September 10 game at Yankee Stadium. *Original art by John D'Acquisto.*

Once the game resumed, everyone was watching Piersall. He usually doesn't play deep so he can catch "would be" base hits. He's one of the best at getting a jump on the ball coming off the bat. He's usually good for at least one circus catch a game. Today was no exception as Blanchard got back in the batter's box and hit a long towering fly ball headed for the Yankee bullpen.

Piersall and right-fielder Willie Kirkland ran to the Yankee bullpen fence and both jumped, attempting to catch the ball before it cleared the fence for a homer. Piersall made the catch and the fans cheered as if he was a member of the Yanks.

Yanks won 7–6.

In the second game, Clete Boyer hit a blast to left field in the sixth inning that appeared to second-base ump Charlie Berry and third-base ump Frank Umont to be a homer. Moments later, both umps gave the universal home run sign of right hand in the air circling in small, counter-clockwise movements.

Understandably, Boyer slowed to a trot, only to be tagged out by third baseman Mike de la Hoz before he reached third base. Confusion reigned among the umps.

Piersall was sitting in the Indians bullpen as he was not playing in the second game. He ran out onto the field to protest to the umps that the ball was not a homer.

Turns out that the ball hit the railing at the 402-foot mark and was still in play. So the umps changed their call and Boyer went from hitting a homer to making an out, which was all the Yankees crowd needed. Just like that, a twenty-minute near-riot unfolded, marked by hankie waving and debris thrown on the field.

The Yankees played the game under protest, but dropped it after winning the game 9–3.

Eventually, the two hoodlums who attacked Piersall were identified. One was fifteen and the other eighteen, which not coincidentally might have been their IQs. They were both from Long Island. They were booked on charges of disorderly conduct and held for fifty dollars bail by Magistrate Walter Bayer, who was quoted in the newspaper upon learning that they were from Long Island, "We don't need your type in New York."

After the game, Piersall mentioned that his dad, who had died the previous week, would have been proud because over the years Piersall had 117 fights and this was the first that he won.

So the Yankees took the doubleheader. Lost among all the hullabaloo, Rog managed only two singles in six at-bats. Now any combination of eight Yankee wins and Detroit defeats will mathematically clinch the 1961 pennant for the Yanks.

After the game, which was the Yankees 145th contest, they went by train to Chicago for the three-game series at Comiskey Park.

Piersall's fielding was inspirational. I had a quick dinner and then met Gary Baker at the Mamaroneck Avenue school field to play circus catches. That's where we try to either throw or hit the baseball so the other guy can catch it before it goes over the fence.

***

When I see guys my age acting in a reckless, irresponsible way as they did at Yankee Stadium, I wonder how does it happen? What sets a kid on a path that results in him becoming a juvenile delinquent?

I realize that life is full of choices. And the result of making those choices could affect your life forever.

Let me explain. Three years ago when I was ten years old, I hung around a guy who lived in my apartment building and had tons of baseball cards. He was a year older than me. I thought he was cool.

When I asked him how he had such a big card collection, he explained that by using the "five-finger discount" he could get any toy for free. We went to the neighborhood candy store together, and he demonstrated his skills. The kid was a thief and was teaching me how to steal.

At the time, the toy I coveted most was the Roy Rogers Chuck Wagon. Keep in mind that this was no small toy that could fit in your pocket like a pack of baseball cards. This toy was over fourteen inches long and had many individual pieces to it—Roy Rogers, Dale Evans, two horses, miniature pots, pans, etc.

The Hobby House toy store was only a few blocks from my apartment building and had the Chuck Wagon out of the box, assembled, and on display.

So the next Saturday morning, when the toy store opened at ten a.m., working alone without an accomplice, I had a plan.

Using the recently learned five-finger discount, I started removing the wagon piece by piece. I pocketed a horse, a wheel, and a miniature frying pan. With my heart racing, I walked out of the store and ran home with my loot.

I returned to the store about twenty minutes later and went straight to the scene of my crime. This time, I abducted Roy, Dale, and another wheel. With each trip, I was getting more confident. I figured I could complete removing the toy by three p.m. at the latest.

On my fourth trip that morning, just before I got to the door to walk out of the store, I heard a stern voice: "Hey, young man, wait a minute."

It was a store clerk who must've been in his forties but seemed older. He escorted me into his office and told me to put everything in my pocket on his desk. I didn't hesitate and figured that my stealing days were over. With sweaty hands I placed on his desk a horse, a wheel, and some assorted miniature pots and pans.

He wanted to know where the rest of the toy was and I gushed, "At home."

"How do you think your father would feel if someone had stolen something of his from where he works?" he asked. But before I could answer, he said that he would have to call my parents. He then asked me what my father did for a living and probably thought that was a simple way to teach me a lesson.

"*Uh, oh,*" I uttered, and in a quiet voice added, "My dad makes plastic toys."

Well, that stopped the interrogation. The clerk was taken aback by my response and quickly figured out that there was more going on than just a ten-year-old kid stealing from a neighborhood toy store. He proposed a deal—that if I brought everything back within the hour, he would not call my parents. I happily agreed, and we shook on it.

I ran home and returned with everything. It was almost noon. My stealing career was officially over. It lasted less than a couple of hours, which must have been a record for the shortest career of thievery in my neighborhood by any ten-year-old.

I never went back to that toy store. Never, ever, ever!

***

Former *Scholastic Magazine* writer Phil Pepe, who now appears in the *New York World Telegram & Sun*, wrote an article published September 10. The headline was, "Roger Maris Going Like 60!" It had the usual bio stuff plus one revelation. Pepe ended the article by writing, "All of us [writers] are more nervous than Roger!"

September 11

Newspapers are now treating Maris as if he was a prize fighter. They are printing the "tale of the tape," which is more appropriate for a boxer, not a baseball player.

Here it is:

Age–27
Weight–200
Height–6'
Neck–16 ½"
Chest (normal)–40 ½"
Chest (expanded)–43"
Waist–35 ¼"
Thigh–24"
Bicep–14 ¼"
Calf –16 ¼"

This stuff makes no sense to me. If Roger was a prize fighter, okay, but he's a baseball player and so his size has little, if anything, to do with success on a baseball field.

If I were in charge of the newspaper, my "tale of the tape" for Maris would have included:

Hits right handers

Hits left handers
Hits curve balls
Hits fast balls
Hits change-ups
Strikes out vs. fastballs
Strikes out vs. curveballs
Strikes out vs. change-ups

***

Outstanding *Daily News* back-page photo taken by Charles Hoff of Rog standing next to the Yankee Stadium center-field Babe Ruth monument. The caption headline read, "So near and yet so far," making reference to the 154-game limit to break Babe's record.

September 12

The *Bridgeport Post* decided to go down Silly Street by sending reporter Dorothy Gribko out to survey people at random about the homer derby and who they thought would beat the record and why.

The responses ranged from a preference for Stan Musial, given by a policeman who wanted to remain anonymous, to one from a frustrated wife: "Maris, Maris, Maris: All I ever hear is Maris."

Elizabeth Lemanski was quoted as saying: "Maris, he's cuter."

Nat Grasso favored Mantle, stating that he thought Maris was too cocky.

Al Domain called Maris a "prima donna."

Maris was favored for his vitality by Murray Weinstein.

Cigar-smoking Jerry Wittenstein said he didn't think it would happen because Mantle has had injuries and Maris is due for a slump.

***

Gene Ward's *Daily News* column, "Inside Sports," started off saying how great Mickey Mantle is, but that Roger Maris was greater. Yet when it came right down to picking the greatest active player of our time, Ward cast his vote for left-handed pitcher Warren Spahn of the Milwaukee Braves.

***

Houk was asked if the home run duel between Mantle and Maris hurt the pennant effort because it emphasized individual effort. Ever the diplomat, Houk told the reporter, "No, because the home runs are winning games, and these are two well-liked guys. Everybody on the club is pulling for them. Nobody is jealous."

***

Because of the home run race, Yankee beer sponsor P. Ballantine and Sons added four games that were not originally scheduled to be televised. So for the remainder of the season, I can watch every game on TV.

***

I have no idea what the numbers of TV ratings mean. But I read where the September 10 Yankee doubleheader with the Cleveland Indians scored a hefty 37.8 rating, which was one of the highest scores in WPIX coverage history. Everyone I knew watched the game.

***

Uh, oh. Rog accused umpire Hank Soar of having a bad night behind the plate at Comiskey Park in Chicago.

Although the Yanks won while Roger walked, singled, struck out, and fouled out, every newspaper carried the story that, according to Rog, Soar miscalled some pitches during Rog's at-bat, as he thought they were outside the strike zone.

As a result of Rog's difference of opinions with Soar, I went back to the July 26 issue of *The Sporting News* that had a front-page story acknowledging umpires in twenty specific categories as voted upon by two groups: writers and managers/coaches. When I read it I thought there's no validity for writers—sitting up in a press box—to judge which umps are best calling balls and strikes. And what fan cares which arbitrator is the biggest grandstander, most diplomatic, most easygoing, or most serious minded?

But did Soar show up in this survey? Yes, by the writers' vote he tied for best at keeping the game moving and tied for easiest to talk to. However, Soar didn't show up in any of the categories voted on by the managers/coaches.

Well, at least for one game we know what Rog thinks of Soar's ability in calling balls outside the strike zone as strikes.

September 13

The September 13 edition of the *Daily News* had a photo of their home run contest $1,000 winner—Mrs. Lilian Passner, who works at Passner's Sweet Shop, a luncheonette, and is the grandmother of five. She was quoted as saying, "Records are made to be broken." She explained that her winnings will go a long way toward paying off heavy medical expenses she incurred following surgery last May.

***

Baseball fan Al Cam of Verona, New Jersey, wrote a letter to Dick Young of the *Daily News*. Cam claimed that if the new home run record is established, it wouldn't last for thirty-four years as Ruth's did. As a result of the livelier ball, he predicted that the record would be broken in 1962 before Labor Day.

***

Weighing in on the home run race was the *Revolución*, Fidel Castro's official newspaper, which began publishing in 1959. The two-column story by the sports editor essentially sneered at the efforts of Maris and Mantle while supporting Ruth.

***

Prior to the game in Chicago, a telegram signed by several hundred fans from Fort Lauderdale was delivered to Mantle and Maris. This was a perfect prop for photographers to get their shots as the ten-foot long telegram was draped over the shoulders of the M&M Boys.

***

In the Yankees' September 13 game against the Chicago White Sox Rog got up once and hit a single in the first inning. He was coming to bat in the third inning with the Yanks leading the White Sox 2–1 when the game was delayed for an hour and twenty-two minutes by the driving rains of Hurricane Carla. Eventually the umps cancelled the game.

Since this is the last time the Yanks will be in Chicago this season, the cancelation means they will play a doubleheader against the White Sox tomorrow, September 14. Which also means the Yanks will play back-to-back doubleheaders in two different cities—first in Chicago on September 14 and then the next day in Detroit.

September 14

Mantle and Maris get to play two games today, noted Joe Trimble of the *Daily News*. He then climbed on board the Frick boat and wrote that any homers hit after 154 games should come with an asterisk.

In the eighth inning of the first game, Maris faced a drastic defensive infield shift. That's where the White Sox shortstop Luis Aparicio moves over to the first-base side of second base and second baseman Nellie Fox is two-thirds of the way toward first base but is standing on the outfield grass.

With the left side of the infield wide open, Rog went the other way as he poked a run-scoring single to left. However, the Yanks lost both games to the White Sox.

For the three games against Chicago, Rog got up eleven times, hit four singles, scored twice, batted in a run, and struck out twice.

***

The magic of the Mantle vs. Maris home run derby has not gone unnoticed in the marketing world. An ad in the *Daily News* promoted comic Joe E. Lewis appearing at Jules Podell's Copacabana on 10 East 60th Street with the headline: "Going Like 60! Shows at 8 & 12 with 3 shows Friday and Saturday, 8, 12 and 2. For reservations call PL 8-9000."

***

American League President Joe Cronin disagrees with Commissioner Frick and was quoted that if sixty-one homers are hit in 162 games, the feat must be regarded as a new record.

Frick's response: "You don't break the 100-meter record in the 100-yard dash. There will be two records. The most home runs in a 162-game schedule and the most in a 154-game schedule."

***

Back in late August, Ralph Houk made news by promising that once the Yankees won the pennant, he would move Maris and Mantle to the No. 1 and No. 2 positions in the batting order. However, he quickly changed his mind. "Many people would call it a cheap record," said the skipper. He worried it might seem that inappropriate consideration had been given to the two players, perhaps at the expense of the team.

***

TV station WPIX has been collecting videotape recordings of Mantle and Maris homer heroics for the purpose of putting together a possible special in the next few weeks, according to a *Daily News* TV notes column. Man, I'd love to see those homers again.

***

The *Daily News'* Jimmy Powers explained in his column why Yogi Berra is more like Ruth than Mantle and Maris. He wrote: "That line, 'Stone walls do not a prison make,' has been running through my cerebral hemispheres. Lately, it has metamorphosed into a paraphrase: Home runs do not a hero make. A celebrity, yes, but a hero only maybe. If someone asked me to name right off which Yankee, from a standpoint of affection as well as ability, most resembled Babe Ruth, it would not be Roger Maris or Mickey Mantle. I admire them and like them, but my choice would be Yogi Berra."

***

Dick Young wrote in his *Daily News* column about choosing the hero of the day: "It is the curse of our business that we are frontrunners....That's the way it is; that's the way it must be in this what-have-you-done-lately business."

Not Scott Free—Frank Scott began representing baseball players in the 1950s as their business manager. He hit a homer representing the M&M boys in 1961. L to R: Roger Maris, President Kennedy, Frank Scott, and Yankee Public Relations man Bob Fishel in the oval office. *Photo by Robert Knudsen, White House Photographs. John F. Kennedy Presidential Library and Museum, Boston.*

Frank Scott, who represents many baseball players in their business dealings off the diamond, is the focus of the *Chicago Tribune*'s David Condon column, "In The Wake of the News."

It turns out that this is the same Frank Scott who handles Mantle's and Maris's business dealings. He explained to Condon that he got his start as the manager of Jock Sutherland's University of Pittsburgh football teams. He then became the Yankees' traveling secretary in the early 1950s.

It was there that he noticed how players were being taken advantage of in their business dealings. Once Scott left the Yankees, he began representing athletes on a commission basis.

He explained in detail what he does for Mantle and Maris. Scott bragged, "I sold Maris and Mantle to *The Perry Como Show* for $15,000. That's the highest price paid for a sports celebrity."

For companies that can't afford Mantle and Maris prices, he offers up other players.

Scott detailed the three types of business categories.

The first consists of offers where he knows there's a ceiling on the client's ability to pay. The garment industry, for example, can't pay the kind of money a cigarette company could give.

The second category is "risk adventures." These are businesses that offer a flat sum if either player breaks the record, but only guarantees a much smaller amount if they don't. Scott knows that most of these fellows will be back after a record is broken, and they'll go higher. With risk ventures, he's passing up token payment and going for the limit.

The third category consists of deals that offer "X" number of dollars now, take it or leave it. He admits, "Those are the deals we can afford to pass up."

Scott provided the current bottom line for the M&M Boys: "We've had 40 deals offered, with about eight signed."

Scott explained that Mantle and Maris are the most sought-after sports personalities he's represented since the Yankees' Don Larsen pitched a perfect game in the 1956 World Series.

He alluded to the fact that businesses that are interested in Mantle and Maris understand the unspoken connection to the most famous sports personality of all time: "Babe Ruth is the silent partner in these $500,000 deals."

***

Today's *Daily News* had a Ford dealer's final clearance display ad with a baseball theme, including the bold headline: " '61 HOME RUNS!"

***

Newspaper reports that the Yanks will go to Australia and Japan after the World Series to play exhibition games were denied by Roy Hamey, the Yanks' general manager.

***

The *New York Times* ran an ad for author J.D. Salinger's new book, *Franny and Zooey*, which was available starting today at Doubleday book shops.

I wasn't familiar with that book, but was somewhat aware of his 1951 book, *The Catcher in the Rye*.

One of my book-smarty friends told me he thought the book's main character, Holden Caulfield, and I had the same attitude about life, girls, the same sense of humor, and an abhorrence of people who were phonies.

He showed me a couple of pages in the book. I wasn't into reading books back then, nor am I into reading books now. I just somewhat remember thinking as I read a few pages that Caulfield had a good sense of humor but not in a ha-ha sort of way. He made you laugh in your head. Caulfield was rebellious, but not like he wanted to pick up a gun and join a revolution or anything. Above all, he wasn't a conformist. The bottom line, he was a lost soul. Was that really me? I don't think so.

There was one part of the book that knocked me over. It was when I read Holden's description of his brother Allie in chapter 5, about how he would write poems in green ink on his baseball glove, a left-handed fielder's mitt. No way, man! That was a total kick in the ass for me. You mean, Holden's brother was as obsessed about baseball and the color green as I was? Get out of here!

I figured the *Catcher* book's popularity was because every jerk who read it thought this Salinger is a genius because he really "gets" it. He gets me. Sorry, but I don't have time to read any goddamn book that isn't required reading for school. Perhaps when I'm older, during the winter, I'll read *The Catcher in the Rye* and then maybe *Franny and Zooey*.

But, honestly, I doubt it.

***

The *Akron Beacon Journal* new-products writer Polly Paffilas was in Chicago on September 13 for the food writers convention. Coincidently, the Yanks were in town to play the White Sox. The newspaper arranged for Paffilas to have breakfast with Maris at the Del Prado Hotel before the September 14 doubleheader. However, the thought of interviewing a big-league ballplayer gave her a bad case of the jitters, so she only ordered a cup of coffee and didn't write her story.

She shudda called me.

September 15

Oy gevalt!

I only use that Yiddish exclamation that means amazement when I'm trying to sound like an old Jewish man of 50 to get laughs from my friends.

Besides the Yiddish accent, the key to sounding Jewish is to say everything in a question.

Why you ask?

Did you know the September 14 *New York Times* had a note that Israeli radio in Tel Aviv is keeping American tourists posted daily on the home run race between Maris and Mantle?

Wouldn't you think I should know that?

Am I losing it? Will this home run thing ever end?

Honestly, who knew?

Go figure?

Right?

***

Roger appeared on WOR-TV Channel 9's "Golf Tips" tonight at nine p.m. Didn't see it, and I don't like golf.

***

"The Inquiring Photographer" is a semi-regular *New York Daily News* feature that usually asks a question of the "man on the street."

Today the question was posed instead to big-league hitters: "What pitcher gives you the most trouble?" Mays, Mantle, Gentile, and Frank Robinson were asked along with Maris, who was first to answer.

"All of the opposing pitchers give me trouble, particularly during these crucial days of the pennant race and the home run competition. However, if I had to name one pitcher, it would be [Camilo] Pascual of Minnesota. When he's got his stuff, I might as well leave my bat in the rack."

***

After the September 13 rainout in Chicago against the White Sox, two of Roger's friends, Nat Brunk and Henry Rosenthal, took him to the Playboy Club. That visit became public today when a note appeared in Herb Lyon's *Chicago Tribune* column, "Tower Ticker."

"Man on a pogo stick: Roger Maris, the mighty Yankee man, scored a circuit clout with the Playboy Bunnies after the rainout of Wednesday night's game. Then, a performer introduced him to the audience and Rog scrammed angrily."

In a *Chicago Tribune* article, "Radio TV Gag Bag," culled by Larry Wolters, it was noted that Ivan Bunny—the name used as a source by another writer, Irv Kupcinet—thinks that Rog is going too far: He's demanded that the No. 60 be put on his uniform next season!" (That's a gag, son!)

This confused me, so with a little checking it became even more confusing, because I found out that Ivan Bunny was actually two brothers, Jimmy and Ivan Colitz. This means that a Chicago newspaper is publishing information from another writer who is using two guys as a source who have an alias. Have I lost you?

***

In his column, "Little Old New York," in the *Daily News*, Ed Sullivan writes about Mantle commenting to Joe Moore after watching Ruth swing a bat on a special TV show: "By contrast, the hands and bats of Maris, Blanchard, Howard, Skowron, and me, on the backswing, are much higher." Mick elaborates: "All of us idolized Ruth. The fact that he hit 730 homers and had a twenty-two-year batting average of .342 proves he was in a class by himself."

Mantle's noting that Ruth hit 730 homers intrigued me. I figured out that if you add the 714 during his twenty-two regular seasons to the 15 he hit during the ten World Series he played in, along with one in an All-Star Game, that equals 730. But who the hell is Joe Moore?

***

Sportswriters covering the Yankees say that Rog was avoiding them after a dismal doubleheader against the Tigers. He managed one single in nine times at-bat. After the game, Rog ducked into the trainer's room, which is off-limits to the scribes.

***

The September 15 *Daily News* back-page headline: "MANTLE & MARIS FOILED," in reference to the game the previous day when both players failed to hit homers in the two games against the White Sox.

***

The typical question now being asked of Maris by reporters who don't cover baseball: Which would you rather do, bat .300 or hit sixty-one homers? Are they kidding? No one is that stupid. Well, maybe they are.

September 16

Roger admitted to reporters that he avoided them yesterday but he said it was not because of his poor performance in the doubleheader. Instead he was "burned up" at some of the things that fans were shouting at him through both games. He was afraid that he might pop off, which would only make things worse. "I felt so lousy that I didn't want to talk to anyone," Rog admitted. "What was there to say?"

***

In the third inning today, September 16, at Detroit, Rog connected off right-hander Frank Lary for home run No. 57. The ball traveled 400 feet, hitting the facing of the roof and bouncing back onto the field where Tigers right-fielder Al Kaline picked it up and threw it into the Yankee bench so that Roger could keep the souvenir.

After the game that the Yanks lost, Rog commented on what Kaline did: "It was a nice gesture, very nice of him to think of it."

***

Elston Howard tied Babe Ruth's home run record today when he hit the sixtieth home run of the Yankee catching staff. It was Howard's twentieth home run of the season, joining Blanchard and Berra, who have each hit twenty home runs. I'm kind of stretching the facts on this because while all three players are primarily catchers, they have hit homers while playing other positions.

September 17

The *Daily News* has a back-page photo of Roger's wife, Pat, holding their son Randy, who was born four weeks ago. Pat is holding the baby in her right hand and showing four fingers with her left hand, indicating, according to the newspaper caption, that Rog is four homers away from breaking the record.

From the many articles I have read about Pat, I don't think that caption is correct. Pat's personality is not one that would be so bold as to signify a home run countdown.

Pat is either signifying that Randy is four weeks old or it's their fourth child (joining Susan, Roger Jr., and Kevin).

Take your pick.

**

The last line in Cleveland Amory's syndicated newspaper column, "Wish-Of-The-Week" (Damn-Yankee department): "That both Maris and Mantle end the season with a total of 59 homers."

**

For whatever reason, I noticed that among the top four best-selling fiction books listed in the *Daily News* are *To Kill A Mockingbird* by Harper Lee and *Franny and Zooey* by J.D. Salinger.

I'm not interested in fiction books because they are made-up stories, just like *Dick and Jane* books. If I'm going to spend time reading something, I want to know that it's true and not make-believe.

**

Dick Young in his *Daily News* column reveals the most obvious business endorsement opportunity is with M&M candies. Young writes that an offer was made toward the end of August to sign up the two Yankee sluggers, but their business manager, Frank Scott, decided to wait because if either one breaks sixty the money would be four times greater. Young speculated that as a result of the party of the first part waiting, the head honchos at M&M Candies are no longer interested.

It appears that this tasty opportunity melted in Mantle and Maris's hands before being consummated.

**

I know everybody is entitled to their insightful opinion, but I didn't understand why it was important to print *Surfside Six* TV star Margarita Sierra's response when asked if she thought Mantle or Maris would hit sixty. The actress, who plays the nightclub singer Cha Cha O'Brien, responded that there was no reason why they couldn't if they take care of themselves.

I imagine that soon after Sierra answered the reporter's question, she asked, "Sixty what?" and wanted to know which one is Maris and which is Mantle.

***

On September 17, the Yanks took on the Tigers in Detroit.

In the top of the fifth with New York leading 3-2, Rizzuto mentioned that he couldn't get over the number of photographers at the game and where they'd position themselves every time Maris got up.

"It's amazing, one second you look down on the field and it's clear and the next second you look down and those eleven photographers are out again."

As the seventh inning is about to begin with Bill Stafford up and Jim Bunning on the mound, Rizzuto hands over the mic to Mel Allen, who admitted, "You know, so often you switch over from television after six innings and come over to radio, you just sit and watch awhile.

"Then you get into a more descriptive mood. Here's the pitch. Swung on and fouled back. Strike two. Nothing and two."

Mel continued, explaining the differences of doing radio as compared to TV.

"You catch yourself sitting back, waiting for something to happen, instead of going into the details."

Up to that moment, I never gave it a thought about the difference between broadcasting TV and radio games. Kind of makes sense.

Four batters later, Rog just missed hitting number 58 when he tripled off the top of the screen in right field, which wasn't there last season.

It was Roger's fourth three-bagger of the season.

After nine innings, the game was tied 4-all.

With two outs in the 12th inning, Rog came to bat and Mel mentioned the distraction the Yanks' right fielder was going through as a result of the eleven photographers on the field crowded around home plate.

"I know it bothers him," he added, "out of the corner of his eye."

This may be a poor comparison, but there are times when I'm at the urinal in the school's boys room, standing next to a couple of other students trying to go.

Without looking directly at them, I can see them out of the corner my eye and, well, it's hard to go, if you know what I mean.

But the Yankee game continued.

Terry Fox ran the count to 2 and 1. Rog then pounded one against the upper deck for home run number 58.

The ball bounced off the right-field facade back onto the field, and second-base umpire Hank Soar picked it up and tossed it to the Yankee dugout for another homer keepsake.

Allen excitedly said the homer travelled 425 feet.

This homer placed Roger in select company with Jimmie Foxx and Hank Greenberg, who also hit fifty-eight homers in a season.

That Maris home run made the score 6-4, which is how the game ended.

I hope those eleven piss-poor photographers got their shot of Roger's shot and are happy snappy.

***

Just how far-reaching is this home run race? The Copley News Service ran a story today out of Montevideo, Uruguay, that began with, "Were Roger Maris a member of the Buenos Aires Bisons of the Argentine League, one of his longer home runs might carry into the suburbs of Montevideo in neighboring Uruguay."

Then the unnamed writer poorly attempted to explain the mention of Maris by stating, "This is only a slight exaggeration. Baseball isn't played in the Argentine, and Roger Maris is an unknown in soccer-conscious Buenos Aires."

This doesn't make sense to me other than the writer in Montevideo is a fan of Maris and desperately wanted to work his name into the article so that the world outside of baseball would see his name.

September 18

The Associated Press reported on September 18 that Maris asked manager Ralph Houk for a day off after hitting his fifty-eighth home run yesterday. Houk refused, explaining that he is focused on clinching the pennant.

***

The American Broadcasting Company's Tom W. Moore, vice president of programming, announced that ABC bought the nationally televised broadcast of the Wednesday, September 20, Yankee game from Baltimore. It is game No. 154.

***

United Nations Secretary General Dag Hammarskjöld was killed in a DC-6-B airliner crash in Africa. He was on a peace mission to the breakaway Congo state of Katanga. It is believed that anti-aircraft damaged the plane and caused an explosion.

This was a peace mission that ended in death! How is that possible? We've got to find a way to bring some understanding here today. We can't go on like this.

***

I read in Earl Wilson's September 18 syndicated column, "On Broadway," that movie bombshell Ava Gardner went incognito to Yankee Stadium, met Rog, and had dinner with him Sunday night. I figured that his reference to Sunday was September 10. Now, I don't want to say that Wilson is not telling the truth, but I just can't believe that Rog would go out after an exhausting doubleheader that took almost five-and-a-half hours to play and would do something like that because it would attract undue attention...especially since it was his birthday and married.

September 19

Pittsburgh Post Gazette sports editor Al Abrams met up with Rog three hours before the twi-night doubleheader against the Orioles. Maris had the clam chowder at the Lord Baltimore Hotel, but there was no mention if it was New England or Manhattan clam chowder. In his "Sidelights on Sports" column, Abrams writes that Maris revealed there are three things that bother him: 1) Some of the letters he receives; 2) stupid questions; and 3) profanity of loudmouth fans.

Maris pointed out a few of the stupid questions he gets asked, such as did he wish Ruth was never born. Or the time a magazine writer asked if he went out on dates or played around, to which Rog explained that he's "a married man." The reporter then explained he was married, too, but that he "plays around." Rog ended the conversation by saying, "That's your business."

It also irked Rog that in gossip columns he reads things that are not true, including being linked with Ava Gardner, explaining he doesn't even know her.

***

Photographers on the field are a distraction for players and spectators. Consider the photographer who was just a few feet behind Rog after he hit his fifty-eighth homer and fell on his face with camera in hand as Rog stepped into the Yankee dugout.

***

Former major leaguer Guy Bush, whose career began in 1923 and lasted until 1938, was the "guy" who gave up Babe Ruth's last two regular-season career home runs, Nos. 713 and 714. "I look for Maris to break the record in the full season—but not in 154 games," Bush told the Associated Press in a widely circulated story.

He felt strongly that "the public will accept Maris or Mantle as home run champion if they hit 61 or more in 162 games."

***

In the ninth inning of the second game of the doubleheader against the Orioles in Memorial Stadium on September 19, Red Barber noted that after Roger's last at-bat, in which Hoyt Wilhelm struck him out, most of the fans headed for the exits.

Barber pointed out in his broadcast, "As if somebody gave a signal. Boom. Exodus." The Yanks won, beating Baltimore 3-1.

***

It was announced today that at forty-three, Ted Williams (Maris's favorite player when he was growing up) married model Lee Howard, who is thirty-six years old. This is the second marriage for both. I never understood why it is important to list a person's age and not include their height or weight.

***

New York is on Hurricane Esther alert, which means baseball games on the East Coast are also on alert.

***

Yom Kippur, the Day of Atonement, the most solemn day in the Jewish liturgical calendar, begins at sundown and will end at sundown tomorrow, September 20.

***

As noted in the *Daily News*: When and if Yankee slugger Roger Maris equals or breaks Babe Ruth's record of sixty home runs in 154 games, CBS will interrupt its regular programming to present taped coverage of the event. The network will take a feed from the Yankees' TV broadcast partner, WPIX.

***

The home run derby continued to make news across the Atlantic Ocean. The *London Sunday Observer* from England had a thousand-word story about the home run race. The headline read: "Babe Ruth Legend Under Siege." Paul Gardner wrote the article as he tried to put the game of baseball in terms the English could understand. "In cricket terms," he pointed out, "a home run is roughly equivalent to a six hit in front of the wicket." He compared Ruth to Jack Hobbs, who, so I'm told, was a legend in English cricket.

***

I'm thirteen years old and just discovered that you can't always believe what you read in a newspaper.

In Joe Trimble's September 19 *Daily News* "Quips 'n' Quotes" column, he writes about the home run record and Ford Frick's decision about the number of games needed to break Ruth's record of 154 games. Trimble points out that it is not within Commissioner Frick's domain to make statements regarding what constitutes a record.

He explains that a seven-man rules committee is empowered to decide what constitutes a record. In other words, Frick has usurped the duty of that committee in stating the 154-game limit for the home run record.

The column goes into detail how, over the years, the rules committee had made decisions and corrected errors in scorekeeping. An example would be that for years, Lou Gehrig's lifetime homer count was listed at 494, but the committee's research showed a triple had been scored as a home run and the total was revised to 493.

Trimble gives other examples of the committee's involvement as it pertains to baseball accomplishments. Among those, he writes that the committee stipulated that a consecutive-game playing streak cannot be prolonged merely by a manager putting a name in the lineup. Which makes sense to me.

According to Trimble, the committee further stipulated that a player must play the field for at least one play or go to bat once for it to count as a game played. This happened once during Lou Gehrig's streak of playing in 2,130 consecutive games.

Trimble explains that during Gehrig's streak, Yankee manager Joe McCarthy listed Lou as a leadoff batter for a game on the road and his position as shortstop because he had a raging fever and was too weak to hit. In the first inning with the Yankees at bat, before Gehrig stepped into the batter's box or played on the field, he was pulled out of the game and sent back to bed at the hotel. A pinch-hitter took his place in the lineup.

That was enough information to send me to the public library where, for the first time ever, I did research on something other than a school project.

After hours of searching *The New York Times* microfilm (which caused my eyes to view everything as if it was rolling), I found the Gehrig game that fit the newspaper's description.

In an article written by James P. Dawson, who covered the game in question, it was played in Detroit at Navin Field against the Tigers on July 14, 1934, and printed in *The New York Times* the next day. Sure enough, the box score had Gehrig leading off playing short, but it listed that he had one at-bat and got a hit.

The article had two paragraphs that explained the circumstance: "Lou Gehrig got into the game for a brief spell, just to avoid snapping his consecutive game string. He insisted on this to protect his mark and boost his string of consecutive games to 1,427, though he is still suffering acutely from a cold in the back that makes breathing difficult and swinging a baseball bat torture."

Dawson added: "Designated as shortstop and leadoff man, Lou slapped a single to right to start a four-run Yankee rally in the first, then gave way to Red Rolfe as pinch-runner, and returned to his hotel quarters."

This contradicted what Trimble had written in his column to make his point about the committee.

Who am I to believe? *The New York Times* day-of-game report from 1934? Or today's *Daily News* column by Joe Trimble?

In my opinion, there are certain records that will never be challenged, such as Cy Young's 511 victories, Joe D's hitting streak of fifty-six games, or Johnny Vander Meer's consecutive no-hitters.

But what if, years from now, a player challenges Gehrig's consecutive-game record of playing in 2,130 games? According to what the *Daily News* printed about the rules committee and that they changed the rules after the fact, is Gehrig's consecutive game record 1,426 games—or 2,130?

So...just because it's printed in the paper doesn't mean it's a fact.

Trimble ended his column by stating that there was one thing for sure: "If Maris hits 61 homers, the public is going to accept him as Ruth's successor." He concluded, "There aren't enough asterisks in the world for Frick to demean that."

***

I knew that Hurricane Esther, with 150 mile-an-hour winds, was headed toward the Atlantic seaboard and could be a problem for the Yankees games in Baltimore when I read that at least sixty ships were being moved from the Norfolk, Virginia, Naval Station.

September 20

In the South Carolina *Greenville News*, columnist Jim Anderson's "Top of the Morning" column included comments by contestants who had sent in entries to the paper's home run derby guessing game:

"Maris is playing for the club and Mantle is playing for the grandstand."

"Maris has more determination."

"Maris pulls the ball better to short right field at Yankee Stadium."

"When Mantle hits it, he hits it a mile."

"If Maris knew the pitchers like Mantle, he might have more homers than he has."

"When Maris hits the ball, it is usually over the plate. Lots of Mantle's home runs are on bad pitches."

"Maris swings for home runs on every trip to the plate."

As a result of reading fan's comments, I wonder sometimes if we are all watching the same games.

***

Today, buried in the sports section of a couple of newspapers, was a small boxed article providing accounts that, with little fanfare, Maris visited a gravely ill four-year-old boy at Johns Hopkins Hospital yesterday, September 19.

The child, Frankie Sliwka, Jr., was suffering from neuroblastoma, a type of cancer. It was reported that the child was obsessed with baseball as a result of his father's passion for the game.

He was struggling to stay alive, but as a result of Maris's visit he was able to attend tonight's game at Memorial Stadium wrapped in blankets with his parents, Frank and Hedwig.

The article said that Rog agreed to make the visit as long it was done without publicity. However, word leaked and the story appeared today along with a photo of Frankie with his nurse.

***

Before the game, Maris and Mantle signed contracts with Frank Coniff, national editor of Hearst Newspapers, for exclusive World Series coverage, which means that some reporter is going to ask them questions and then write it as if the players actually wrote it themselves.

***

The Orioles game against the Yankees was being broadcast around the country. However, Major League Baseball telecasts are not received in Kansas City for general viewing due to league rules that blackout games of those cities having Major League teams.

Kansas City's KMBC-TV station management invited Roger's wife, Pat, who stayed in Raytown, Missouri, to their studios so that she could watch the Yankees-Orioles game in a special viewing room.

Maris entered the September 20 game against the Orioles in Baltimore with fifty-eight homers. This was the only ballpark that—with the exception of the four-bagger Rog hit on July 17 that was lost due to a rainout—had held Maris homer-less this season.

During the season, the baseball writers noted that Maris was ahead of Ruth's home run pace by nine, eight, seven games, etc., and based on the 154-game schedule, this was his last chance to tie and then break Babe's record.

The number of newsmen covering this game ballooned from the normal forty-five to seventy-one.

Maris was up against more than just the tough Orioles pitchers. In addition to the ever-present ghost of Baltimore's own Babe Ruth, Memorial Stadium is a big ballpark—309 feet down the right-field foul line with a 14-foot high grandstand that curves sharply away from the foul pole and measures 380 feet to deep right from home plate.

Ruth Tied Up—In the Yanks' Game 154 at Baltimore's Memorial Stadium, Maris No. 9 walks back to center field after hitting his 59th homer, which tied the Babe's 1921 total when the Bambino "only" hit 59 homers that season.

As a result of Hurricane Esther, the weather is bad, with howling winds blowing in toward home plate, dammit. This was the god-almighty 154th game of the season, which meant that, according to Baseball Commissioner Ford Frick, Maris had to hit three four-baggers to officially break Ruth's record of sixty homers in 154 games. That would be a monumental feat because Rog hadn't hit three homers in one game in his entire big league career.

As for the team, the Yanks needed to win this game to clinch the American League pennant.

For this game, I decided to listen to the radio broadcast and watch the TV telecast simultaneously, which isn't easy to do but I didn't want to miss anything.

In his first at-bat, Rog faced Orioles right-handed pitcher Milt Pappas and lined out to right field.

Coming out of the commercial break in the bottom of the first inning, former Yankee shortstop (and now broadcaster for the Bronx Bombers) Phil Rizzuto was behind the radio mic. Rizzuto acknowledged Memorial Stadium public address announcer Roger Griswold as being the most dramatic in the big leagues.

The Scooter, as Rizzuto was affectionately called by fans and players, added to his Griswold description: "He does a wonderful job." Then he explained, "You think you are listening to *Highway Patrol* (a popular TV show) or the drama of the month."

Shortly after, in the Yankee radio broadcast I could hear an announcement in the Orioles press box.

"Attention all Orioles traveling party. Please bring your bags to the ballpark when you come to the game tomorrow night." This was not meant to be heard over the air, as it was instructions for those members of the media who would be traveling with the Orioles team by plane to Chicago.

Rizzuto giggled and asked his radio producer, "Did they hear that over the air, Joe? Well, that doesn't concern us."

For whatever reason, I enjoy hearing those things that are not intended to be heard by the fans. I guess it's the closest I get to a behind-the-scenes baseball experience.

With one out and nobody on base in the third inning, Rog came to the plate for his second at-bat.

The Scooter announced, "And here comes Roger Maris, who lined to right field in the first inning." The former Yankee apologized to his radio audience, explaining that he was rooting for Roger Maris this night.

Me, too.

Meanwhile, on the television, with the count going to one ball, one strike, the TV cameras couldn't help but show the photographers who were allowed on the field every time Rog came to bat. Mel Allen's terse comment about the shutterbugs said it all: "There they are."

The photographers were a distraction for me watching TV, and they had to be a hindrance to Roger's concentration at the plate. They were on the field near the Yankees' dugout, close to the Yanks' on-deck circle, perhaps no more than twenty feet from the batter's box down the third-base line. They were everywhere except in Roger's underwear.

The next pitch was a ball, which brought the count to two balls, one strike.

In front of 21,032 fans, Pappas got the sign from his catcher and quickly went into his windup as Mel was talking: "I imagine after all of this is over someone may write about the month-long, day-in and day-out excruciating pressure...."

Pappas throws Rog a fastball.

Rog swings and connects.

Allen called it with the cadence of a runner jumping hurdles: "There's one, it is going, it is going, it is gone. Number fifty-nine!"

On the radio side, Rizzuto identified the pitch as headed to the plate, "Two-one pitch," then burst into an excited description of the blast, "Drive deep to right, way back there. Way back and there's number fifty-nine for Roger Maris!"

Rizzuto followed with a personal message of congratulations to Maris, exclaiming, "That a boy, Roger. Fifty-nine home runs."

Rizzuto then quickly described the onslaught of more photographers on the field trying to capture the moment as it played out.

With a pause, perhaps to collect his thoughts, Rizzuto went back to describing the Maris homer: "Man, he really creamed that one," then adding some historical context: "Roger Maris really hit one for his fifty-ninth homer of the year and that puts him in a select field of just two men who have hit fifty-nine homers—Babe Ruth, who also hit sixty, and Roger Maris. He steps ahead of Jimmie Foxx and Hank Greenberg. And there was no doubt about that one. Man, he creamed it."

Field Interference —Once Maris passed the fifty home run mark, competition among local newspaper photographers in each American League city increased; they were all jockeying for position. In Detroit's Tiger Stadium and Baltimore's Memorial Stadium, unlike other ballparks, this meant they were allowed on the field when Maris came to bat.

At the same time, Mel Allen allowed the crowd's cheers to escort Maris as he circled the bases. After Rog crossed home plate, Allen said, "And the Yankees are claiming number fifty-nine and so he becomes the second man in history to ever reach that total, surpassing Jimmie Foxx and Hank Greenberg."

Back on the radio broadcast, realizing that Maris had two, maybe three more times up, Rizzuto described the possibilities: "Can you imagine? One more homer and he'll tie Babe Ruth's record!" Just then, the next batter, Yogi Berra, hit a homer, making it back-to-back homers.

Pappas kept getting hit hard by the Yankee batsmen, which led to him being replaced by Dick Hall in the top of the third inning with one out, Elston Howard at second base, and the score 4–0 Yankees. While the pitching change was taking place, Rizzuto spent time talking about Maris's fifty-ninth homer.

To keep his listeners statistically in the know, Rizzuto mentioned that Maris had hit two homers in one game seven times this year. He then added that Maris had hit fourteen homers in games that the Yankees right-hander Ralph Terry pitched in, including tonight. Just before Hall was ready to pitch to Bill Skowron, Rizzuto acknowledged that the odds were not as near as great against Maris as they were before the game started.

Routine Routine—During Game 154 in Baltimore, Roger's teammates keep their usual game routine, even though Maris needed three homers, according to the commissioner, to break Ruth's record and a win for the Yankees to become 1961 American League champs.

Roger's fifty-ninth homer meant the world to me because of all the odds against him, plus the fact that Mantle was not hitting behind him, which, according to the doubters, was the only reason Rog was getting "fat" pitches to hit. This meant that the pitchers were willing to let Rog take a hack at a pitch rather than put him on base with a walk and then have to face Mantle.

That home run was also significant because it meant that Rog had hit a homer in every American League ballpark this season.

In the fourth inning, as Maris stepped into the batter's box, he was one swing away from hitting No. 60.

Rizzuto announced that, once again, the photographers were out on the field and the fans were holding their breath.

Later, it was reported that Maris admitted to Orioles catcher Gus Triandos as he approached the plate, "Don't think my collar isn't tight."

After four pitches, Maris struck out swinging against the 6′ 2″ right-hander, Dick Hall.

The Yanks led 4–2 in the seventh inning with Hall still on the hill when Rog came to bat again.

Rizzuto then traded mics with Mel Allen, who was doing TV play-by-play on WPIX.

During Roger's at-bat he hit a long fly ball to right that was going, going, going…to be caught by Orioles right fielder Earl Robinson.

In the ninth inning, for his last at-bat, Roger faced Hoyt Wilhelm, who for ten years in the big leagues was known to throw practically nothing but knucklers. Triandos had to get a larger glove to catch it, due to the fact that when that pitch is thrown properly, the movement of the ball traveling to the plate is unpredictable. It darts, flutters, dips, moving up and down erratically in slow motion like an old, beat-up Wiffle ball.

So not only was it hard to catch, it was harder to hit.

As Wilhelm was warming up, Rog displayed his dry sense of humor by asking home plate ump Ed Runge out of the side of his mouth while looking at the pitcher, "So, Ed, what does this guy throw?"

Wilhelm stoically looked in for a sign. Everyone in the ballpark, listening to the radio, and watching on TV knew that every pitch would be a knuckleball.

I moved closer to the TV and turned up the radio volume. With no emotion in his voice, Allen announced, "Up comes Roger Maris."

Up comes Roger Maris?

Is Mel kidding? I'd be screaming if I was doing the play-by-play. Other than Ruth, how many players have ever stepped into the batter's box having hit fifty-nine homers for the season? None.

Allen quickly reviewed what Rog did in his previous at-bat. He then described the first pitch, which was fouled back on a check swing for strike one.

The next delivery, according to Allen, resulted in a slow tap down the line on a half swing. Wilhelm came over, picked up the slow roller, and tagged Rog out as the Yankees were retired.

On TV, I had watched as Rog started to swing at Wilhelm's second pitch, then held up as the ball floated in. The pitch found Maris's bat. Ever so slowly, as if the baseball itself was disappointed, it trickled harmlessly down the first-base line in fair territory.

I watched as the expressionless Wilhelm picked up the ball and softly pressed it against Rog's uniform as he appeared to be half-heartedly jogging to first base for the out.

It was a damn dribbler, nothing more than an "excuse me" swing. So instead of Roger's bat hitting the ball, the ball hit the bat in his last possible at-bat in game 154.

Allen explained to the radio audience that the Baltimore crowd was giving Rog a standing ovation, which pleased me. But unless the game goes into extra innings, it was over.

Since Maris was the last out of the inning, Johnny Blanchard brought out his teammate's Spalding glove and told Rog how proud he was to be on the same team as him.

Second base ump Charlie Berry stopped Rog as he was jogging to his center-field position and said, "Son, you've had a fine year. Just keep up the good work."

Three Oriole outs later, the Yanks won the game 4–2 and clinched the 1961 American League pennant for the twenty-sixth time.

In order to capture the celebration, WPIX had a TV camera to broadcast events live from the Yankee locker room.

This truly is "inside baseball," and I'm imagining that I'm off to the side in the Yankee clubhouse, taking it all in.

The first player interviewed by Allen was Elston Howard. Yogi was next and expressed his wish that Rog had hit one more homer in the game. Manager Ralph Houk said that everyone on the team was pulling for Rog. Then a series of interviews with whomever Allen could get to talk to him: Rollie Sheldon, Jim Coates, Luis Arroyo, Bobby Richardson, Clete Boyer.

Then Allen paused to read a telegram from "the good folks at Ballantine Beer," congratulating the team for winning the pennant.

Allen then corralled Rog for an interview. He began by offering his congratulations and adding, "I'm sorry you didn't get No. 60."

Maris: "Well, I was trying."

Allen then mentioned the earlier "washed-out homer" game back on July 17.

Allen: "How do you feel to come so close?"

Maris: "Well, it always feels good to come close, and I'm in some pretty good company with Ruth, Greenberg, Foxx, so I'm very happy."

Allen interrupted Rog and said, "You are in company with just Ruth." Then he switched subjects, asking, "You won't mind the asterisk, will you, from here on out?"

Maris: "No, I'm sure I won't."

Allen: "You going to keep swinging? You're not going to take a day off, are you?"

Maris: "No, I'll keep playing and see what happens. I'll just take my chances."

Allen: "You have been under severe pressure."

I could hear exasperation in Roger's voice as he replied, "That, you are right on."

Allen brought up the pressure question, focusing on the photographers who crowded around home plate.

Maris: "It does get to you after a while."

Allen: "Do you feel relieved?"

Maris: "Right now, yes. Very relieved. Winning the pennant and the 154-game limit is over with."

Allen: "No regrets?"

Maris: "No regrets."

Allen: "God bless you. Great team man, Rog." Allen then noted how Rog on a number of occasions would bunt to get a runner from third to home.

Mel let Rog go as the photographers were begging for one more shot. Mel continued to do interviews with General Manager Roy Hamey, who said, "What a ball club. I'm proud of this club. Wonderful, wonderful, wonderful. Tremendous spirit."

More Allen interviews: Ralph Terry and then Moose Skowron, who said, "The greatest ball club I ever played with," and Wally Moses, who said, "This is the best club I was ever on."

For the purpose of getting a sponsor's name into the broadcast without going to a commercial, Mel read another congratulations telegram, this one from P. Ballantine and Sons and the R. J. Reynolds Tobacco Company.

Then back to the interviews, first with pitcher Bill Stafford, who during the off-season is the deputy sheriff of Athens, N.Y. Then Ralph Houk, Yankee trainer Gus Mauch, Whitey Ford, Hector Lopez, Billy Gardner who said, "This is a great ball club," Bob Hale, Johnny Blanchard, Tex Clevenger, Hal Reniff, and Yankee public relations director Bob Fishel.

Mel had time to read one more telegram, this one from "your neighborhood Ford dealers."

Throughout the interviews, I could hear celebratory hooting and hollering as Ballantine beer and New York State Gold Seal champagne was consumed and sprayed in every direction.

At one point, Rog lit up a cigar as if he was just informed that his wife had given birth to a baby, which pleased the photographers because they needed one more shot. "Hey, Rog, look over here."

After the game, the fan who nabbed home run No. 59 was aware of Sam Gordon's offer of $5,000 for homer No. 61, so the fan offered to sell No. 59 to Rog for a figure close to that. Rog turned him down.

And for all those lame excuse naysayers, Rog hit home run No. 59 without Mantle batting behind him.

However you spell the sound of sticking out your tongue or the Bronx cheer, insert here, because it makes my point about those guys

Was it possible that with eight games remaining, Rog could hit one or more homers? Man, I hope so.

Holy Toledo. I've got school in a few hours.

***

Claire Ruth was quoted after the game: "The Babe loved that record. He wanted to be known as the King of Home Runs forever."

***

An unidentified fan was interviewed as he left the stadium in Baltimore. "I came in here hoping the guy would never hit another home run, and I left pulling for him to tie Ruth. I never would have believed it possible, but he gave it such a try he converted me."

***

The Yankees' pennant-winning party was covered by Dick Young of the *Daily News*. It began shortly after midnight and ended after four a.m. Wally Moses was doing a lot of singing, and Spud Murray provided the music for a few team members to sing "Goodnight Irene" to Ralph Houk's wife, Betty.

***

Do I wish Rog would hit another tonk to make it sixty? Yes. But fifty-nine homers in 154 games was more than okay, as I didn't want to be greedy.

***

Mayor Wagner sent Yankees club president Dan Topping a telegram: "Congratulations to you and all the Yankees on winning the pennant. Our city is proud of the Yanks and hope they take the World Series in character-istic style—that is, four straight. All best wishes."

After Wagner sent the telegram, he announced that the city would honor its team with a ticker tape parade—on either October 2 or 3.

***

With the game televised to many parts of the country and the American League pennant all but decided, I was curious as to how many people attended games tonight.

The Red Sox were in Chicago and drew 8,610 fans to Comiskey Park.

The Indians hosted Kansas City in their last home game of the season and drew 2,632 fans in their ballpark, which has a capacity of more than 75,000.

I can't imagine what that was like for the few fans who sat in an empty ballpark. Oh, wait a minute. I remember that the Yanks drew 1,947 fans at

Yankee Stadium earlier this season when they played the Kansas City Athletics on April 17.

September 21

The September 21 *New York Times* was filled with Maris stories. Writer Richard J. H. Johnston surveyed fans with the question: Should Maris be credited with breaking Ruth's record if it takes him more than 154 games to do it?" Of the twenty-four asked, fifteen agreed with Commissioner Frick.

My favorite response posed a question I hadn't heard before: "Do the Yanks have to win the pennant in 154 games?" Bartender Pat Flood answered his own question with a "No," which made the point that the season's American League pennant will be decided on a 162-game schedule, not 154 games, and therefore so should the home run record.

Meanwhile, baseball fans in Tokyo, Japan, were also polled on September 20. They were divided as to the controversial 154-game schedule deadline.

Fans polled in Havana, Cuba, were unanimous in their opinion, simply summed up with, "Ruth *si*, Maris *no*."

***

Jim Murray of the *Los Angeles Times* wrote a column about Rog that was titled, "Failure At 58?" Murray elegantly pointed out all the challenges Maris faced, from the height of the wall at Baltimore's Memorial Stadium to the pitchers to Ford Frick.

Murray ends his column by saying, "The fence, the pitchers, the commissioner of baseball, the ghost of Ruth will be picketed out in right field for Maris—the toughest shift in history. I hope he hits that ball right through all of them and into that glass case at Cooperstown."

Too bad Murray doesn't write for a New York paper.

***

U.S. Representative Melvin Price from Illinois, a former newspaper sports editor, was at the White House when President Kennedy, upon seeing him, remarked, "Well, he didn't make it."

***

The New York Times ran a short piece from Toronto with the headline, "Canadians for Maris."

***

A United Press International headline asked, "Did Frick Pull A Boner In HR Record Ruling?" Well, you can imagine how seeing the word *boner* in the newspaper set off giggles from my buddies...and me. I'm sorry, but there are certain words that make me giggle, and boner is one of 'em.

The article referenced an informal poll conducted among the Baltimore Oriole players. Without reservation, fourteen of the fifteen players felt that Maris should be entitled to a home run record if he hit sixty-one within the Yankees' next eight games.

***

As a result of Maris falling short of tying Ruth's sixty home run mark, a photo of sixteen-year-old baseball fan Richard McCue polishing the "Babe Ruth Plaza" sign outside Baltimore Memorial Stadium was printed in Pennsylvania's *New Castle News*.

***

Earl Wilson's September 21 *Daily News* column, "It Happened Last Night," mentioned that Roger had some friends visiting him, including his barber, Frank Garzaniti of the Stage Barber Shop and Max Asnas, owner of the Stage Delicatessen.

***

Roger revealed to Joe Reichler of the Associated Press today that a Baltimore doctor told him his hair loss was caused by stress from his assault on the home run record.

"I was afraid it was some kind of disease," he said, "but the doctor assured me it was none of the sort. He said it was just a case of nerves, caused by strain and tension."

***

Maris's failure to hit his sixty-first home run in his 154th official game last night had at least one side effect. It might have been slightly obscure, but it was a side effect: It proved that, similar to humans, Casey the Computer is not infallible.

On August 30, Casey, an IBM 1401 electronic computer, calculated the chances were fifty-five out of one hundred that Maris would hit sixty-one homers in 154 games.

There is no joy at IBM, as mighty Casey has struck out.

***

Steve Myhra of the Baltimore Colts grew up in Wahpeton, N.D., which was fifty miles from Maris's Fargo high school. The two were reunited before the game at Baltimore Memorial Stadium.

While both were in high school, they competed against each other in football, basketball, baseball, and track.

In 1951, they both made the first team North Dakota All-State Grid Squad, Myhra as a tackle and Maris as a back.

***

I'm a big fan of the Marx Brothers and have done my best to imitate Groucho when the opportunity presents itself. Tonight is the last show of the TV program *You Bet Your Life*. That means I'll never again hear Groucho remark, "Say the secret *woid* and win a hundred dollars."

Well, dat's da most ridiculous ting I ever *hoid*.

***

Before the September 21 Orioles game, the Oriole Advocates civic booster club honored Roger by presenting him with a trophy for his sportsmanship. Oriole radio broadcaster Herb Carneal, the master of ceremonies, said the award was "not for hitting fifty-nine home runs, but for sportsmanship."

Described as being several feet tall, the trophy was inscribed for Roger earning the "ultimate respect and admiration of Oriole fans."

***

The Associated Press reported that Maris's fifty-ninth homer traveled 390 feet. Yet Al Abrams of the *Pittsburgh Post-Gazette* reported that the fifty-ninth homer traveled 450 feet.

Am I supposed to add them and divide by two to get the average?

***

The two players who hit fifty-eight homers watched the game last night. Hank Greenberg watched from an ABC-TV booth at the game, and Jimmie Foxx was in an ABC studio in New York.

***

The day after Maris hit his fifty-ninth homer, many newspapers carried a story about Pat Maris, who felt that she was responsible for her husband's feeble last at-bat when he rolled out to Wilhelm.

According to the report, Pat was watching the game on a special TV feed at the Kansas City TV station KMBC. In the ninth inning she exchanged seats with another viewer to get closer to the TV.

She recalled that she and Roger have a superstition that whenever she leaves her seat while watching a game it puts a hex on him.

Pat was quoted as saying, "Moving my chair jinxed him. I did the same thing earlier in the season, and he struck out."

***

United Press International's Oscar Fraley penned an article about Maris that was inappropriate, as it disparaged Roger's actions in the locker room, physical appearance, demeanor, and character, rather than providing his readers with insightful information pertaining to baseball.

I'm guessing Fraley was trying to draw attention to himself by taking a point of view that other writers wouldn't lower themselves to argue.

It was apparent that Fraley was misguided and quick to judge while not considering the stress of the intense media interest along with the physical grind of 154 baseball games.

Here are a few samples of his snarky descriptions of Maris after Rog hit his fifty-ninth home run:

- "He was impassive as someone living in a vacuum."

- "He was a man with the cold poise of a Mississippi steamboat gambler holding a royal flush."
- "The face was as expressionless as those cut into the unyielding rock of Mount Rushmore."
- "His deep-set eyes gazed forth on a watching world with the flinty, unwavering stare of a house detective checking a spurious credit card."
- "The voice was the flat, level monotone of a train announcer reading a part in 'Othello.'"
- "He shrugged, still without cracking the veneer."
- "He didn't look happy, or sad, or relieved. You'd see more expression on the fish who stole your bait," he wrote.

If Fraley was trying to describe Maris's post-game appearance, then one of these descriptions would have made the point. He went overboard in performing a one-man verbal "dog pile." Anyone who read Fraley's words was cheated.

I had to wonder how Fraley would have reacted if someone had reviewed his journalistic writing while at the same time calling him a disingenuous, loudmouth, ill-mannered, egotistical, self-centered, overweight, mean-spirited slob with poor personal hygiene who is a friendless, stingy, beady-eyed, foul-smelling, misogynistic, nose-picking farter who never has a kind word to say about anyone. And that even on the good day, he's infested with moral rot, and his verbal communication skills are peppered with coarse profane language.

On the chance that I haven't made my point clear, Fraley can invest a dime and pick up the phone and call me anytime weeknights after 6:30 p.m. I'm in the book but here's my number: WH 6 2062. You obviously need help, and I'm the guy who can give it to you.

*** •

Mary Jane Porter, a journalist from the *Messenger Inquirer* of Owensboro, Kentucky, wrote a story titled "Women to Be Happier Now, With Home Run Race Ended." Her point was that women were not interested in baseball, and only faked interest to please their husbands.

It just so happens I know a couple of girls who, same as me, like baseball. And they aren't married and don't have boyfriends.

***

The *Daily News* ran a photo of Rog holding four-year-old Davey Herzog, son of Orioles outfielder Whitey Herzog, on the back page of their September 21 issue that was shot prior to last night's game. Rog and Whitey were teammates when they both were with the Kansas City Athletics in 1958 and 1959. Currently they are Raytown, Mo., neighbors.

A Crowning Moment—Roger was awarded the 1961 Babe Ruth Sultan of Swat Award by the Maryland Professional Baseball Players Association. The award recognized the player with the greatest "slugging average"—combining home runs and runs batted in—while at the same time honoring Babe Ruth, who grew up in Baltimore.

September 22

It was announced today that Maris will return to Baltimore on January 15 to receive his second Babe Ruth Sultan of Swat award, which is a bejeweled crown that looks like the crown on the head of a king in a deck of playing cards.

I don't understand why an award such as this is announced before the end of the season? Does anyone remember what happened last year at the World Series?

Let me remind you. Before the game was over and it appeared that the Yanks would win, Yankee second-baseman Bobby Richardson was voted the series MVP. Then, in the bottom of the ninth inning, the Pirates' Bill Mazeroski hit the most dramatic World Series home run to win it for the Pirates.

So what would happen if, before this season ends, Willie Mays hit an unprecedented six homers in one game? Perhaps it's another example of taking advantage of the national spotlight on Rog.

***

On September 22, the *Daily News* upped their home run contest cash award to a $4,500 payout, of which $3,000 goes to the winner. The offer was good for the time period of September 26 to October 1, but only hand-delivered entries to the Information Bureau in the lobby of the Daily News Building on 42nd street are eligible.

***

In Robert Sylvester's *Daily News* "Dream Street" gossip column, he wrote: "I told you Roger Maris wouldn't come close."

Obviously, there are some people who are going to gloat in the face of Maris's failure to break Ruth's record. I think the descriptive word would be "petty."

***

Maris was named the August winner of the S. Rae Hickok Pro Athlete of the Year poll. Maris received fifty-eight first-place votes, Warren Spahn twenty-seven for second place. Mantle placed third.

***

Ed Sullivan's *Daily News* column, "Little Old New York," had this "One Man's Opinion" item: "Yessir, I was rooting for Babe Ruth defending that. It wasn't because of his age but because Babe did it the hard way—against a slower ball, larger playing fields and bats that were inferior to those used by Mantle and Maris."

"Old Stone Face" left out that Maris—unlike Ruth—faced greater challenges, such as better pitching, night baseball, the increase in defensive talent due to the integration of Negro stars, larger ballparks, jet lag, and a slew of media that contained some nasty, unethical reporters instead of drinking chums.

***

One of my favorite quotes from Roger appeared in a number of newspapers: "I was hired to play this season for the Yankees and not employed to play against Babe Ruth."

***

There are plenty of newspaper stories about funding for a new government project launched by President Kennedy called the Peace Corps. I don't know what it's all about, but I like the name. It makes me wonder what would this world be like if peace on earth was given an opportunity to thrive.

September 23

I'm getting a kick out of the extent to which non-sportswriters are including Maris's name in their columns: In Charles McHarry's *Daily News* "On The Town" column, he writes sarcastically: "Grandma Moses' wire to Roger Maris reads: 'Wait till you try for 102.'"

***

In the *Daily News'* September 23 issue, they ran an ad promoting that Dick Young would straighten out what's been going on with Maris, Ruth, Frick, asterisks, 154- and 162-game schedules, record books—by writing an entertaining tell-all story on Sunday, September 24.

Oh, my god, will this asterisk thing ever go away?

***

Dick Young's *Daily News* column "Young Ideas" pointed out that "Frick said nothing of asterisks or footnotes. He did not intend, then or now, that Maris's achievement should be relegated to footnote status."

***

For me, every day is a perfect day to play baseball, and Saturday, September 23, was no exception. In fact, it was better than perfect because I didn't have school, and we were experiencing one of those rare, warm and unseasonable New York days of fall.

I called my classmate Marc Satenberg, who lived a few blocks from my house, and asked him if he wanted to meet me at Ralph Avenue field, not far from where we both lived, and hit the ball around.

I knew Marc wasn't obsessed with baseball like me because his first love was music. Mostly folk music.

Marc is an immensely talented guitar player and singer. There was no question in my mind that Marc was going to be a famous folk singer someday soon. In addition to his musical talents, he surely looked the part. With his un-schoolboyish, manly good looks, he appeared beyond his thirteen years with a day-old unshaven beard and curly black hair complemented with thick sideburns.

It was Marc who got me interested in motorcycles. We talked about them, drew pictures of them, then decided that we should take out a classified ad to purchase an old one that didn't run just so we could take photos sitting on it.

The closest we could get to actually riding a motorcycle was riding our bicycles. Rather than put baseball cards in the spokes to sound like a motor, we put partially air-filled balloons in the spokes, which resulted in a much more ominous sound.

While riding, we developed a game in which we would jump our bikes over chains that were no more than three inches off the ground as if that was a fifteen-foot tall barbed wire fence.

We also created a game in which—while riding our bikes in circles in a parking lot—we would pass a small broomstick handle to each other. That was it. Nothing more than a handoff riding at breakneck speed. Naturally, we called the game "Bystick."

Once during this past summer, when Marc was at a sleepover in my house, we stayed up late watching TV.

Since I knew Marc was smart, I asked him what he wanted out of his life. He didn't hesitate, explaining that he wanted to be a famous folk singer, make a lot of money, own a Harley-Davidson 350cc motorcycle, have beautiful girlfriends, and travel around the world.

When Marc asked me the same question, I also didn't hesitate: "I'd like to have one of Roger Maris's bats and one of his home run baseballs, play for the Yankees, have the best baseball card collection in the world, live in a nice house with a wood-panel den and a leather sofa that smells like a baseball glove, and be happy."

Marc looked back at me with a furrowed brow and said slowly, "Man, you are so square."

But on this perfect day, it was all about playing baseball. Fortunately for me, Marc always seemed to be receptive to play some ball at a moment's notice.

Since there were only two of us, it was "fungo" time, which meant that the batter would toss the baseball into the air and hit it before it landed on the ground.

The rumor floated around that the name "fungo" came about because, once you hit the ball, it was "fun to go" get it.

Marc was first up. He wasn't really that good of a hitter because he couldn't place the ball where he wanted to hit it.

For me, I love easy fly balls where I don't have to run a long way to catch them. Those balls are called a "can of corn." That name came about as a result of those cans of corn stacked so high—almost to the ceiling—on shelves of grocery stores that shoppers needed a stick to topple the top can so that it fell straight down and they had to catch it before it hit the floor.

After Marc took a few cuts, one of his swings pulled the ball and it veered drastically away from me, rolling near some other kids who were playing catch. Marc yelled to a kid who was closest to where the ball landed: "Hey, how 'bout a little help! Can you get the ball for us?"

The youngster waved and asked, "Where is it?"

Without hesitating, Marc responded and pointed, "It's between me and Banana Nose,"—referring to me.

The kid ran over, picked up the ball, and threw it to Marc.

Ahh, yes, another endearing and descriptive nickname created on the spur of a moment by a beloved friend.

September 24

Dick Young is never shy when it comes to sharing his opinion about most things in sports. In today's *Daily News*, he writes, "The [baseball] rules committee of seven are, in the main, newspapermen. By tradition, newspapermen are dedicated; also lazy. If this particular committee has met twice within the past three years, it has strained itself."

***

In Gene Ward's *Daily News* column, "Inside Sports," he notes that Frick was one hundred percent correct about the 154-game schedule. He added that the majority of baseball fans agreed with Frick.

This would have been a lot more credible if it had been published before the 154th game was played.

***

The Boston Red Sox were out of first place by more than thirty games, but the team smartly offered a trade: an autographed Maris ball, plus two tickets to their 1962 opener—to the fan who catches a Maris homer in Fenway when the Yanks come to town for two games Saturday and Sunday.

Rog didn't connect, but Mick hit his fifty-fourth.

***

Dick Young's column occasionally prints letters from readers. Obviously, Young picks those letters that he can answer and make for good reading.

Naturally, with the home run race nearing its finale, many of the letters were about Maris.

Sy Evans of New York City writes: "Please find room in the shed next year so Maris and Joe Trimble can make sure they break Babe Ruth's record."

Young's response: "Please stop picking on Joe Trimble. He belongs to me."

Frank Mancaruso of Brooklyn writes: "If Maris hits 61 homers in 162, why not add the homers Ruth hit in the first 8 games of the following season."

Young's response: "Ruth hit 1—and I'm sure you can come up with a better idea than that."

James P. Cassidy of Bergenfield, NJ, writes: "Use the ratio 162 to 154 which translated means that Maris would have to hit 63.1 homers to dethrone Ruth. If he gets 63, no dice; if he gets 64, a coronation."

Young's response: "Your formula appears to be mathematically equitable, but I'm afraid such equations would not receive public acceptance, due to complexity."

Clarence M. Davis of Hempstead, NY, writes: "M&M had an advantage as a result of the strike zone being different when Ruth played, which was the shoulders and eventually lowered to the armpits."

Young's response: "You seek Utopia. The world changes and conditions are never the same. But if Maris were to be given Ruthian record recognition on the basis of 162 games, there certainly would be something smellier than armpits."

Philip J. Levandoski of Brooklyn writes: "I agree with Frick 100%. I would like to see the number of plate appearances to qualify for a batting title be adjusted for catchers since they experience more injuries than other players." He made his case because it appeared that Elston Howard will not come to bat the necessary 502 times.

Young's response: "It does appear that catchers are being discriminated against. However, any rule which makes different requirements for different cases is a weak rule. Why not simply lower it to 462 for all?"

***

Roger managed to hit a single but failed to hit No. 60 at Fenway Park in four at-bats. The Red Sox crowd of almost 31,000 showered Maris with cheers and a standing ovation after he flied out in his last plate appearance of the game. Boston won 3–1.

***

T. Norell, a postal employee from Simpsonville, South Carolina, was the winner of the *Greenville News* contest. His entry was not the only correct guess, but was postmarked an hour earlier than Steve McAllister's entry.

***

The *Daily News* reports that Ford Frick took umbrage with American League president Joe Cronin, who will accept the new home run record regardless of the number of games.

You're killing me, Frick.

September 25

In a speech at the United Nations, President Kennedy talked about nuclear disarmament, declaring: "Today, every inhabitant of this planet must contemplate that day when this planet may no longer be inhabitable. Every man, woman and child lives under a nuclear sword of Damocles, hanging by the slenderest of threads, capable of being cut at any moment by accident or miscalculation or madness. The weapons of war must be abolished before they abolish us."

This speech confirmed my belief that we are all doomed. I need a beer. We've got to find a way to bring some loving here today, or I'll never reach eighteen when it's legal for me to drink.

***

In Charles McHarry's "On the Town" *Daily News* column, he wrote that even though Maris didn't break the Bambino's sixty mark, the Yankees catchers did. Yogi Berra, Elston Howard, and Johnny Blanchard have hit a cumulative total of sixty-one homers this season.

***

The most obscure note about Mantle and Maris is appearing as a one-line filler in newspapers: "A stripper adopted the name Mickey Maris."

So let me guess. Next week Sheb Wooley will come out with a song about the M&M Boys that will eclipse his "Purple People Eater" song from a couple years ago.

No, no wait, I've got a better guess. The Chipmunks will release a baseball song next March during spring training.

***

Wisely anticipating the deluge of business offers headed his way, Maris became incorporated. Henry McLemore, a sports columnist for the Hearst Newspapers, had some fun with the prospects of Maris's testimonials and endorsements in his column, "Looking 'Em Over."

"We will see (I am sure) Maris drinking Hoopla Cola, munching Krispy Krunkles, building a wall with Never Crack bricks, playing golf in Toe Delight shoes, using Never Slip chalk on his pool cue, shaving with a Man's Best Friend razor, saying 'Yum, Yum' after a bite of cake baked with Split-Second Mix, grinning from ear to ear after a sip of All Ready coffee, and inhaling blissfully after a puff of a Himalaya cigarette ('cool as snow and mountain tall').

"He will also (I am also sure) show us what shirts wear the longest, which trousers are cut the best, which ties never wrinkle, and will advise us on where to spend our vacations, what car to drive, what cereal to gulp in the morning, what soap keeps us cleanest for the longest time, and suggest the type of linoleum for our library floor."

If McLemore really knew Maris, his personality and on-field baseball accomplishments, he would have mentioned endorsements for a product such as All-Star Fly Chaser that catches anything in the air, or that when traveling Maris stays at one of the 142 Runs Batted Inn hotels, or that Maris enjoys a "to die for" dessert of Sacrifice Bundt Cake. The writer might have considered to include how Maris makes a point to always sign autographs with a No Bull Pen and keeps his growing collection of trophies in a Safe At Home.

September 26

The *Chicago Daily Tribune* takes a cheap shot at Rog when they titled the Yankee-Orioles box score and purposely misspelled his first name—Rigor Maris.

That rag is for the birds.

***

Barry Goldwater, the senator from Arizona, commented on the speech

JFK gave yesterday at the United Nations in which the president warned the delegates they would be remembered for either turning our planet into a flaming pyre or bringing it peace.

Goldwater remarked, "Based on history, I have no faith in disarmament. There is always one…in the world who won't go along with it."

The three dots represented a word which newspapers did not want to print and I don't think the word was idiot. I'm going to guess that the word was "ass."

***

Another offer popped up for the fan who catches the record-breaking golden gopher: An all-expenses paid trip to the World's Fair next year in Seattle.

***

Led by player representative Whitey Ford, the Yankees held a players-only meeting at three p.m. to discuss World Series shares.

***

National Football League Commissioner Pete Rozelle weighed in on the asterisk situation as it pertained to football. Over the past twenty years, the NFL's regular season has expanded, going from eleven games to twelve games and now fourteen games.

He was quoted by *Daily News* sportswriter Dana Mozley in a September 26 article, making it clear that he wasn't second-guessing Ford Frick: "It must be our policy to take the best performances as they come, regardless of the number of games, if the records are to mean anything."

***

I read that to keep his hand-eye motor skills sharp while improving his concentration and patience, Roger enjoys playing Labyrinth before a ball-game. That's the small wood-box game with knobs on the side to balance a steel ball the size of a marble rolling through a maze, while trying to avoid the holes along the path or the ball drops through the hole and you need to start over again.

***

Throughout my life, one of my idiosyncrasies is to give inanimate objects personalities and names. Not just stuffed animals like "Smokey Bear," "Jocko," "Sleepy," "Smiley," and "Throw Up Monkey," but things like a spoon, a pencil, my bicycle, a blanket, my baseball mitt, radio, and even my pillow.

I don't know why, but I do. I'm sure that some shrink would be able to explain it in a couple of seconds. But I live with it every minute that I am awake. Such was the situation for the baseball that Rog would hit for home run No. 60.

Watching the game on TV, I immediately thought how fortunate that specific baseball was to play such an important role.

I thought about that baseball's existence long before it got into the September 26 night game at Yankee Stadium. His beginnings can be traced back to the A. G. Spalding factory in Chicopee, Massachusetts, where elements of baseballs are assembled, a process that includes the cover being stitched by hand. However, it probably would be more appropriate at this point for "Homer No. 60" to tell his story in his own words.

Thanks, Andy.

Ahh, yes, I relished the immense satisfaction of that 108th double-stitch, red-lace thread connecting my two horsehide panels that were carefully sewn together by A. G. Spalding & Bros. chief stitcher, Beryl Gauthier. Oh, how good that feels. She completes me. I'm now a big league baseball. And once that official indicia stamp is applied, I'm an official American League baseball.

Allow me to share with you my genetic history. Uniform specifications for the ball began in 1872, when our official size (nine inches in circumference) and weight (five ounces) were established. Our center was changed from rubber to cork in 1910. A cushioned cork center, with a rubber layer wrapped around the cork, has been used since 1931. For nearly a century, every ball has included four layers of wool yarn and each of our horsehide white-leather panel covers are secured with 108 hand-sewn stitches.

The final touch is the application of the light-blue stamp that reads "OFFICIAL BALL AMERICAN LEAGUE" with a facsimile Joe Cronin signature and his title, albeit abbreviated, "PRES." That stamp is my official birthmark, which proclaims that I have "THE CUSHION CORK CENTER" and below that, "THE SIGN OF QUALITY" as part of the legendary REACH logo.

Once completed, I'm carefully wrapped in white tissue paper and placed in a colorful red, white, blue, and yellow Reach-designed single-baseball box. I'm then inserted in a larger box that contains eleven other boxed American League baseball brethren. We are then shipped, usually by truck, to a ballpark.

Fortunately for me, my destination was the Bronx, specifically Yankee Stadium at East 161st Street.

Once there, we waited patiently for the light of day. I'm guessing that it might have been a couple of weeks before I was removed from the Reach box along with seventy-one lookalikes and tossed into a ball bag.

My ultimate fate could be any number of possibilities. Likely scenarios include being thrown around by Yankee players for the purpose of "warming up" their arms, or possibly being just another baseball in batting practice, which in both cases means not participating in an official American League game.

Then there's always the chance that I could be selected and placed on one of the old vintage picnic tables in the Yankee clubhouse so that every Yankee player could write his name in ink on my horsehide. I would then become an autographed souvenir instead of a blank baseball, a prized possession for someone associated with the team.

But my greatest desire, like any other baseball worth its yarn, would be to get into an official American League game. However, I need to explain that merely getting into a game doesn't guarantee my fate would be memorable.

There are many stories of baseballs in years gone by who entered a game only to have an experience that lasts one pitch as a result of being fouled off into the stands. That would be heartbreaking. To be so close, but yet so far away from what I have desired for my whole life.

In preparation for the September 26 night game—the Yankees facing the Baltimore Orioles—I, along with dozens of other balls, was delivered to the umpires' locker room that afternoon just after lunch.

It was there that each one of us baseballs was rubbed up with Lena Blackburne mud, named for a 1920s infielder who initiated the practice. This removes our white sheen and slickness so that a pitcher can get a better grip. The mud originates from the New Jersey side of the Delaware River, but its exact location is a secret.

Moments before the singing of our national anthem, I was in the Yankee dugout, patiently waiting with the other baseballs for the game to begin.

All of us baseballs were bursting with anticipation, excitedly hoping to get into the game in a memorable and meaningful play.

I knew that the ultimate experience would be for one of us to be pitched to Roger Maris at-bat because we all knew that he began the game with fifty-nine home runs.

Bill Kinnamon was the home-plate umpire and Gus Triandos was the Orioles catcher for Jack Fisher, the starting pitcher for Baltimore.

In the first inning Roger Maris singled up the middle.

Patiently, I waited for my time to arrive.

In the third inning with the Orioles leading two to nothing, Roger came to the plate with two outs and nobody on base. Under the arc lighting of Yankee Stadium, the pitch sequence from right-hander Jack Fisher to Maris was:

1st pitch: Lined foul down the right-field line (new ball, not me, is put into play)

2nd pitch: Pop foul into the stands (another new ball, not me, is put into play)

3rd pitch: Outside for ball 1

4th pitch: Low for ball 2

5th pitch: Grounder foul.

The count was two and two. That's when I felt umpire Bill Kinnamon's fingers grasp me and toss me to Fisher, who caught me with his A2000 Wilson glove.

Needless to say, I was as nervous as Fisher, who, for whatever reason, didn't go to the rosin bag. Instead, he immediately rubbed me up, either because it's a habit he has when a new ball is put into play or for the purpose of getting a better feel for my horsehide covering. This was it.

Fisher read Triandos's sign for the next pitch. I knew that it was the ultimate game-situation pitch as Fisher placed his right index finger and middle finger to the left side of my seam and his thumb on the back seam. I knew instinctively that I was supposed to curve on my way to home plate.

I was hoping that I wouldn't veer outside the strike zone for ball 3 or—as a result of being in the strike zone with Maris not swinging—become strike 3. Then there was the possibility that Maris would swing and miss me completely for strike 3.

The possibilities are endlessly mind-boggling. Oh, how I wanted to be hit. I was praying that if I was hit, I wouldn't go foul.

The Baltimore right-hander went into his windup and swoosh....I'm on my way to home plate. I did curve but not enough to fool Maris as his bat hit my seamless fat-side solid, changing my direction by thrusting me violently toward right field.

For a fraction of a moment, as I was hurtling toward Yankee Stadium's upper-deck stands, I had a monumental concern that my trajectory would take me to the right of the right-field foul pole for, dare I think it, a foul ball.

Then...uh, oh...yikes...humph...thud...bang...ouch...owwwie.

My ascent was stopped by a concrete step no less than four feet from the right-field foul pole in fair territory in the upper deck.

Hooray for me! Yippee! I did it!

Not only did I get into the game, but Roger Maris hit me for a home run. Home run No. 60! I was elated, bursting with pride. Can you blame me?

As a result of hitting the upper deck façade, I ricocheted harmlessly back onto the right-field grass in front of the Yankee bullpen.

Orioles right fielder Earl Robinson ran over and picked me up. He tossed me to second base umpire Eddie Hurley, who then relayed me toward the Yankees dugout so Maris could have me as a keepsake. Thanks, Earl and Eddie, for your thoughtfulness.

On my way to the Yankee dugout I watched as Maris circled the bases in a brisk, non-celebratory jog, just as he had done fifty-nine times earlier during the season.

Then, as Maris rounded third base, I caught a glimpse of Frank Crosetti, the

Yanks third-base coach, back-pedaling toward home plate so that he could congratulate No. 9 with a handshake and pat on his back.

All the while, I couldn't help but listen to the fans cheering.

As Roger's right foot stepped on home plate, he shook hands with Hector Lopez, the next batter, and grabbed Yankee batboy Frankie Perdenti's left hand with his own left.

Maris kept the same jogging pace and proceeded into the Yankee dugout while removing his batting helmet. Yogi Berra, who was heading to the on-deck circle, shook his hand and then patted him on his right shoulder.

As if it was meant to be, Roger and I entered the Yankee dugout at the same time. He entered at the home plate end of the dugout, while on the other end of the dugout I was handed over to the Yanks assistant clubhouse man, "Little Pete" Previte.

Maris tried to make his way through the swarm of players in the dugout who wanted to congratulate him as the fans' cheering was replaced by applause for his accomplishment of hitting sixty homers in one season.

My ears were filled with Roger's Yankee teammates urging him to step out of the dugout and onto the field to acknowledge the fans' applause.

To appease his teammates, Maris reluctantly moved to the top step of the dugout and then briefly removed his Yankee cap and waved it to the fans in a shy manner.

The Yanks won the game 3–2, after all three of the Orioles batters struck out in the ninth inning to end the game.

Maris jogged in from center field with an unprecedented escort of three Yankee Stadium cops and six Yankee Stadium ushers wearing bow ties.

As the Yankee locker room swarmed with players, reporters, and photographers, I was comfortably resting on some folded, fresh-laundered towels on a shelf in Roger's locker. Nearby was a pack of Camel cigarettes and an empty Ballantine beer can.

Roger's locker was filled with fan mail, a bottle of cologne, and a shaving razor. I couldn't help but notice that to my left in the shelf above me was high-priced haberdashery such as a Dobbs Fifth Avenue New York hat box that sat on top of a few Robert Bruce boxes of Antron knit shirts.

I overheard someone, I think it was "Big Pete" Sheehy, the longtime Yankee clubhouse manager, say that Roger's sixtieth (that would be me) hit very close to where Ruth's sixtieth was hit in 1927. He should know 'cause he was there for that one, too.

The reporters were relentless with their questions, and every photographer needed just one more shot.

As Rog removed his pinstriped Yankee jersey, he revealed that he was wearing a Yogi Berra Yoo-Hoo T-shirt, which made me smile. I was photographed a couple of times with the man of the hour holding me. But not one reporter interviewed me.

After the Yankee locker room emptied out and the lights were turned off, I had trouble falling asleep, thinking about how fortunate I was to be a part of baseball history.

What an incredible experience. As you can well imagine, I had a ball today, September 26, 1961.

***

After hitting homer No. 60, Rog went on Red Barber's postgame TV show with Mrs. Claire Ruth. "I'm glad I didn't break Babe Ruth's record in 154 games," he stated in a shy manner. "This record is enough for me."

***

It's obvious that Rog was now dead-even with Ruth for homers in a season. What wasn't so obvious was that Rog hit No. 60 in his 684th plate appearance, while Ruth hit his sixtieth in his 689th plate appearance. Looks to me like Rog crossed that Ford Frick hundred-yard-dash finish line before Babe.

No Bluffing—The first ballpark my father brought me to was the Polo Grounds in Harlem. The experience of seeing the field's green, green grass, the Giants' bright white uniforms and the Phillies' oversize uniform numbers—plus the aroma of cigar smoke and beer—have stayed with me to this day. *Photo by Leroy Eischield.*

My aspirations of catching a foul ball date to 1957 when my dad took me to my first big-league game. The Phillies played the Giants at the cavernous Polo Grounds in upper Manhattan.

With envy, my eyes followed balls hit into the stands as those fortunate fans pocketed the ultimate souvenir.

At nine years old, I had already figured out the components for such a baseball experience to happen—seat location, number of games attended, ability to catch a ball in the air with or without a mitt, plus an enormous amount of luck.

My conclusion: It was not going to happen for me.

If catching a foul ball was out of my reach, certainly catching a home run was way beyond likely. And catching a Roger Maris home run wouldn't be in the cards for me in a zillion years.

After Maris hit his fifty-ninth home run on Wednesday, September 20, I read with a great deal of interest the accounts of a thirty-two-year-old baseball fan from Baltimore named Bob Reitz. In the third inning of the Orioles-Yanks game, he had out-scrambled dozens of fans to snag Maris's fifty-ninth homer in the right-field bleachers at Memorial Stadium. For his efforts, according to newspaper reports, he suffered a skinned and bruised right arm.

The newspaper photogs had Reitz, an unemployed can company machine operator, meet Rog under the stands between innings.

As if they were best pals, they posed together with the baseball with Maris's left hand resting on Reitz's left shoulder.

That lucky stiff.

In anticipation that Reitz would hand over the ball, Rog called for some-one in the Yankee clubhouse to bring him a couple of baseballs that he could sign and trade for the home run ball.

Reitz quickly nixed the proposed trade.

Maris seemed puzzled. "You gonna keep that?" he asked. Reitz nodded. Maris said, "Good luck to you," and headed back to the game in progress.

A reporter asked Reitz, "Suppose Maris hits his sixtieth home run his next time up, what will you think of your ball?"

"He can hit sixty, it won't make any difference," Reitz replied. "They'll want both of them, you can count on that."

Before Reitz could get away, Ducky Cassese, the Memorial Stadium umps locker room attendant, interceded as an unauthorized negotiator for Maris. He told Reitz that if he handed over the ball to Maris and showed up for the first two games of the World Series at Yankee Stadium, he would get him two tickets for each game.

No deal. Seems Reitz wanted his trip to New York to be all-expenses paid.

Reitz then said about his brief meeting with Maris, "If he wants the ball, he can come to my place and we can make a deal."

The next day, Reitz displayed the ball at a Polish sausage factory, where he worked to help his cousin until he could find a full-time job.

That night after the game, which the Yankees lost 5–3 to the Ori-oles—quite possibly as a result of too much celebrating the night before when they clinched the American League pennant—Maris attempted once more to get the ball.

Lou Grasmick, a former major leaguer who pitched a couple of games for the 1948 Phillies and was now a successful Baltimore businessman, drove Maris over to Reitz's house at 1803 Aliceanna Street. Roger sat in the car as Grasmick went in to see if he could work out a deal.

Right off the bat, Reitz declared that he wanted the grand sum of $2,500, so Grasmick returned to the car and told Maris of Reitz's demand, to which Maris promptly said, "No dice, let's go."

When I read that, I couldn't imagine how great it was that Roger Maris would actually go to a fan's house. That could've been me!

The next day, Reitz said he couldn't sleep.

Meanwhile, a Baltimore sportswriter named Frank Colley wrote in his Friday column, "The Colley-See-Um of Sports" (*Coliseum*, get it?), that Reitz should have just given the ball to Maris, explaining that the publicity that Reitz received should have been satisfaction enough.

Three days after making the catch, according to Reitz's cousin, he was smoking six packs of cigarettes a day and not available for comment. He was taking aspirin, not feeling too well, and annoyed by the insistent questioning by the press and television reporters.

By Sunday, a local newspaper described Reitz as so harried and upset that he decided not to sell the ball. "I don't know what I'm going to do, but it'll either go to Maris or the Hall of Fame," he said. "When I decide, I'll let everyone know. I just want to be left alone."

He added: "You can't imagine how much this ball has upset my personal life."

Articles about the ball and the many offers Reitz received were showing up in newspapers across America. One of the offers was for $500, which came from Daniel L. Wagner, who lived at 12 Northwest 117th Street in Miami.

Another offer was more substantial. Michael Vitello, president of Garwood Baltimore Truck Equipment, was willing to pay $2,500.

Vitello said that if he purchased the ball he would keep it for about thirty days and then have it mounted at Memorial Stadium as a memento to the man who came close to breaking the home run record of Babe Ruth, who was born in Baltimore.

Reitz said that he was offered $5,000 by a television station in Sacramento on the condition that Maris didn't hit any more homers.

Five days later, newspaper interest in the ball was waning.

Finally, Reitz announced his decision: He would accept the $500 offered by the Sports Boosters of Maryland and turn it over to the Associated Catholic Charities of Baltimore.

Michael Fox, president of the Sports Boosters of Maryland, said that both Maris and Reitz would be invited to attend the group's eleventh annual dinner in November. Reitz would officially present the ball to Maris and the check for $500 would go from Fox to Reitz to a representative of the charity.

Wait...I couldn't believe it. You mean to tell me that Reitz gave away that cherished and historic baseball? Perhaps catching a home run ball hit by Roger Maris was not what I had imagined it to be.

September 27

Roger's parents were both quoted about No. 60 by the Associated Press.

Roger's father, Rudy Maris, said: "I feel great. I hope he gets another one. I felt he'd get a tie when he got back to Yankee Stadium. The pressure is off now."

Ann "Connie" Corrine Maris, Roger's mother, said she'd predicted he would tie the record. "Whenever he'd hit a homer, it brought tears to my eyes," she added.

***

Newspapers all over the country celebrated the historic moment. The best was the *Daily News*, which ran a front-page headline: MARIS GETS 60 IN 159 GAMES, alongside a photo of Rog kissing the Babe's widow, Claire Ruth.

***

With greenbacks dancing in his head, Roger's agent, Frank Scott, was quoted in newspapers around the country as saying that Maris's sixty-first homer would be worth $300,000 in royalties over a three-year period.

***

Maris was the eleventh player to hit sixty homers in organized professional baseball. The first was Tony Lazzeri for Salt Lake City of the Pacific Coast League in 1925, when he clouted sixty in 197 games. Of the eleven players, Joe Bauman hit the most homers—seventy-two homers in 1954 for the Roswell Rockets in the Longhorn League.

***

On September 27, Ken Smith of the *New York Mirror* wrote that although Maris didn't hit sixty homers in 154 games, he did break one record. "Certainly no man in baseball history has ever talked half so much to the newspapermen as has Maris."

***

Maris was given a twelve-gauge Winchester shotgun from the Connecticut Sports Writers' Alliance in recognition of his contributions to baseball. The presentation was made in the Yankee clubhouse by Pat Boldug of the *Hartford Courant*, along with more than thirty sportswriters.

"It's a beautiful gun and I'll find good use for it in the off season," said Maris.

While I can understand giving Rog an award or trophy for his on-field accomplishments, this gift makes no sense to me.

***

Rog sat out the Wednesday, September 27, game, explaining that he was exhausted and that he and Yankee manager Ralph Houk had agreed ten days earlier that he would take off the game should he hit No. 60.

Writers and fans were in disbelief that Rog gave up at least three at-bats to try to hit his sixty-first homer.

Rog was at Yankee Stadium but didn't participate in batting practice or throwing. In fact, he never put on his spikes and walked around the clubhouse in stocking feet. Yankee owner Dan Topping suggested that he leave before the game was over, which he did. Maris would actually have two days off as there was no game scheduled for Thursday, September 28.

Rog could now prepare for the final home stand against the Red Sox. The *Daily News* listed the three Boston pitchers, all righties, scheduled to start: Don Schwall, Bill Monboquette, and Gene Conley.

***

Harold Rosenthal of the *New York Tribune* reported that Angels manager Bill Rigney's players refer to Mantle and Maris as "Thunder and Lightning."

September 28

The incredibly talented sports artist Bill Gallo drew Roger's face using the dates he hit homers and the names of pitchers who threw those pitches. He titled the drawing "It Took a While, But Here It Is!"
It's a beauty.

***

I read an article written by Jim Elliott in the September 28 *Baltimore Sun* saying that Yankee coach Frank Crosetti said the ovation Roger received after hitting his sixtieth home run was the greatest he's ever heard. That's quite a compliment, seeing as Crosetti played with Ruth for a couple of years and was around Joe DiMaggio for his entire career.

September 29

United Press International revealed in 1920 they had a deal with Babe Ruth: After each homer he would either call or send a telegram describing the sort of pitch he hit. The Bambino would get five dollars per homer.
Some days Ruth would provide a descriptive account of no less than two hundred words. Other times fewer: "low outside...Babe."

***

The *Journal-American* took out a display ad in the *Daily News* with pictures of Mick and Rog promoting that they would be writing exclusive World Series articles for the *Journal-American*.
I'm trying to understand why one newspaper would allow another newspaper to advertise in their paper. Perhaps the answer simply is, business is business, regardless of who wants to spend the money.

***

The Monkey Club had something to celebrate today: The heroic chimp Enos made two orbits around the Earth and was safely recovered after a splash-down in the Atlantic south of Bermuda. Hooray for Enos.

***

A friend of my mom sent me a *Great Falls Tribune* clipping from Montana about Maris. At least, I thought it was about Rog because it had a cartoon drawing of two generic baseball players flipping a coin. The headline read: "Who are these guys Maris and Mantle?"

The story told how Montana's State Board of Regents plans to fix a uniform "wage scale" of $1.50 an hour for athletes at Montana colleges who hold campus jobs.

How's that for a reach?

***

It was announced today that former Yankee manager Casey Stengel would once again manage a baseball team in New York City. Nope, not the Yanks. This time, "The Ol' Perfessor" signed a one-year contract to skipper the 1962 Metropolitans, the infant entry in the National League.

***

This week's *Life* magazine had a one-page article allegedly written by Rog about game 154 when he hit his fifty-ninth homer. I'm pretty sure this was another deal that Frank Scott put together. Even though Rog got the byline, he was probably interviewed over the phone by some copy boy who wrote the article. The title told me all I needed to know: "I Tried Not To Think About It."

***

Before heading to Yankee Stadium for the game against the Red Sox, Roger and Mickey were scheduled today to videotape their guest shot on Perry Como's *Kraft Music Hall* program. Each player would receive $7,500 for the appearance. The show will air October 4.

***

In anticipation of Maris breaking the sixty-homer mark, a crowd of

21,485 fans were on hand for the game. With the incentive of $5,000 to the fan who caught his next home run, the right-field stands at Yankee Stadium were full, in contrast to the other parts of the ballpark.

It was a quick game, taking only two hours and seven minutes.

The Yankees won, 2–1, with Rog going to bat four times, resulting in a couple of walks and pop-outs to shortstop and to first base in foul territory.

September 30

In Saturday's *Daily News*, the Yankee ad that featured the patriotic top hat in conjunction with the "Y" of Yankees for today's game appeared just below a note that prominent Indian composer, conductor, and sitar virtuoso Ravi Shankar landed in New York yesterday for a ten-week, ninety-city tour. I'm pretty sure the newspaper made a mistake when they spelled *guitar* as *sitar*.

***

I realized that today is the anniversary of Ruth hitting his sixtieth homer. How ironic yet appropriate it would be if Rog connected for No. 61.

It was not meant to be, as Rog walked in his first at-bat, grounded out to second base in his next two at-bats, then singled to right field in his last at-bat.

Jack Reed replaced Rog in the top of the ninth, which meant that tomorrow would be the last chance Maris would have to break the season home run record.

The Yanks won the game, which took two hours and fifteen minutes to complete. But I noticed something curious in the box score: The attendance was listed as 19,061.

Hey, I don't mean to be a donkey's ass, but I find it hard to believe that the attendance for the game turned out to be 19,061. Come on. Someone is playing around with the attendance figures.

***

From reading a *Sports Illustrated* story on Rog I learned that his favorite male singer is Frank Sinatra, but he doesn't have a favorite female warbler. When a reporter asked if he could put down Doris Day as his answer. Rog told him, "How could you write in something else when I told you I don't have a favorite female singer?"

***

After the game, Maris sat next to his locker and acknowledged to the horde of sportswriters that there was only one game left for him to break Ruth's record. "It's sink or swim now," he said. "It will all be over tomorrow."

***

Pondering the last game of the season, I thought about the one washed-out homer on July 17, the extra-inning August 23 triple that missed going out of Wrigley by a foot, and the ball he hit in Detroit on September 17 that failed to clear the screen by a foot, which also wound up a triple.

Yeah, I know. It's a game of inches.

***

My friend Gary Baker went to the movies and saw *The Guns of Navarone*. He told me that the newsreel that was shown before the film was about Maris hitting his sixtieth homer. "Bake" said it showed Maris connecting for No. 60 and was probably about a minute long.

Naturally, I called the theater and was told that the newsreel was titled "Hour of Baseball Glory" with commentary by Peter Roberts.

Boy, I'd love to have a copy of that film so I could play it over and over again in my bedroom anytime I wanted.

How cool would that be?

OCTOBER 1961

"I started to cry tears of joy. My guy did it."

October 1

It didn't take long for the photo of Rog posing with the twelve-gauge Winchester shotgun presented to him by the Connecticut Sports Writers' Alliance to appear in a newspaper ad. The October 1 issue of the *Scrantonian Tribune* was promoting a local radio station by graphically inserting the number "61" at the end of the barrel of the shotgun. The headline read: "Will Roger Hit #61 Today? Hear it on radio WSCR."

***

I know, I know, I'm too old to still be reading the Sunday funnies. At least my fascination with using Silly Putty to make reverse images of comic strip panels has worn off.

Nonetheless, here's my brief summary of today's colorful world of Sunday funnies with an emphasis on my favorite comic strips.

The Lone Ranger: In a continuing story, Jenke proves to be a stubborn prisoner.

Archie: Herbert Orbit's scaled-down atomic sub "P-10" model is launched, only to sink as a result of an open hatch.

Bugs Bunny: Elmer Fudd buys brushes from Bugs and Sylvester.

Dennis The Menace: Mr. Mitchell sees an optometrist thinking he needs glasses.

Joe Palooka: Mr. Walsh is diagnosed with an illness that will prevent unwanted guests from visiting him.

Mickey Finn: The only comic today with a baseball theme has everyone thinking that Uncle Phil is at the World Series, but instead he's watching a kids' ballgame with a friend.

Nancy: Nancy goes door to door trying to sell a bar of soap.

Peanuts: Lucy reads "Goldilocks" to Linus.

Steve Canyon: One of Canyon's pilots has crashed because he unknowingly took a tranquilizer.

Superman: Lois Lane receives a mirror with magical powers that reveals people as who they really are and not as what they pretend to be.

Li'l Abner: Never could understand what they were saying and what the comic was about.

Pogo: Don't like it, didn't read it.

***

Understanding it was a creepy thing to do, I glanced at the names of people who recently passed away in the obituary column, realizing that they would never know if Maris hit his sixty-first homer today.

***

The *Daily News Coloroto* magazine had a great picture: A full-page color photo of Rog hitting either home run # 47 or #48 off left-hander Billy Pierce of the White Sox on August 16 at Yankee Stadium. Hard to tell which homer it is because he hit two off Pierce that day. The photo was taken from the centerfield bleachers.

***

According to a couple of New York newspapers, the Red Sox' probable pitcher for today's game has now been changed to either Tracy Stallard or Gene Conley.

Both are right-handers, but Conley is the vet, having been around since

1952, while Stallard is a rookie after a cup of coffee last season when he threw just four innings.

***

Rog and Pat went to St. Patrick's Cathedral in Manhattan in the morning, then headed to Yankee Stadium. Unlike other games, Maris decided not to eat prior to the regular-season finale.

***

Last night I watched the big Magnavox console television in our den. My favorite Saturday night show is *Have Gun — Will Travel* on Channel 2.

Our den is 15' x 10'. Because it is a corner room, it has four windows, two on each side that face out into the back yard. Because this is the most-used room in our house, it contains a strong and very stale cigarette stench. The walls, originally white, are discolored with a light nicotine film.

In the middle of the room is an old worn area rug that partly covers a creaky wood floor. In the corner is a radiator that is cranky and noisy every winter when turned on for much-needed heat.

Along the wall is a sofa that is also a pull-out sleeper bed. I spent three weeks there recuperating from the fire in which more than twenty percent of my body was burned on August 26, 1960, at Camp Kiowa in Pennsylvania.

As you walk into the den immediately to your left in the corner facing the TV is a large green Naugahyde recliner whose best days stopped just before the Giants left for 'Frisco after the 1957 season. That armchair, my dad's, lords over all activities in the room.

The den often serves as my dining room. As I watched the tube, I would eat lunch and dinner on thin metal trays partially framed in rusty edges. I devoured a lot of Birds Eye fried-chicken TV dinners in our den.

This morning, the first day of October, began with my usual breakfast of choice—heavily buttered Thomas' English muffins washed down with a glass of milk.

Knowing that the Sunday newspapers would be full of Maris articles, I rode my Schwinn to the closest store in White Plains that carried the New York *Daily News* and *The Times*. I bought a copy of each.

Over the years, I noticed that my dad went to the sports section first when he read a newspaper. And when he read a tabloid like the *Daily News*, *Post*, or *Mirror*, he started by looking at the back page, which was always covered with sports photos.

So I began reading the *Daily News* starting from the last page. As I looked at each page, making my way to the front page, I noticed a small display ad for today's Yankee game at 2 p.m.

As it has been for years, the ad is simple. Included is the stylized lettering for the Yankee name, as well as the distinctive use of the customary Uncle Sam Stars-and-Stripes top hat that has been around since before I was born. I did notice, however, that it changed in 1958 from topping the bat that was part of the "K" in the word Yankees to supporting the front part of the "Y" in Yankees.

The ad had no hype to jazz up it up, such as that the Yanks were the 1961 American League Champs or that Roger Maris was going for his sixty-first home run and that the fan who caught it would get five grand. It looked like every other small, to-the-point ad promoting a 1961 Yankee home game.

My dad wasn't a *New York Times* reader, so I assumed that guys who read that paper probably didn't start on the last page, but went first to the editorial section.

Trying to act like a grownup, I turned to the *Times'* boring, nothing-but-words, pictureless editorial section on page 8. The type was smaller than any other New York rag.

To my surprise, there sandwiched between "Letters to The Times" and "Topics" was a column titled "The Asterisk That Shook the Baseball World," written by James Reston and datelined Chapel Hill, North Carolina.

What was a baseball story doing in this section of the newspaper? Did someone make a mistake when they put the paper together?

Reston began his column by noting that in Congress's last session 2,783 bills had been passed for the relief of injustice or undue hardship to private citizens of this country. He then stated that nobody introduced a bill for what he called "the relief of Roger Maris," which made me wonder: Was this really about baseball?

Sure, his column mentioned Babe Ruth, but it also contained the names of Nikita Khrushchev, John F. Kennedy, Richard Nixon, Adlai Stevenson, Thomas Dewey, Al Smith, William Jennings Bryan, Henry Clay, Jefferson Davis, Trotsky, Malenkov, Molotov, Ponce de León, Ahab of *Moby-Dick*, Ophelia, Hamlet, and Casey Jones.

The article might have been more relatable to me if Reston named Maynard G. Krebs, Jughead, Zorro, Paladin, Clarabell, Groucho, Elvis, Moe, Larry, and Curly.

The only sentence that made any sense referred to the 1961 home run record chase, during which Maris had to worry about Ruth, while Ruth didn't have to worry about Maris. In fact, Ruth probably didn't have a care in the world back in 1927, except for maybe where he'd get his next hot dog after the game.

Reston wrote that baseball commissioner Ford Frick's decision about the record having to be set in the same 154 games as Ruth showed the worst judgment since Sherman Adams took that rug from his old friend Bernard Goldfine of Boston. Whoever they were.

Well, that's where Reston lost me because not only did I have no idea who Sherman Adams and Bernard Goldfine were, I didn't care. Obviously, this was not written for thirteen-year-olds like me.

So I kept searching the pages of *The Times* for more Maris articles. Fortunately, I found a lengthy story related to Maris, even though it wasn't in the sports section. It was about Frank Scott, the business manager for Mantle and Maris.

Gay Talese, a staff reporter, provided details about who Scott was and about his firm, Frank Scott Associates. Turns out that "Scotty," as he was known among big leaguers, represented sixty of baseball's best players. He took ten percent of their earnings for negotiating appearances, product testimonials, and endorsements.

I was aware that players did commercials for cigarettes, cereal, and shaving blades so they would look sharp, feel sharp, and act sharp. But I had no idea about the amount of money they made or their other endorsement opportunities that ranged, according to this article, from pants to peanut butter.

In the article, Scotty was described as a small, imaginative, amiable, and sometimes pushy forty-three-year-old man who often smiled with a face-full of dollar bills. Can't imagine what a face-full of dollar bills looks like.

Scott provided a jaw-dropping example of how his business worked. To make his point, he used the pitcher Don Larsen's 1956 World Series perfect game.

Talese quoted Scott, though Scott misidentified the historic game Larsen had pitched. Luckily for both guys, the article wasn't on the sports page, so naturally I assumed that nobody who read it would catch the error.

Scott explained: "In 1956 before Larsen took the mound at Yankee Stadium against the Brooklyn Dodgers for the sixth game [as every fan knows, it was the fifth game] of the World Series, he was getting paid $150 for an appearance. By the sixth inning, Larsen was pitching hitless baseball, raising his fee to $300. Going into the ninth inning and only three outs away from a no-hitter perfect game, the price was $500. Three outs later Larsen's fee was no less than $1,500." Scott emphasized his point by dramatically stating, "And getting it."

Scott had been the Yankees' road secretary in 1950, but as he became too "buddy-buddy" with the players, the Yankees' front office decided to go in another direction and replace him. It was then that Scott began negotiating off-the-field deals for players.

His business didn't take off until 1956, when Mantle had a Triple Crown season, leading the American League in batting average, RBIs, and homers. Scott was able to generate $70,000 of added income for "The Mick" as a result of close to a dozen product endorsements that included the logical Batter Up pancake mix.

Frank estimated that his take in commissions for 1961 would be more than $80,000, thanks in large part to the M&M Boys.

Interestingly, not all of Scott's deals had been for players who had a great season. He explained that when an incident with a player made the news, he tried to earn a buck or two off it.

This was the time when batters first started to wear protective batting helmets, so if a player was hit on the head by a pitch he'd avoid serious injury. Almost before one of his clients reached first base as a result of getting bonked in the noggin, Scott had hustled up three paid TV appearances to talk about it.

Without mentioning specific players or their stats, Scott explained that an endorsement fee started at around $750 if a player had a so-so season. For a player who had a good season, it was no less than $1,000. But if they won the Most Valuable Player award, it was no less than $1,500 for a one-year deal.

"There's absolutely no limit to the amount of outside money big-name athletes can make providing they're hot," he boasted.

I'm guessing that the hottest players ever had to be Rog and Mick.

***

Before the game there was talk in the Yankee Stadium press box about the possibility of a fan catching No. 61. Red Barber said that to avoid confusion and fighting for the ball, if it were him and he caught the historic agate, he would run out onto the field so there wouldn't be any doubt that he caught it.

***

For me, Sunday morning TV consisted of the 9 a.m. Chuck McCann show, *Let's Have Fun*, on WPIX Channel 11. Chuck's sense of humor aligned perfectly with mine. His portrayal of characters was ironically silly and irreverent with a touch of slapstick and a dash of absurdity, which equals funny and made me giggle out loud.

Because of my parents' imposed restriction that I couldn't go to Yankee games unless I had adult supervision—and because neither parent was interested in a trip to the Bronx—I had no alternative but to stay home and catch the Yankees' last game of the regular 1961 season on TV.

Unlike the September 20 Yankee-Oriole game when I listened to *both* the TV and radio at the same time, for this one I'll be watching the tube only.

I'm counting on the fact that some company like Ballantine Beer will produce a record of the radio broadcast if Maris hits one out and sell it at Manny's Baseball Land across from Yankee Stadium.

I figured that practically no one would watch the other TV channels at the same time as the Yankee game.

NBC Channel 4 was showing the "Protestant Fund Appeal" program, whatever that was. There was a football game between the Redskins and the Giants on CBS Channel 2, and ABC Channel 7 had the movie *Captain January*, starring Shirley Temple.

With my father at work, my sister and mom left me alone to watch the game, which would provide me the opportunity to think out loud while strategizing, managing, and coaching the team. I could also bait, chide, groan, cheer, and scream at the TV, which on occasion I do.

As I had done throughout the season while watching Yankee games, I would alternate reading newspapers and magazines while searching for and—when found—meticulously cutting out articles about Maris, then carefully stapling them on scrapbook pages.

Thinking about the future, it was my hope that when I was older and could afford it, I would have my Maris scrapbooks professionally bound.

With great anticipation, I situated myself in front of our TV by 12:30 p.m. to watch Red Barber's Yankee pregame show on WPIX Channel 11 beginning at 1:40 p.m., with the game starting at 1:55 p.m. I often don't pay attention to what's on TV as it's just to keep me company. I switched the channel until I found a cartoon show that I didn't watch, as my focus was on cutting out newspaper articles about Maris.

For the last couple of weeks, the Yankees were filming every one of Roger's at bats and, if he hit a homer, playing it again during the broadcast.

I had read in a Yankee publication that the Yanks' concept of film replay began on July 17, 1959, when Ralph Terry was pitching a no-hitter against the White Sox at Yankee Stadium. In the ninth inning, a Terry pitch resulted in a ground-ball single up the middle by Chicago's first batter, right fielder Jim McAnany.

At that moment Yankee broadcaster Mel Allen asked TV director Jack Murphy to re-show the hit that had just happened live. Murphy obliged and the viewing audience was introduced to a replay of a hit.

If Rog connects today, wanna bet WPIX will show it a jagazillion times, maybe a tagazillion times?

The visiting Bosox were in sixth place, thirty-two games behind the Yanks. So the only thing the teams were playing for was pride and personal stats.

Personal stats? None was bigger than what Maris was attempting to achieve in the game, which was actually game No. 163 for the Yanks due to a game that ended in a tie after seven innings on April 22, when the team was in Baltimore.

The umps had called that game at 11:30 p.m. after two rain delays. It would be played over again in its entirety, but all the stats counted. Had it been ruled a suspended game by waiting until the 11:59 p.m. curfew for the official halt, it would have been resumed from that point on and played prior to another game.

It was a bright, sunny autumn day in the Bronx with the temperature in the mid-seventies. It was warm for that time of the year.

The game began much like every other game of the 1961 season. The Yankees starting pitcher Bill Stafford struck out the side in the first inning.

On the mound for the Red Sox was twenty-three-year-old right-hander Tracy Stallard, who had a 2–6 record. In Stallard's rookie season in 1960, he only pitched four innings in four games. One of those games was against the Yankees exactly a year ago on October 1, 1960, at Yankee Stadium. Stallard faced Maris once in that game and struck him out.

For those watching TV, Phil Rizzuto described Roger's first at bat as he made his way from the on-deck circle to home plate.

"And here comes Roger Maris."

Phil summarized Roger's batting statistics to date. "Roger, batting .268, 16 doubles, 4 triples, 60 homers, a hundred and forty-one runs batted in. He's tied right now with Jim Gentile for the American League lead in RBIs."

Once the WPIX TV cameras swung around to show Red Sox right fielder Lou Clinton backing up to the warning track, Rizzuto announced, "There's the right-field stands waiting for homer No. 61. The most heavily congested spot in Yankee Stadium right now. You know, it's worth a lot of money."

But on the first pitch thrown to Rog, "The Scooter" was startled, quickly saying, "And he hits to left field."

"Yastrzemski (pause) he's got it. A beautiful catch by Yastrzemski. Kubek back to first."

"And the fans in right field are moaning. That fooled Yastrzemski for a moment. Maris very seldom hits the ball to the left side of second base."

"Not many more chances left for Roger."

It was very rare to see Rog hit the ball to left field, as he was a dead pull hitter. I thought he was nervous and overanxious. I know I was.

I figured Rog would have two, maybe three more at bats unless the game goes into extra innings.

During the game, the three Yankee broadcasters (Rizzuto, Red Barber, and Mel Allen) rotated mic duties. When time permitted they thanked a bunch of behind-the-scenes people who work for the team. Those people must be thrilled to hear their names mentioned on a Yankee broadcast. I know I would be.

In the fourth inning, Red Barber was calling the shots. He pointed out that sitting in the front row behind the plate were Cincinnati Reds pitcher Joey Jay and catcher Darrell Johnson, along with former Yankee pitching coach Jim Turner, now the pitching coach for the Redlegs. They had the best seats in the ballpark, Section 8, and were scouting the Yankee lineup for the upcoming World Series.

Red talked about Mantle and whether he would be well enough to start in the series. He had been out of the lineup with a bad cold since he pinch-hit in the first game of a doubleheader back on September 19.

Barber also mentioned that starting October 2, a special World Series newspaper column written by Mantle and Maris would appear in the *New York Journal-American*.

Knowing that Rog was heading to home plate, I paused from browsing through *Sport* magazine. "Wally Moon, The Dodgers' Dynamic Pro" was on the cover. My eyes were now transfixed by our TV. I crossed my fingers on both hands for good luck, holding them up near my shoulders as Maris stepped into the batter's box against Stallard with Bosox catcher Russ Nixon flashing signs.

Barber, whose broadcasting style is to understate the obvious, told the TV audience as Rog approached, "Okay number 9." To me it sounded as if Barber was saying, "Maris, this is your chance to try and break the Babe's record. Let's see what you can do."

Barber then explained to fans watching at home what happened in Roger's first at bat: "Roger did what he rarely does in his first at bat. He hit one to left field. Yastrzemski went back and pulled it down."

Rog was wearing his Yankee pin-striped jersey, custom-tailored with sleeves cut short to give his biceps more room.

As was his ritual, Rog smoothed out the dirt in the batter's box first with his right foot, swaying back and forth from the catcher toward the pitcher, then finished up with his left foot doing the same.

Rog then hitched up his pants by the belt near his hips while still holding his Louisville Slugger bat in his right hand as he had done in his previous 695 plate appearances.

His butt stuck out as he balanced on his feet, which were perfectly per-pendicular to home plate. He took a couple of practice swings and then cocked his hands away from his body and perpendicular to the ground. He held the bat still and concentrated on Stallard's right-hand release of the American League Spalding baseball with league president Joe Cronin's name stamped in light blue on it.

Stallard began his windup and released his first offering.

That first pitch, according to Yankee TV broadcaster Red Barber, was a fastball, wide: "Rog laid off it for ball one."

Rog stepped back from the plate but stayed in the batter's box. Before getting set for the second pitch, he lifted his right spike to his left knee, balancing himself with his bat in his right hand as he picked the infield clay from his right spike with his left hand.

Once both feet were on the ground, Maris wiped his left hand on his left thigh uniform pants. Then, as was his habit, he knocked the inside portion of his right spike with the barrel of his bat, just to make sure it was entirely devoid of clay.

Before getting set in his straight-up batter's stance, Roger reached up midway of his 33-ounce and 35-inch Louisville Slugger A92 model ash wood bat to the pine tar with his right hand, then his left hand so as to get the sticky substance in his palm and fingers for a better grip.

Then, once again he hitched up his pants at the hips. He took a quick practice swing and got set for Stallard's next offering.

The second pitch was announced by Barber as low. Ball two. Barber explained to the TV audience that the fans were booing because they wanted Maris to get something he could swing on.

I was disappointed that Barber was doing the play-by-play. His voice was too dry and choppy for my taste. He lacked the personality I wanted from a baseball broadcaster.

I would much rather have had Mel Allen behind the mic. He was a welcome and frequent audio visitor in our home and in my dad's car. I always enjoyed Allen's garrulous descriptions during a game, especially during rain delays when Mel was the show. I learned a lot from his stories during those precipitation breaks.

For the third pitch with the count two balls and no strikes, Stallard looked in for catcher Russ Nixon's sign.

The Yankee Stadium scoreboard's giant Longines clock in right-center field showed 2:43 P.M. (Which, if you add them up, equals nine, Roger's jersey number.)

Rog went through his same ritual, tapping his right spike with the barrel of his bat, grabbing the pine tar portion of the bat with both hands, hitching up his pants, followed by three quick practice swings.

On Roger's third practice swing, Stallard was already in his wind-up with both arms swayed and extended behind him. The pitcher then brought his hands together in the "ball in glove" position over his head. Stallard then took his normal forward stride and delivered his thirty-fifth pitch of the game. It was a waist-high fastball that never reached Nixon.

Roger's grooved, slightly upper-cut swing that had produced sixty homers that season sent the Spalding baseball rising off the bat on a great towering arc fly to right field. It sailed over Red Sox right-fielder Lou Clinton's head and to the left of the black painted 344 FT sign on the teal-colored, 40-inch-tall Yankee Stadium cement right-field wall.

Let's Face It—In this photo of Maris hitting his 61st homer, Cincinnati Reds pitchers Jim O'Toole and Joey Jay, and catcher Darrell Johnson along with Reds pitching coach Jim Turner can be seen watching the ball heading to the right-field stands. I studied the expression of ninety-four distinguishable fans' faces in the photo and gave many of them nicknames. *Courtesy National Baseball Hall of Fame.*

The record-breaking homer landed in the outstretched right-hand palm of Sal Durante, a nineteen-year-old fan from Brooklyn, who was standing on seat No. 4 in Section 33, Box 163D, eight rows back from the right-field wall.

That was No. 61 and would have been a home run in Babe Ruth's day, too.

"He did it! Oh, my God, he did it!" I yelled in uncontrolled exhilaration. At the same moment, I gleefully tossed the *Sport* magazine toward the ceiling and over the moon. "My guy did it!"

Maris had broken Ruth's record that had stood since 1927 for 12,420 days…but who's counting.

As Rog circled the bases with his head down in a deliberate, emotionless pace, I moved closer to the TV and got down on the floor. As he rounded third, Yankee third-base coach Frank Crosetti uncharacteristically shook Roger's hand, which he also had done for Maris's sixtieth homer.

As Rog jogged down the third-base line approaching home plate, he moved from a brilliant October spotlight of sunshine into a shadow. It was as if the curtain was coming down on his one-man, six-month theatrical baseball play, *Chasing 60*, in which he had the lead role.

Maris's right foot unceremoniously touched home plate as he shook the right hand of Yogi Berra, the next batter, while at the same moment his left hand grasped the left hand of Yankee bat boy Frankie Perdenti.

Red Sox catcher Russ Nixon stood still with his right hand on his hip and his left hand in his catcher's mitt, and looked down to make sure that Maris's foot touched home plate.

As the Yankee crowd kept roaring its approval, Rog continued to jog to the Yankee dugout with his head still down. Before Roger reached the corner of the dugout, a young fan—who looked to be in his late teens and overcome with excitement—ran onto the field to shake Roger's hand and pat him on the back.

Oh, how I wanted to be that lucky-dog fan.

Barber gave the crowd the opportunity to cheer and continued to narrate without much emotion about the historic moment. Joining him was Mel Allen, "The Voice of the Yankees."

Red Barber: "There it is."…"Sixty-one."…"$5,000 somebody."…"He got his pitch."…"$5,000."… "And here is, eh, the fellow with sixty-one."…"You are seeing a lot today."

It was at this point that Barber engaged Allen, asking, "Well, you haven't seen anything like that, have ya?"

Allen replied, "Nobody ever has, Red." He continued, "Nobody has ever seen anything like this. Not much you can say. You just look and listen and watch."

Barber once again brought up the financial aspect of the home run ball, "I see two figures…61 and $5,000."

With excitement in his voice, Allen tried to bring the audience back to what was going on by asking Red, "Did you see that boy going up the runway? He had the ball."

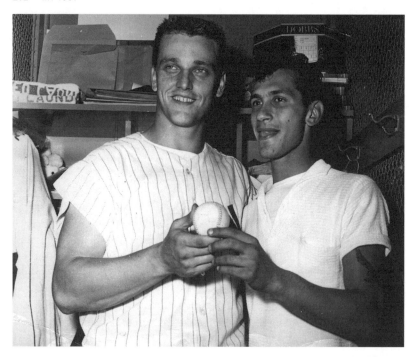

The Catcher—After the season's last game, Sal Durante, who caught the 61st homer, stands next to Rog in his locker for newspaper writers and photographers who have been waiting for this moment since mid-summer. *Photo courtesy of National Baseball Hall of Fame.*

I started to cry tears of joy. My guy did it. I was pleased that the Yankee fans awarded Maris a standing ovation. The sound was not that of simple cheering, but more like appreciative applause acknowledging his season in total, much like a faithful audience that had sat through a two-and-a-half-hour Broadway play sixty-one times.

Roger's teammates were there to congratulate him as he ducked into the dugout and took off his batting helmet. Yankee trainer Gus Mauch was the first to greet him, then Bill Skowron and Clete Boyer, and clubhouse men Big Pete and Little Pete.

It looked like Rog was trying to make his way to the far end of the dugout as Tony Kubek reached out to congratulate him. But Hector Lopez and Johnny Blanchard pushed Rog out to the dugout's top step, where he took off his Yankee cap and quickly waved it, acknowledging the fans' cheers. Rog tried twice to get back into the dugout. But Elston Howard joined Lopez in straight-arming him to keep him from returning to the semi-privacy of the Yankee bench.

Then, while standing on the top step as if embarrassed by the fans' accolades, he looked into the dugout with his arms outstretched, as if to say, "Come on, guys, let me in!"

The next batter was Berra, who waited before he stepped into the batter's box, giving fans the opportunity to shower Maris with applause. As far as I was concerned, the remainder of the game was meaningless…unless, of course, Rog hit No. 62.

Barber continued to broadcast the game after Stallard threw two pitches to Berra. "Well, it is one ball and one strike to Yogi as the game goes on."

"Friends, you are seeing something that has never happened before in baseball. A ballplayer hitting sixty-one home runs in a regular season. And he really hit it."

Yogi then hit a grounder to the Red Sox second baseman, who threw over to first.

"And we have two outs."

The TV camera showed Rog in the dugout and Barber noted, "There's Roger."

"Well, when that ball went into the stands, I know three people that got off the hook or thought they were off. That was Dan Topping and Roy Hamey and the Ol' Redhead because in the pregame show we all said that we thought he'd do it today."

Johnny Blanchard was batting and Barber had to play catch-up on his at bat.

"Strike two," Barber informed the TV audience.

Then Blanchard swung and hit a pop up.

Barber called the play, "High foul ball. That's Pete Runnels moving under it. There's Nixon the catcher. First baseman for the out."

Once the ball was caught, Barber summarized the inning. "One run. One hit. And that's history."

"Well, for Maris as he goes to center field."

The camera caught second base umpire intercepting Rog, Barber noted, "There's Jim Honochick congratulating him."

In turning over the mic to Mel Allen, Red segued into acknowledging that his broadcast partner would be doing the World Series, "And now, friends, I want to congratulate my good friend Mel Allen, who not only turned in a fine year's work here at The Stadium but is all tuned up to be on the television of the World Series that starts Wednesday. Mel, all the luck in the world. And on you it looks good."

Allen graciously accepted the nicety and then softly tossed a compliment back to Red. "Thank you very much, Red. God bless you, and it's been a great thrill working with you all year and the past several years as the time has flown."

With all the pleasantries completed, Red moved the spotlight back on Maris, indicating the noteworthiness of what happened: "We've got the technicalities straightened out now. The score at the end of four innings is Maris one and Boston nothing."

Barber appeased me with that last comment because this game's major significance was at least 61 percent about Roger Maris.

WPIX replayed the film a few times while the broadcasters kept feeding the audience information about who had caught the homer and what was happening under the stands out of view of the TV audience.

With the game still in progress, beneath the stands stood the fan who caught the homer, Sal Durante, an 18-year-old fan who lived at 1418 Neptune Avenue in Brooklyn. He was offered a lamb sandwich, a glass of milk, and a piece of blueberry pie in the Yanks press room after he made the catch. He took a bite of the sandwich but admitted he was too excited to eat.

His girlfriend, Rosemarie Calabrese, had gone to the game with him. She wore a blouse and semi-toreador pants. She mentioned that this was the second baseball game she had ever seen, counting last Tuesday's game against the Orioles.

Sal explained that he was originally going to play sandlot baseball with his cousin John Tortorella, but decided to attend the Yankee game instead. The last Yankee game Durante had attended was when Rog hit No. 60.

When introduced to Roger, he said emphatically, "Rog, this is your ball. You hit it, and it belongs to you and every baseball fan."

Rog was taken back by the offer and suggested that Sal collect the $5,000.

It was then that Durante admitted that it was meant to be, because his family was in a financial hole and he wanted to marry his girlfriend, Rosemarie of Bensonhurst.

I wondered if Rog would hit another homer and break his own record. I thought, is Sam Gordon really going to pay $5,000 for that ball?

***

Yankee's public relations man Bob Fishel spoke briefly on the broadcast, explaining that after Rog connected the attending sportswriters rose from their seats and applauded, which is unprecedented, going against the unwritten rule that there is no cheering in the press box.

***

Barber mentioned that Maris actually hit sixty-two homers this year. The "Redhead" was alluding to the July 17 rainout in Baltimore. But he did it as an afterthought, without any significance.

I thought Barber did a poor job of acknowledging the moment. There was almost no enthusiasm, compared to the way Phil Rizzuto probably handled the play-by-play on the radio. As Rizzuto would say, "Holy cow!"

I'll bet one of my 1960 Topps Roger Maris baseball cards that Scooter hit it out of the park calling that home run.

Before the sixth inning got underway, Sal Durante, the fan who caught the homer, was ushered into the TV booth so that Mel Allen could interview him.

I could see Mel and Durante getting set for the interview when Yankee Stadium PA announcer Bob Sheppard said, as if on cue, "Your attention please, ladies and gentlemen."

Then Mel began the interview.

Mel Allen: "What's your name, son?"

Sal Durante: "Sal Durante."

Allen: "And is that the ball that was hit out there?"

Durante: "Yes, sir, that's the one."

Allen: "Yeah. And where you from?"

Durante: "Coney Island."

Allen: "And what were you just doing, taking pictures?"

Durante: "Yes, sir. I don't know."

Allen: "Huh?"

Durante: "I don't know. I don't know what to say."

Allen: "Well, what time did you come out today?"

Durante: "About 12:30 I got here."

Allen: "Yeah. And you had your seat out there, huh?"

Durante: "Yeah."

Allen: "Well, okey doke. I just wanted to say hello to you and you established the fact that you got the ball? Eh?"

Durante: "Uh, huh."

Allen: "Okay, Sal. Where you from? Coney Island?"

Durante: "Coney Island."

And then once more as if on cue, I could hear Sheppard announce, "Your attention, please...."

Allen ended the interview, "Thanks for coming up. Thank you."

Now I think the world of Mel, but he dropped the ball and did a piss-poor interview.

Normally, when Mel interviews someone I feel as if I'm listening in on their private conversation. But not this time. His voice was filled with hesitation and contrived.

Frankly, I could have done a better job. I would have started off with, "So, tell me, Sal, with the crack of the bat, did you know you were going to catch the homer? Anybody get in your way or try to take the ball from you? What was the first thing you thought when you caught the ball?"

Anyway....

In the sixth inning, with Tony Kubek on first and one out, Roger faced Stallard again.

I felt that this was going to be anticlimactic for everyone at the Stadium, watching or listening.

For Roger's first swing, he took a cut at a curve and fouled it off for strike one.

As if he had read my mind, Mel stated what I was thinking. "I wonder how much pressure is on him now. He's trying to break his own record."

Before Mel continued with the play-by-play of this at bat, he did a quick summary of Roger's first two at-bats, "Maris flied to left and hit his 61st in the fourth inning."

Rog then hit the next pitch on the ground in foul territory down the first base line for strike two.

Mel called it, "Foul ball."

Before the next pitch, Mel informed the viewers, "Bob Sheppard, our public address announcer who is a schoolmaster and likes to dabble in a little poetry, just handed this over, a poem. We'll read it to ya. No balls, two strikes. One out in the sixth inning. One to nothing, New York."

But before he read the poem, Mel called the next pitch, "Low and inside." He took a breath and began in his inimitable fashion reciting Sheppard's poem:

They've been pitching me low and wide and tight.
I've been tense and nervous, drawn and paillard.
But my prayers are full of joy tonight.
Thank you, Lord, for Tracy Stallard.

Mel finished up by acknowledging the author along with the poem's title. "That's by Bob Sheppard. 'Thoughts of Roger Maris.' "

Then Mel returned back to exclusively doing the play-by-play of the game.

"One ball, two strikes."

"That's up high, a change-up. Two two."

"Two balls, two strikes."

"And ball three. Three and two."

Now with the count full, Allen, perhaps thinking about viewers who were also football fans, he decided to pass along the score of the game being played in Washington, D.C.

"In the second quarter, Redskins 21, Giants 14."

Thankfully, Mel returned his focus to the probability of the next pitch.

"Well, I imagine if this ball is anywhere near the plate Rog may be swinging. It'll have to be a real bad pitch for him to take it."

"Strike three."

"He went for it."

The next batter, Hector Lopez, ended the inning with a deep fly ball to right field.

In the eighth inning, Rog came to the dish for what would more than likely be his last at bat of the regular 1961 season. Left-handed Chet Nichols replaced Stallard on the mound.

Mel was still doing the play by play. "And here is Roger Maris."

"His 60th homer came in Game 158 and 61 in Game 162."

"Ball one."

Mel then got into the math with regards to number of games, "You can add one to each total for a tie game, in which he did not hit a homer."

"Foul ball out of play."

"The one game washed out by the records in which he did."

"Yankees of '27, when Babe hit 60, also played one tie game where the records counted."

"One ball. One strike."

"A little outside ball two. Two and one."

I was hoping that Mel would talk about plate appearances rather than games but Rog hit the next pitch.

"It's a high fly ball to very short right. Schilling's out under it. And the side's retired. No runs. No hits. No errors. No one left on. At the end of eight innings, New York 1 and Boston nothing."

The Yankees won 1–0. Roger's home run was the difference. With that homer, Rog also won the American League RBI title with a mark of 142. The new single-season home run record was now sixty-one homers, and Roger Maris owned it!

I was not disappointed that I wasn't there in person because I rationalized that there were two benefits of staying home and watching the game on TV. To begin with was my ability to see the film of Rog hitting No. 61 a couple of times. The other was watching the Red Barber Post Game Show, which I anticipated would be the greatest post-game show ever in the annals of the game.

Red opened the show with, "Well, friends, our post game guest for today is Johnny Sain and he's here."

"But a young man has also gotten himself on the show and there he sits there. And I'm glad to see him sitting there relaxed and, ha ha, and of course you know that he had done something that no ballplayer has ever done, 61 home runs in a pennant season. And sitting with him is his manager. And we're looking forward to having a little chat in a moment and letting Roger see home run 61 that he hit."

Red then turned his attention to the Yanks' skipper.

"Manager Houk, fans of course were wildly excited in the fourth inning and, even the case of hardened professional baseball writers, as I understand Bob Fishel tells me, got very emotional and all stood up and applauded. Was there much interest in the Yankee dugout?"

Ralph Houk responded, "Well, we were all excited, Red, and of course I'm just happy Roger was on our side all year and I'd like to take this time to congratulate you, Roger, for doing something that no other man in baseball has ever done. And it was great for all of us. And it was a real climax to a wonderful year for you and the Yankees."

Roger spoke in a low-key, almost shy, reserved voice, "Thank you very much, Ralph. I enjoyed it myself."

That response got everyone on the Red Barber show to laugh out loud.

"I'm sure you did," confirmed Houk.

Barber chimed in and asked Rog a question: "Well, I'm sure you enjoyed 61 more than those last few ahead of it."

"Yes, I have Red. This was, like I say, my biggest home run I ever hit," Rog responded.

Barber uttered an affirmative, "uh-huh," then, wanting to have Rog see for the first time his at bat added, "And now, let's, ah…the film isn't quite ready yet, huh? Okay, as soon as the film is ready, Roger, we'll crank 'er up. We'll want you to see it on the monitor and give us your reactions as you faced this young right-hander who was throwing hard out there.

"And see, he started you off first inning with an outside pitch and you went to left, huh?"

Rog explained his thought process. "Well, he threw a pitch that I didn't think he threw, it was sorta like a sinker. When he threw the ball it was like a fastball, but it tailed away from the plate. Away from me. And, of course, my natural reflexes, I guess wanna go right with it. I don't know. I wasn't trying to hit to left. But I know that."

Keeping the ball rolling, Barber asked, "And your next time up, I think he tried to start you with the same type of pitch, didn't he?"

Rog did his best with his response: "He threw, I think, one outside and came inside with the other one. I'm not sure."

Satisfied, Barber added his confirmation, then an explanation and ended with an introduction. "Okay. But you can be sure now. We'll give you a look at it. And then we will release you to the press and the photographers and your teammates over in the clubhouse. Film is coming up. And let me ask you as we wait for it to come up. Were you thinking that maybe this would be it?'

So as not to be misquoted, Maris said honestly, "Well, I was hoping it would be it. I wasn't thinking maybe it would be it."

Barber pressed Rog, "You didn't have a hunch?"

Maris answered again, "Well, no, I didn't, Red. I was hoping that I could get a pitch to hit."

Barber acknowledged Maris's answer with "uh-huh," then continued, "Well, you did. And now you are going to see the first one. Well, then. I thought that was the same type of pitch that he gave you the first inning."

Maris answered: "Well, that was the pitch that was high and outside and the other one was low and outside."

Again another "uh-huh" from Barber, followed by, "Well, you are going to see the other one. Did you expect to get a pitch to hit right now with the count 1 and 0?"

"No, I didn't," Maris said, and then pointed out: "Of course, you have to be ready just by chance he does throw one in there and I was trying to be ready for anything. Just hoping to be over the plate where I could pull it."

Barber continued with one more affirmative "uh-huh," and said, "Well, now on this next pitch. I think you saw it when it left his hand."

Maris concurred, "I must have 'cause I met it right here."

Respectfully, Barber instructed Rog: "Well, take a look, Mr. Maris, it's yours. And look at the scramble around the five thousand dollar baseball."

Maris chimed in, "Yeah, they were scrambling there."

Barber added, "Well, the kid that caught it said he was really pressed in."

Rog acknowledged, "Well, I'll tell you, I talked to the young boy there right after we completed that inning. And he's a real nice kid."

Barber uttered, "uh-huh," then complimented the new home run king: "Well, Roger, that is very wonderful. You can see the reaction of your teammates, the trainer and the crowd is just wild and, of course, you came out and everyone thought that you handled your bow very simply and just perfectly and it—"

Maris interrupted Red, "Well, if you notice here that once I get out I start to go back in, and they keep pushing me out. They didn't want to let me, let me in the dugout."

Perhaps at a loss for words, Barber said, "Well, look, nobody ever hit 61 before. Very good."

Maris then described his frustration: "I can't get back into the dugout. They just keep pushing on me."

With the film over, Barber ended the interview, "Well, we'll let you get in the clubhouse now because you sure belong in there, Roger."

"Thank you, Red," said Rog.

Barber wished Maris a great series.

Houk added, "It was a great day."

With that, Rog got up to exit, not realizing where he was walking.

Barber explained to the viewing audience, "Well, right across the camera. Walk across my camera any time. Very good."

Red then turned his attention to the Yankees' pitching coach, "Now let's move over here, Johnny Sain. Well, John, thank you for waiting but this was something that we just had to do."

Sain politely responded, "Well, Red it's…of course I expect to take a back seat on something like this. It's a real pleasure because I certainly enjoyed watching Rog operate that bat all year and I think that possibly had something to do with our pitching too."

Barber added, "Well, it doesn't hurt when your pitchers have someone making runs for you."

Sain continued. "Definitely. Definitely. He and Mantle and Yogi and all those boys have done a magnificent job with that bat. Naturally, leading the league in home runs for a club is something else. That is very outstanding, Red.

"You know, I pitched against the New York Giants the year that they set that record."

Barber gave Sain a short, "uh-huh" and Sain went on. "And they had Mize and a few of those boys that hit a few off of me, too."

Barber questioned Sain: "And if you were pitching against a batting order like that, it worries you?"

Sain's retort was to the point. "It certainly does. You have no place to relax or, well, there's very little relaxing on the mound anyway but you, you definitely are going all out all the way."

The Barber show was better than I anticipated.

Watching Rog seeing himself on a TV, hitting his 61st homer for the first time, might have been one of the coolest things I have seen on TV in my life.

After Roger's TV appearance, the reporters buried him with questions.

One reporter asked Maris what he had thought when a fan raced out to shake his hand before he reached the Yankee dugout. "I didn't even know he did it," said Maris. "I was so happy I wasn't paying attention to anything. My mind was a blank."

In a post-game interview, Stallard admitted that he had a simple approach when facing Maris. He explained, "I just throw the ball. I put my stuff against his stuff, and he hit my stuff. It was my best pitch. A fastball."

Russ Nixon, the Red Sox catcher, when asked what pitch he had signaled to Stallard: "It was a fastball, and it didn't get to me."

Thinking about the 1961 Yankee season, it seemed like every other day during the season either Maris or Mantle hit a home run. In actuality, they did better than that. I counted that they hit home runs on 83 days of the 162-game schedule, played in 142 days.

But my guy did it. He hit sixty-one tonks.

Poking Around—This photo of Rog posing in his locker for photogs with a No. 61 jersey and "The Ball" provided me with the opportunity to inspect the photo so that I could snoop around in his locker. *Photo courtesy National Baseball Hall of Fame.*

***

After the game, one of the questions asked of Rog was about the bat he used, which was now perched on two clothing hooks in his locker: would he keep using it for the upcoming World Series? Rog disclosed that he used that bat to hit No. 59 and 60 and would take no chances with it. "I'm keeping it."

***

How's this for a baseball coincidence?

Two hours after Rog connected for his sixty-first homer in Yankee Stadium, his North Dakota teenage sports rival Steve Myhra was playing for the Baltimore Colts against the Minnesota Vikings at Baltimore's Memorial Stadium.

The North Dakota M&M athletes had been reunited in Baltimore the night Rog hit No. 59.

With two seconds on the clock in the final play for the Baltimore Colts, Myhra kicked a 52-yard field goal making the score 34–33 and a win for Baltimore.

***

WCBS-TV Channel 2 aired the film of Maris hitting his sixty-first homer with a one-minute bulletin: "Maris is the single-season home run record holder, comma, end of sentence, period."

***

When I came to my senses I picked up this week's *TV Guide*. It had a picture of Carol Burnett on the cover.

Usually when I visited the bathroom, instead of browsing *Reader's Digest* I would religiously check the guide for baseball movies being aired and any baseball specials, especially around World Series time. I checked to see who Ed Sullivan would have as his guest. Among those listed to appear was Brigitte Bardot. *Va va voom,* but no Maris.

Sullivan had earned a well-deserved reputation for introducing sports celebrities on his show. So I counted on Roger being in the audience or maybe walking on stage and talking with Sullivan.

Therefore, I won't be watching Channel 4's *Walt Disney's Wonderful World of Color* on our black-and-white TV at 7:30 p.m., because I have to see Rog take a bow and wave to Ed Sullivan's 8 p.m. audience on CBS.

Man, was I disappointed. Instead of Maris, that night Sullivan introduced sixty-five-year-old Tom Zachary, who threw the pitch that Ruth hit for his sixtieth homer.

As Ed raised his right arm looking out into the audience, he encouraged those seated in front of the stage and those watching from home: "Let's hear it for Tom Zachary." Respectfully, but disappointed, I barely clapped.

***

That evening, Roger and Pat had dinner with friends Julie Issacson and his wife, Selma, and sportswriter Milton Gross of the *New York Post*. Rog had a shrimp cocktail, a steak (medium), a mixed salad with French dressing, a baked potato, two glasses of rosé wine, a sliver of cheesecake, two cups of coffee, and three cigarettes.

What struck me as interesting was that Rog was only a few blocks away from the theater where Ed Sullivan's TV show was broadcast and could easily stand for a moment before an appreciative audience while picking up a handsome fee.

I wondered what had prevented Rog from appearing on the show.

***

This was indeed the season of the home run as the major leagues set a new record by hitting 2,730. The National League hit 1,196 round-trippers. The Yanks led all teams by clouting 240, and the expanded American League hit 1,534 homers. The Kansas City Athletics were last in total homers with 90.

***

Of all the congratulations Maris received for breaking Ruth's record, the one that I thought was the most incredible was from President John F. Kennedy: "My heartiest congratulations to you on hitting your sixty-first home run. The American people will always admire a man who overcomes great pressure to achieve an outstanding goal."

***

Mayor Wagner's telegram to Maris: "Heartiest congratulations. Our city is indeed proud of you, and I am sure every baseball fan in the country is equally so. We're particularly glad that a Yankee player was the first to hit 61 homers in a season. All the best luck to you and the team in the Series."

***

Pope John made an unpublicized visit to the Vatican's radio station today. The message of his broadcast was peace, truth, and unity—but no mention of congratulations to the Yanks or Maris.

A Mirror Image—It's obvious that this Bronx street "newsie" was not thrilled that the Babe's home run record was broken.

***

Later that evening, The Orioles, not the baseball team but the singing group, were performing "Come On Home" in Harlem. They accompanied Sonny Til at the Apollo along with Little Anthony and The Imperials, who performed "Shimmy, Shimmy, Ko Ko Bop."

***

Throughout the season I heard and read from critics the advantage that Maris had batting in front of Mantle, which resulted in not walking him intentionally or unintentionally because Mantle was in the on-deck circle. I couldn't argue with that. I thought that the last time Mantle batted behind Rog was September 17 which—according to that assumption—pitchers would not give him anything close to hit and not worry about walking him. So with that logic, Rog should have been stuck on fifty-nine homers.

October 2

The next day, October 2, Roger's accomplishment was on the front page of every New York newspaper as well as around the country. Searching for anecdotal tidbits about Maris, I combed through every page of every New York newspaper—and even those out-of-town papers—I could lay my hands on.

Of all the photos printed that day, the shot taken by Mel Finkelstein of fan Sal Durante "eyeing up" Maris's home run baseball is one of my favorites. It appeared on the front page of the October 2 *New York Journal-American*.

I studied the box scores, noticing that attendance for the Yankee Stadium game was 23,154. Instantly, the "154" jumped out at me. My first thought was, "Uh, oh. No way, man."

To me, that figure obviously came from a Yankee ticket office "wise guy" who didn't think that Maris's home run record was legit because it was accomplished in eight more games than Ruth played. To make his point, the jerk inserted a hidden message so that the last three numbers in that day's announced attendance were the same as the number of games Ruth had to hit sixty homers. It was a cheap shot at my guy's accomplishment.

***

There was no doubt in my mind that I had to get a copy of the video and radio broadcast of the game.

I knew that Phil Rizzuto was behind the mic for the Yankee radio broadcast when Rog connected, but wondered who the Red Sox radio announcer was that called Maris's record-breaking at-bat and how did he describe it?

During school, when I could sneak it in, I began writing a draft of a letter to WPIX, the TV station that had carried the Yankee game, requesting a copy of the videotape.

I took a shot knowing that even if WPIX had sent that three-inch videotape, I didn't have the machine to play it. I later found out that the machine was the size of a piano and cost tens of thousands of dollars. Silly me.

I did, however, receive a response from the WPIX production manager, Edward M. Roberts. He advised me that he couldn't sell a copy of it to me, but added, "Even if we did, a copy of the film would cost about $50."

He ended his letter with a suggestion: "I know you will be very disappointed at this news, so I stopped in a Peerless Camera store to inquire if any of their movies sold for home use might include shots of Maris's home run. They said nothing has been released yet, but there probably would be soon. The clerk was busy, and I am not sure he checked very carefully, so why don't you go to a local camera store and ask again."

As for the Red Sox radio broadcast, if one was recorded and existed, I had to have a better plan than just writing a simple letter from a thirteen-year-old kid politely asking for a copy. I needed more time to figure out how to own that recording. Someday I know I'll get it.

Selfishly, I wanted to experience the thrill over and over again of Maris hitting his sixty-first homer.

In many ways that recording would provide me with indescribable feelings, similar to those I experienced when I bought a seven-inch vinyl record earlier this year that started with the first song I just had to own: "I Like It Like That." The only difference would be that when I heard the recording of Rog, my heart would be dancing instead of my feet.

I knew one thing: I'd need more than one copy of that at-bat because I didn't want this record broken.

By the way, of the sixty-one homers Rog hit this season, this homer on the last day of the season was the only game he won with a homer being the only run for the Yankees.

That deserves another Mel Allen, "How about that!"

***

The latest edition of *Sports Illustrated* had Maris in mid-swing on the cover in a Yankee-gray road uniform. Unfortunately, the photo of Rog was so large that it did not include the bat he was swinging, which was disappointing.

Let me give you an example of what I mean by disappointing.

You know the guy on the Ed Sullivan show who, with the Ray Bloch Orchestra playing fast music, spins five plates on sticks at the same time without one of those plates crashing to the ground?

Well, imagine the plate-spinner guy getting his picture on the cover of *Life* magazine.

There he is, wearing his tuxedo and a large bow tie, standing behind one of those long sticks in which a plate is balanced and spinning. He's looking up…but the photo does not show the plate.

You see what I'm talking about?

In the upper right-hand corner of the cover, in the shape of a football with a red, white, and blue horizontal stripe, were the words "World Series Preview." It would have made a lot more sense if it was in the shape of a baseball, don'tcha think?

Attached to the cover was a 3 ¼" × 4" small red-paper flyer promoting an article in the magazine: "No. 60 FULL STORY OF THE LONG CHASE."

Knowing that Maris had already hit his sixtieth and sixty-first homers, I'm guessing the magazine was printed and hit the newsstands prior to or on September 26.

The inside article, written by Roger Kahn, provided some delectable Maris tidbits such as:

- Elston Howard's locker is next to Roger's Yankee Stadium locker.
- When the Yankee players were in Minneapolis to play the Twins this season, they stayed on the eighth floor of the downtown Hotel Radisson.
- Kahn describes Maris in great detail, including the points of Roger's upper lip and how it curls toward his nose, creating a Cupid's-bow effect.

My eyes drifted over to the adjoining page, which was a full-page photo of a bare-chested Roger listening to reporters' questions. I zeroed in on his lips. Kahn was correct.

Toward the end of the article, Kahn wrote eloquently about that game in Baltimore: "No one who saw Game 154, who beheld Maris's response to the challenge, is likely soon to forget it. His play was as brave and as moving and as thrilling as a baseball player can be." I'll bet Kahn did real well in his junior high English class.

Once done with the Maris article, I continued reading the magazine and came across a Rex Lardner story about the Comiskey Park ushers provided by Andy Frain Services.

Frain talked about Maris. He mentioned that if Maris had come to bat with fifty-nine homers at Comiskey Park a couple of weeks earlier, Frain would have dispatched 125 experienced ushers and 25 chiefs to the edge of the field to make sure none of the fans considered jumping from the stands to offer their congratulations, or in Frain's words, "tear him to pieces."

Which reminded me that, according to Kahn, "Maris is being covered more intensely than any other figure in sports history. Not Ruth or

Dempsey or Tilden, or Jones was ever subjected to such interviewing and shadowing for so sustained a period."

The cost of that *Sports Illustrated*—twenty-five cents—translates to five packs of baseball cards. It's my new math. I calculate the cost of everything based on a five-cent pack of baseball cards.

***

Sam Gordon, who announced that he would pay $5,000 for the home run ball, and Sal Durante, who caught the ball, made a brief appearance on the 10 a.m. CBS-TV show premiere of *Calendar*.

***

Hey Ralphie Boy—The friendship between Roger and Ralph Kiner began in the mid-1950s when they were both working for the Cleveland Indians. Kiner was the GM for the Indians' Triple-A farm team—the San Diego Padres. *Photo courtesy of Cleveland State University.*

Hy Gardner wrote a story on October 2 for the *Boston Globe* about the night before the Yanks' last game. Roger and a former minor-league player–first name, Joe–had dinner at Danny's Hideaway in Manhattan. Before they left, they went over to say hello to two other diners, Hank Greenberg and Ralph Kiner. Hank told Roger that they would be at the ballpark tomorrow to watch him hit another homer.

Roger responded, "I'll sure try but they've been getting tougher to hit every day."

Gardner quoted Greenberg: "That fellow with Roger played in the minors with him but didn't quite make it. It proves though what a nice kid and modest champ Maris is. At the peak of his glory, instead of going out with a big name, Maris goes out with a ballplayer who's so completely forgotten even I can't recall Joe's second name."

***

The *Indianapolis Star*'s weatherman reported: The pitcher who served up Roger Maris's sixty-first home run ball probably will be signed up to endorse Brand X products. Fair and a little warmer today and tonight.

"I, Pat Maris, have been following the baseball career of Roger Maris ever since he entered professional baseball in 1953. We and his family are extremely proud of his accomplishment. Such as his being named Most Valuable Player in the American League in 1960 and particularly the fact that he is the only man to have hit 60 home runs in one season since the great Babe Ruth.

Pat Maris

No Lie—Roger's agent Frank Scott slays me. I'm convinced that he was the one who made arrangements for Roger's wife, Pat, to be a contestant on *To Tell the Truth*. Here's the affidavit wording, as read by host Bud Collier.

This evening, Roger's wife, Pat, appeared on the TV show *To Tell the Truth*. Bud Collier hosted. The panel members: Tom Poston, Dina Merrill, Johnny Carson, and Kitty Carlisle. Two other contestants claimed they were Pat Maris. Frank McConnell, a retired brigadier general in the United States Army, said he was Roger's father. Peggy Alderman, a private secretary for a company that fabricated precious metals and their alloys, said she was Roger's sister.

The affidavit read by Collier:

I, Pat Maris, have been following the baseball career of Roger Maris ever since he entered professional baseball in 1953. We and his family are extremely proud of his accomplishment. Such as his being named Most Valuable Player in the American League in 1960 and particularly the fact that he is the only man to have hit 60 home runs in one season since the great Babe Ruth.

Signed, Pat Maris

This show had been filmed on September 26, the day Roger hit No. 60.

***

Thanks once again to Frank Scott, Hearst Headline Service enlists Rog and Mick to become byline sportswriters for the 1961 World Series. Great cartoon of them swinging a bat and a typewriter.

According to newly employed sportswriters Mantle and Maris, the Yanks will win the series in seven games.

***

Phil Pepe of the *New York World Telegram & Sun* reported today that during batting practice before the October 1 game, Rog hit two balls into the seats, but said "I don't feel too sharp" when asked how he was feeling.

***

Boston Globe writer Douglas S. Crocket surveyed fans in Bean Town about Maris's accomplishment. The article was titled, "But Local Fans Not All Thrilled." The results were predictable as they are from Boston. Those surveyed included:

Charles Poulcs, 39, of Arlington: "I think everyone agrees that Maris will never be another Babe Ruth."

Clinton Hibbard, 51, of Cambridge: "He's not the greatest clutch-hitter in baseball history, though. Joe Cronin was."

John Curtiss, 29, of Cambridge: "If Ted Williams had Mantle batting behind him, he'd have 80 homers."

Kenneth Sargent, 24, of Billerica: "No matter what Ford Frick says, I think that Maris has broken Babe Ruth's record."

***

Showing off when there is no reason to show off twists my shorts in a knot. *The New York Times* wrote about the legitimacy of the home run record as it relates to the schedules of 154 games versus 162 games in an article, "Aggression in the Bronx."

As best as I can tell, they used contrived, overly elaborate sentences to summarize each side's position.

In the article the *Times* made reference to Maris's Louisville Slugger by writing "...whose bat has all the deadliness of a rocket launcher....Those who feel that record books should not be cluttered up with a lot of asterisks indicating the differing conditions under which high-water marks are set will demand that the new champion be enthroned with no flyspeck on his claim to preeminence. Babe Ruth's partisans will be no less adamant in insisting that no one who failed to match him in 154 games is entitled to usurp his title."

Throughout my school years, I was quite familiar with people—usually one of the girls who lives in the Highlands area—who showed off their writing and vocabulary skills.

This was a perfect example of some guy at *The New York Times* who has his pen stuck way too far up his ass.

I have, at thirteen years of age, come to the conclusion that the final arbitrator will be Father Time. It will be interesting to see on which side of the fence this home run debate will fall in five, ten, or twenty years from now when I'm thirty-three years old.

***

The New York Times is late coming to the "Maris-in-Depth-Article" party based on what I read in their paper today.

Here it is the day after Maris hits his sixty-first homer, and the article entitled "Angry King of Swat" is about his demeanor and his personal history. None of the quotes about Rog were attributed to an identified source other than a "teammate" or a "Kansas City executive," which may explain why the writer of the article was also not identified.

But one nugget caught my attention: When Rog played for the Indianapolis Indians in the minor leagues back in 1956, he beat out eighteen of nineteen drag bunts for hits.

***

In the same edition of *The New York Times*, Macy's took out a full-page ad that showed a photo of Babe Ruth about to hit a pitch. The copy next to the Ruth image was complimentary to the Babe, acknowledging that his record still stands after thirty-four years.

Then it offers a backhanded compliment to Maris with the explanation that his record is different. The ad goes on to challenge Maris to become a hero like Ruth to small boys and their fathers.

"We're all proud of Roger Maris, proud that the home run record still belongs to the home team. For when records are rolled up, they're rolled up here…and when they're broken, they're broken here, too. That's what makes New York so exciting…."

The last line uses the word hurrah for Roger Maris and the Yankees.

It's apparent to me that the copywriter who penned the wording must have spent time writing about housewares or shoes and should leave sports to someone who knows what they are writing about. Specifically, I didn't understand what was meant about records being "rolled up."

***

The New York Times had a full-page ad, "WE JOIN YOU IN THE PEACE RACE," that supported President Kennedy's proclamation that man must put an end to war, or war will put an end to man. It went into detail about disarmament. Mercy me, things ain't what they used to be.

***

On page 2 of the *Journal-American*, Dime Savings Bank of Brooklyn took out a quarter-page display ad promoting loans for those who want to build a fallout shelter, which begs the question: What's going on?

***

Jimmy Cannon of the *Journal-American* wrote a column that touched my heart: "I wonder how many kids today think of themselves as Roger Maris? It is not an impossible dream. Once Roger Maris wanted to be Ted Williams."

***

The United Italian-American League wanted to honor Roger by having its president, Paul Rao, present him with a custom-made silver plaque at City Hall on October 3. The news media showed up, as did Mayor Robert Wagner, albeit late, but unfortunately the plaque didn't.

With news photographers shooting, Rao explained that the plaque was still at the silversmith, which got Rog to break up laughing, a moment the photogs caught on film and printed the next day. The photo caption contained the additional information that the plaque was delivered to Maris later that day in his hotel room.

October 3

Ah, Watson, as in Sherlock Holmes, the "Maris No-Show Ed Sullivan Mystery" is solved.

I read in today's October 3 newspaper about why Maris wasn't a guest on Ed Sullivan's Sunday night October 1 show. On September 5, Maris and Mantle signed a limited exclusive TV appearance for the Perry Como fourteenth-season show opener taped on September 29 and airing tomorrow, October 4.

Also appearing on the Como show with Mickey and Roger are Buddy Hackett, Fran Jeffries, and Mel Allen. Plus, a regular cast that includes Don Adams, Kaye Ballard, Jack Duffy, Paul Lynde, and Sandy Stewart. The featured musical number that had everyone singing, "Take Me Out to the Ball Game."

***

George Weiss, formerly the Yankees general manager but now the Mets GM, explained in an Associated Press October 3 article how he made Maris a Yankee. It started back in 1955. Maris was with Reading (Pennsylvania) in the Eastern League and belonged to the Cleveland Indians. When Maris joined Cleveland in 1957, Weiss knew he couldn't make a trade with Frank Lane, the Indians GM. Instead, Weiss told KC Athletics owner Arnold Johnson that if Johnson ever landed Maris, Weiss would make him a real deal to bring Roger to the Yanks. Weiss deserved more credit than he received for putting together the 1961 Yankees.

***

Here's a Maris statistic you won't find anywhere else in the world: 1961 Roger Maris Congratulatory Homer Handshakes. After reviewing each box score, I determined that Mantle, being the next batter, shook Roger's hand after fifty-three homers (including the four tonks he hit on July 25), while Yogi Berra glad-handed Rog four times. Deron Johnson, Tony Kubek, and Hector Lopez each had one congratulatory palm press.

I did not include bat boy homer handshakes, nor did I include Roger's twenty-eighth home run, which was a game winner in the ninth inning on July 1, 1961, against the Washington Senators at Yankee Stadium. In that one, Maris ran straight past Mantle, who according to a joking Rog didn't realize the game had ended.

Other than Mantle, here are the numbered Homer Handshakes: No. 1*—Deron Johnson; No. 4—Tony Kubek; Nos. 8, 9, 59, and 61—Yogi Berra; No. 60—Hector Lopez.

*Rog batted seventh for the April 26 game when he connected for his first homer of the season.

October 4

Before breakfast, as it sometimes happens to me, I felt a bad stomach ache developing. Not the throw-up kind of stomach ache, but enough of an ache so that, as a precaution, I thought it would be best to share with my mom that I also had the chills and felt a bit dizzy. It was Wednesday, October 4.

Being considerate of my classmates and aware that I might be contagious, I suggested to my mom that it could be the start of a bug that's going around, and I shouldn't go to school.

I didn't need to provide any theories how my illness came about, but I was prepared to mention that it was probably something I ate yesterday. Or maybe it was connected to one of my friends being sent home from school last Friday with a bad case of the dreaded Hershey Squirts. Or maybe I caught a bug from our substitute for our gym teacher, Mr. Cropsey, who was not in school last week as it was rumored he had a fever over 101.

My mother suggested that I rest all day. She prescribed that I bring my blanket and pillow into the den and if I had enough strength to watch a little TV.

***

Great *Daily News* photo of Rog smiling with Lefty Gomez and Tommy Henrich, shot yesterday in the Yankee locker room.

Listen to This—As Rog is trying to get ready to play Game 3 of the 1961 World Series, ABC's "Speaking of Sports" host Howard Cosell offers some advice. *Photo by Bob Wood.*

***

Experience counts as the Yanks won the first game of the World Series by a score of 2–0, which made me feel better, but not enough to go back to school.

***

It was noted in today's *Daily News* column "On the Town" by Charles McHarry that Roz Starr—who supplies news of celebrities to movie studios, hotels, TV stations, and newspapers—has memorized five thousand telephone numbers, including those of Jayne Mansfield, Grace Kelly, Anita Ekberg, Jackie Gleason, Marlene Dietrich, and Roger Maris. I'll bet she has Frank Scott's number and not Roger's. I'm just saying.

***

Is this insane? The October 4 *New York Times* published a telephone number, ME 7-1212, that can be called for the World Series score update every half inning. What is this world coming too?

***

Great ad in the *Daily News* promoting Perry Como's *Kraft Music Hall* TV show that included photos of guests Mantle and Maris.

***

I found out that the winner of the *Pittsburgh Press* home run contest was a seventy-six-year-old woman, Mrs. Mamie Wally from Etna, Pennsylvania. Her brother did the guessing, but filled in her name in the entry blank and also submitted one in his own name. The winning entry had it perfect with Mantle clouting fifty-four homers and Maris with sixty-one.

Mrs. Wally explained that she would share her $500 winnings with her brother after paying her income taxes.

***

Norman Atkinson of the Guy Lombardo Orchestra sang the national anthem before game No. 1 of the World Series. The orchestra entertained the fans for an hour before the game started.

***

Reuters had an East Berlin story about a twenty-five-year-old Lothario who was convicted of marriage fraud after proposing to sixteen pretty twenty-year-old girls. All accepted his proposal, so a Leipzig court awarded him two-and-a-half years in the clink.

***

According to the "Stars Today" forecast, the prediction for Roger—who is a Virgo—reads: "Luck is changing. Your fate depends upon moving ahead with confidence despite criticism from the sidelines. Follow an inner voice of wisdom."

***

Maris appears to be a different person to different writers. There is a lack of consistency in their observations. This makes the point that if six people see something, they will more than likely not agree on what they saw.

Dan Daniel writes in his *Sporting News* column that Roger is a quiet, humble, soft-spoken family man, with four kids and a happy wife, and adds that Maris is devoutly religious.

***

The Perry Como *Kraft Music Hall* show taped September 29 aired tonight.

The players wore tuxedos (with their uniform numbers on the back), and when Como mentioned that it was time for a commercial, Rog quipped, "Want us to endorse something?"

Como, who long ago was a barber, noticed that Mantle had a light beard, to which Mickey explained that this would be the tenth commercial he has shaved for today. The beard reference was an attempt to be funny while perhaps acknowledging that Mantle is a manly man.

"He's already broken Bess Myerson's record for commercials," Maris cracked.

Como asked Rog if he had any advice for rookies in the big leagues next season. "Yes, I have," replied Roger. He looked into the camera and delivered the line, "Don't hit sixty-one."

October 5

Still feeling under the weather, it was easy to convince my mom that I should stay home again today, Thursday, October 5.

Even though the Yanks had a combined total of 2,753 innings of World Series experience, the Reds won the second game 6–2. I calculated that the earliest I would feel better and return to school would be October 9.

October 6

I have now trained myself to look for anything that has the combination M&M in it. For example, a story in today's *Daily News* caught my eye because the headline was "Miami's M-M Squad 13 Over Navy Tonight at the Orange Bowl." Upon reading it I realized that the reference was to the

Miami Hurricanes' quarterback George Mira and end Bill Miller and their team being a 13-point pick over Navy.

***

Perry Como's show was reviewed in today's *Daily News*. Regarding the M&M Boys, the reviewer observed their acting was just about what was to be expected from personable, intelligent young athletes. They contributed some entertaining moments.

***

Starting at 8:30 p.m., WPIX aired a thirty-minute show, "Roger Maris, Home Run King," hosted by Mel Allen. It contained videotape of his last eleven homers and an interview with Rog, plus a film clip of Babe hitting his sixtieth homer.

If it takes me the rest of my life, I need to get a copy of that film.

***

Robert Sylvestor's *Daily News* column, "Dream Street," mentioned that the World Series column written by Mantle and Maris in a competing newspaper had sixty-one clichés in it.

October 7

According to an Associated Press article, President Kennedy spoke at a private luncheon for a dozen or so New Jersey newspaper executives on October 6. He advised that any prudent family should provide for fallout protection.

Oh, my dear God. I don't know whether to run, hide, or cry.

***

After Roger's homer made the difference in the Yanks 3–2 World Series win over the Reds in Game 3, I informed my mom that I felt I was getting better.

***

Some of these nuggets about Maris are absurd but they do make me laugh. According to the Associated Press, Rog received one write-in vote to be the tax collector of Old Saybrook, CT.

***

Another silly mention about Roger in Charles McHarry's *Daily News* column, "On The Town." McHarry wrote: "Regardless of how he does in the Series, Roger Maris has it made. He's being sought to cut the ribbon at the opening of a lettuce and tomato emporium in Woodcrest, New Jersey, on October 18. If he shows up and does the job, he'll get all the lettuce and tomatoes he can eat for the rest of his life."

***

Jack Butler, who writes about sports for Brooklyn's newspaper *The Tablet*, pointed out in today's issue that after Maris hit his sixtieth home run on September 26, the so-called imperturbable, experienced sportswriters asked Maris to autograph their scorebooks.

Let me save you a trip leafing through Mr. Webster's pages because I had to look up "imperturbable." It means "self-controlled."

October 8

By Sunday afternoon after the Yanks beat the Reds 7–0 and needed just one more World Series victory, I was most definitely on the road to recovery. But to make sure, I suggested to my mom that just to be safe I should stay home from school tomorrow.

***

Roger's game-winning homer in the World Series yesterday is being labeled by some papers as home run No. 62.

***

Gene Ward printed a letter of complaint from a reader in his column, "Inside Sports." Nick Landsberg of New York City took issue with the fact that on September 11 Ward wrote that Mantle is great but Maris is greater. Ward responded, "Just my opinion, Nick. Maris, in the public eye, is greater right now than Mantle, who is the better player of the two."

October 9

Late today, coincidently, not long after the Yankees had beaten the Reds, 13–5, to take the Series in five games, I was miraculously cured and announced to my concerned mother that I'd be attending school tomorrow without question.

She smiled.

According to reports, Rog was the first Yankee off the field after Vada Pinson's check-swing pop fly to Hector Lopez was caught in shallow left field. Roger quickly showered and dressed and hustled to catch a 5:50 p.m. flight home to Kansas City.

He left behind a disastrous .105 World Series average, getting only two hits in nineteen at-bats for the Series, which was the worst productivity among non-pitchers with more than one at-bat.

When Roger and Pat arrived in Kansas City, they were greeted by a crowd of one hundred fans that included the president of the Raytown [Missouri] Chamber of Commerce, Dr. Dillard Eubank, who presented Pat with a bouquet of yellow and white mums.

Unable to go directly home, they were escorted to Raytown City Hall, where they received a key to the city in a short ceremony. A caravan of about twenty cars escorted by patrolmen convoyed them to their home at 5120 Blue Ridge Boulevard.

October 10

Frank Scott's handiwork showed up on page 66 of the *Daily News*. Camel cigarettes has a full-page ad with pictures of Maris, Ford, Skowron, and Berra all smoking a Camel. The ad included a list of eighteen other baseball clients who presumably are Camel smokers, ranging from Hank Aaron to Warren Spahn.

***

Jimmy Powers wrote in his *Daily News* column that Maris threw no tantrums despite the aggravation of enduring a horrendous slump during the World Series. He was, according to Powers, civil even to rookie writers who asked the most banal questions.

October 12

Cheez, this is silly. The National Macaroni Institute announced that Roger Maris is named Macaroni Sportsman of the Year because he "used his noodle" in setting a new home run record.

***

In a summary of the 1961 season, *The Sporting News* said that one reporter cluelessly asked Ralph Houk, "Did you ever signal Maris or Mantle to hit a homer?" To which the Yankee manager remarked indignantly, "I hope you're kidding."

October 15

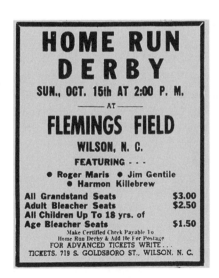

Long Distance Operators—Those lucky stiffs in the South who for a couple of bucks could attend the home run derby at Flemings Field in Wilson, N.C., where they could watch Roger Maris, Harmon Killebrew, and Jim Gentile.

Less than a week after the World Series concluded Roger, who had to be mentally and physically exhausted, joined Harmon Killebrew and Jim Gentile in a five-city home run hitting exhibition tour in North Carolina.

***

Larry Lackman of *The Cincinnati Enquirer* wrote that Rosemary Murphy, the recently crowned Mrs. America, attended a Yankee-Indians game in Cleveland. One of the photos taken was with Maris. When she returned home her son Jeffrey asked, "Mommy, why would Roger Maris want his picture taken with you?"

October 18

Turns out that 1961 was a tough year for Babe Ruth. Whitey Ford also broke a Ruth record—this one when the Babe was a pitcher for the Red Sox and threw twenty-nine-and-a-third consecutive scoreless innings in the 1916 and 1918 World Series. Ford extended his consecutive scoreless innings to thirty-three-and-two-thirds.

***

The Yanks' per-player World Series share of $7,389.13 is announced by Commissioner Ford Fart...er, I mean Frick.

***

The Sporting News also had a note that a female newspaper photographer was asked to leave the field before a World Series game. "Absolutely no women allowed on the field," a spokesman for the commissioner's office tersely explained.

***

There was a full-page ad for "Maris for Camel" cigarettes in the same issue of *The Sporting News*. These testimonial ads are troubling to me because companies know that as a result of a player using their product it will attract others to follow.

Naturally, wanting to be like Rog, I had to give a Camel a try. I got halfway through (cough) one of my dad's (ahem) Camels and thought I was going to (hack) puke my brains out.

***

Earl Lawson's story in *The Sporting News* referenced a quote from Reds manager Fred Hutchinson in the headline: "Hutch's Sizeup of Series—Maris's Blast Ruined Us."

Hutchinson felt that Maris's October 7 homer, which won Game 3 for the

Yanks, was the most damaging blow of the Series. It ruined a fine pitching performance by Bob Purkey, and the team just couldn't bounce back.

**

Remember when Governor Rockefeller said that if Maris hits sixty-one homers he would send Michigan Governor John B. Swainson "One of our prize New York dairy calves"?

Well, he did, and the Michigan governor's wife, Alice, and three-year-old daughter Kristina named him "Homerdale-Clyde-Maris 61."

October 21

Roger, who took up the game of golf a year ago, played in an exhibition at Omaha's Miracle Hill Golf Course in front of a gallery of about three hundred. He shot a ninety-three.

He was teamed with pro Dick Knight against pro Don January and Olympic athlete Johnny Weissmuller, who won five gold medals in swimming in the 1920s, then played Tarzan in the movies in the nineteen-thirties and -forties.

I have never played golf, nor do I have any interest in the game. In addition to the ball being small, it just sits there.

October 22

Maris was named winner of the September poll for the S. Rae Hickok Professional Athlete of the Year Award.

The Hickok Manufacturing Co., a Rochester firm that makes belts, wallets, and other accessories for men, created the distinctive award in the early 1950s, a gem-studded, solid-gold buckle on an alligator-skin belt.

The award, which basically holds up your pants if you so desire, was created by Ray and Alan Hickok in honor of their father, Stephen Rae Hickok, who died fifteen years ago.

October 23

Jack Wheeland of the *Star-Gazette* of Elmira, NY, reported today that during the 1961 World Series a ten-year-old boy from Elmira, Jimmy Kelly, had written Roger Maris asking him to be his sponsor at the Sacrament of Confirmation..

Maris turned him down in a telegram that arrived three days before his confirmation: "I regret I will be unable to attend your Confirmation and be your sponsor Sunday. God bless you on this big day in your life."

Although disappointed, Jimmy was thrilled that Maris responded with a telegram that now can be handled only if you wash your hands and have his permission.

***

Sadly, Frankie Sliwka Jr., the little boy whom Rog visited in Baltimore on September 19 when he had fifty-eight homers, never recovered. He died today on October 23.

October 24

Senator Barry Goldwater wrote an opinion column about the Eighty-Seventh Congress and who was the victor—the President or the Congress?

His piece, which ran on editorial pages around the country, made reference to the recent home run race: "The record of Congress should not be compared to an attempt by Roger Maris to beat Babe Ruth in a home run race." He continued on but lost me by the umpteenth paragraph.

***

In her October 24 syndicated column "Voice of Broadway," Dorothy Kilgallen posed the question: "Is it true that Bob Dale Martin, who has written 'Bring Me a Warm Body' for the Off-Broadway theater, actually asked Roger Maris to star in it?"

***

I kinda guessed that as a result of the home run race some kids would be named after the two Yankee sluggers. Such was the case for a couple in Pensacola, FL, Mr. and Mrs. W. H. Moore. They had a baby boy on October 24. To cover all the bases, they named him Mickey Maris Moore. Mmm.

October 26

Sam Gordon admits in a newspaper article that the idea of paying $5,000 for the sixty-first homer was germinated by his brother and a Sacramento television man who asked him to put up the $5,000. He confessed that he didn't think Maris would make it and that he wouldn't have to come up with the money, so told them "You got my OK."

October 29

Sal Durante, who caught Maris's sixty-first home run at Yankee Stadium, married Rosemarie Calabrese at St. Finbar's Church in Brooklyn today. The bride was given away by her father, Ralph, in front of 300 well-wishers, of whom only 150 were invited to the wedding reception at a Brooklyn hotel.

Having Your Cake, Too—Four weeks after catching Maris's 61st homer, Sal Durante married his girlfriend, Rosemarie Calabrese, at St. Finbar's Church in Brooklyn. *Photo courtesy of the Durante family.*

***

Sportswriter Leonard Shecter of the *New York Post* didn't miss the opportunity to capitalize on Maris's 1961 season. Earlier this month, his book,

Roger Maris, Home Run Hero, was published by Bartholomew House. I'm guessing that the ink is still wet on most, if not all, the copies.

Pop Backing Up Rog—I wanted to get both my father and Rog in the same photo so I moved to the second row of the right-field stands to get the perfect shot.

NOVEMBER 1961

"On the inside edge of the locker were the words BAD DAY."

November 1

The Sporting News ran yet another editorial about Ford Frick's edict that no home run record would be accepted as beating Babe Ruth's unless it was accomplished within 154 games.

Maybe that's where the term "beating a dead horse" came about?

The commissioner's edict created another problem. Turns out he made his ruling without consulting the Records Committee of the Baseball Writers Association of America. Some of the writers thought Frick's decision was arbitrary, capricious, and illegal.

This ongoing discourse, debate, and disagreement demonstrates that baseball's supposedly informed and educated right hand has no idea what the left hand is doing.

Frankly, I'm disappointed, but not surprised.

It got me to thinking that with the expanded schedule of 162 games there were other records that were matched or surpassed but ignored by Frick and the media, the so-called guardians of baseball. Obviously, the focus of records broken in 1961 due to extra games should not have been on Maris alone:

- Jim Gentile of the Baltimore Orioles tied Ernie Banks' 1955 record for hitting five grand-slam homers in a single season.
- Chuck Schilling of the Boston Red Sox eclipsed the record for the fewest errors in 150 or more games by an American League second baseman with eight. The previous record of nine miscues was shared by Bobby Doerr of the Boston Red Sox (1943) and Chicago White Sox's Nellie Fox (1954).
- Dave Philley (Orioles) easily broke Julio Becquer's (Senators) 1957 record of most at-bats in a season for a pinch-hitter—66—with 72 of his own. He also bested the record for most hits by a pinch-hitter—20—with his 24, eclipsing the 1936 record set by Parke Ed Coleman (St. Louis Browns).
- Not all of the records set in 1961 were positive. Rookie Jake Wood of the Detroit Tigers set a new single-season mark for striking out with 141, which bettered (?) Jim Lemon's 138 K's in 1956 with the Washington Senators.

Where's the justice?

November 4

President Kennedy announced today that the United States is getting ready for possible atmospheric testing of nuclear bombs. This is being done to ensure continued U.S. nuclear superiority over the USSR.

I kept looking for a quote, "My dad can beat up your dad."

***

One of my school assignments is to read a book of my own choice. There's a catch, however. The book must be approved by our teacher.

I selected the official 1961 Yankee yearbook that I bought at Yankee Stadium this past summer, not the unofficial publication sold on the surrounding streets. Guess what? My teacher explained that the yearbook does not count as a book. I then argued that it has the word "book" in the title.

Moving on, my second choice, fortunately, was approved. Leonard Schecter's pocketbook *Roger Maris: Home Run Hero*.

I'm way ahead of this read-a-book game because I have already read and reread it a couple of times.

Since I'm not a book reader, I'm now bragging at lunch to my classmates that the last two books I read were *Roger Maris: Home Run Hero* and *Roger*

Maris: Home Run Hero. Then I add, "Currently, I'm reading *Roger Maris: Home Run Hero.*"

It gets a laugh every time. Well, almost every time.

This fifty-cent paperback is Roger's life story. It covers his minor league career and some of the home runs he hit in 1961.

Besides the type being real small, this is the first book in my life I have read that didn't have pictures. It's 160-pages long.

If I was a reviewer, I would give it sixty-one gold stars, which would have broken the old book review record of sixty stars.

***

It was reported that the Sacramento public relations event planned by Sam Gordon in which he would present fan Sal Durante with a $5,000 check and give Roger his sixty-first home run baseball did not go well.

Ignored in accounts of the event was the fact that Rog, one of the most sought-after celebrities, attended with no appearance fee so that Sal could collect his check. Perhaps the reporters covering the event were miffed that Rog didn't schmooze them up so they could write exclusive stories.

The *San Francisco Examiner*'s headline summarized the resentment: "Hello…Goodbye: Maris Snubs Sacto Fete."

Noted in the United Press International story was the fact that Rog was annoyed when a TV cameraman's light fell, scraping his forehead.

The Associated Press article pointed out that the fans attending the event asked Maris to bring Mantle next time.

November 7

Nikita Khrushchev announces that the USSR will continue its nuclear tests indefinitely if the United States resumes atmospheric tests.

This is the adult and very dangerous version of the playground game of "I Dare You" and "You Go First."

November 8

Baseball legend Branch Rickey was quoted in this edition of *The Sporting News*: "Maris would have to hit 180 (homers) to equal Ruth's feat."

Oh, for crying out loud, Branch, ever hear of the words "sarcastic" and "hyperbole"?

***

Dan Daniel wrote in the November 8 edition of *The Sporting News* about the minutes of an October 3 player representatives meeting. At first I was disappointed, then intrigued with the topics discussed. The meeting was supposed to be a secret, but now it's in a newspaper.

To begin with, the players voted to freeze pension payments to the 111 men collecting $175 a month, while not allowing former managers to participate in the pension program. I have no idea what that means, nor do I care. Now I'll have to look up the word *pension*.

Some of the topics included the players' demand that, for All-Star Games, every position player selected—that is, other than pitchers—must be used in the game.

The article listed the players attending, who were all white. The subject of desegregation in housing for Negro players during spring training in Florida as well as during the regular season was brought up. They resolved that it should be addressed in a more aggressive way.

The player reps voted and elected Frank Scott to head up the Major League Players Association. I'm sure that was based on his dealings with the players over the last eight years as an agent and his ability to negotiate extra bucks for many of them.

Another agenda item that caught my eye was the business relationship of Topps and Fleer regarding exclusivity contracts with player-image rights on trading cards. Now, why couldn't the players vote to insist that the card companies improve the quality of their pink slabs of gum in every pack?

The players also noted there was a great deal of concern regarding the heating of Milwaukee's bullpen, along with playing-field sight lines in Philadelphia's bullpen, and the layout of Yankee Stadium's home bullpen, which forced fans to walk to the bleachers through its back end.

They also proposed that infields be dragged in the fifth inning, and that a letter be written to some guy named Mr. Alfred Berry, who is attempting to add his pitching rating calculations as an official part of records.

Mention was made that Scott will continue his research about the possibility of off-season employment for players. Players were reminded that all dues be collected and paid to the Major League Baseball Players Association central office after the June 15 team cut-down date.

What are they paying dues for?

November 10

Sadly, I informed all members of the Monkey Club that an Atlas missile carrying a small squirrel monkey named Goliath exploded after it veered off course following liftoff from Cape Canaveral.

Those of us in the Monkey Club bowed our heads in a minute of silence.

November 11

In a solemn Veterans Day tribute at Arlington National Cemetery, President Kennedy asked that the nation join him in prayer, "That there will be no veterans of any further war."

***

In Dan Parker's November 11 *New York Mirror* column, "Broadway Bugle," he took umbrage with Roger's older brother Rudy accompanying him to Sam Gordon's Sacramento restaurant for the sixty-first home run ball event with Sal Durante.

Parker pointed out that Gordon paid the Maris brothers' round-trip air fare of $672.28 from Kansas City. He further pointed out that Rudy was overly protective and worked to prevent anyone from taking advantage of Roger. It was evident that Parker wasn't sensitive to everyone wanting a piece of Rog, and didn't understand that Rog was there as a personal favor for Durante and Gordon in exchange for just the cost of a flight from Kansas City. That's a major-league steal.

In hindsight, I'll bet that if Rog could have paid $672.28 to not attend—and if Sal could still collect his dough— he would've in a New York second.

I have the feeling I'm going to be defending Rog against the ill-informed for the rest of his baseball career.

***

Baltimore Orioles outfielder Whitey Herzog, who resembles Maris and lives in the same Kansas City suburb of Raytown, Missouri, was in a local bowling alley when he was stopped by a female admirer and asked if he was, indeed, Roger Maris.

Herzog, who hit five homers the whole season, said, "I wish I was. We both hit baseballs, but his go a lot further than mine."

November 14

As if the March edition of *MAD* magazine issue announcing that 1961 was going to be a *MAD* year wasn't enough, the Superman comic book of May 1961 had a story titled "The Night of March 31st."

As a prank, the staff of DC Comics decided to have fun with their readers by having the story take place the day after March 31, which is April Fool's Day.

The comic book story is intentionally filled with mistakes in lettering, goofs in coloring, incorrect artwork and boo-boos in the story plot.

Stuff like Superman wearing only one boot, a Bizarro-looking Perry White, Supergirl's unusually long hair, Clark sleeping with his glasses on, and the Leaning Tower of Pisa placed in Metropolis.

On the last page of that issue, readers were asked to list as many of the errors that they can find in the Great Superman Boo-Boo Contest.

This was my type of contest. I'm convinced that by winning this contest it will change my life.

I figured no one on this planet would examine each comic panel like me.

I must have looked over every conceivable aspect of the contest story a couple hundred times. I had my sister type out my list of boo-boos and then I mailed it in, hoping, thinking, and praying that I would win the top prize of an original Superman drawing.

No way can I lose, as I came up with 85 boo-boos.

I rode my bicycle six blocks from my house to the mailbox. With fingers crossed, I kissed my entry envelope for good luck and dropped it in the mailbox slot.

As Bizarro would say, "I hope me am not going to win."

Every day I checked the mail hoping to receive my letter of congratulations.

When did DC post the names of the winners? It wasn't until issue #149, November 1961.

There were 12,000 entries. I'm a loser but here's the interesting part. I found a boo-boo in the announcement of winners. The contest rules indicated that there would be 10 winners but when the winners were listed there were only five plus nine honorable mentions.

For crying out loud, the guys at DC comics made a boo-boo in acknowledging the correct number of winners because five is not ten and five plus nine is not ten. This must be the new math I've heard so much about.

November 15

Rog, his wife, Pat, and their friend Jim Cosentino were driving to Kansas City for a day of shopping when they heard on the radio that Rog had won his second consecutive American League Most Valuable Player award.

As voted by the twenty members of the Baseball Writers' Association of America, Rog polled 202 votes to Mantle's 198.

Rog received seven first-place votes, six second-place votes, three third-place votes, three fourth-place votes, and, believe it or not, one sixth-place vote. This prompted the "dean" of American baseball writers, Daniel Margowitz, to wonder and then write in *The Sporting News*, "...who gave Rog a sixth-place vote?"

I also wondered who, and why?

November 16

Before, during, and after Yankee games in 1961, Roger Maris was often the target of professional news photographers.

As a result of my obsession of examining newspaper photos of Maris from the 1961 season, I detected that—in addition to Maris's Yankee jersey sleeves being tailored short—the top button of his jersey was often unbuttoned. As best as I could determine, that was an idiosyncrasy that began with Joe DiMaggio, who always kept his top button unbuttoned for no significant reason.

Rog was often photographed in his Yankee Stadium locker after games in which he had hit a homer. As his home run total increased, photographers had him hold up the back of a Yankee jersey, displaying a uniform number that corresponded with the home run number he had hit. Or they'd have him hold up the appropriate number of fingers signifying his latest home run number.

The day after he hit his fifty-second and fifty-third home runs of the season, the September 3 *Daily News* had a front-page photo of Rog. Staff photographer Charles Hoff shot the photo.

I'm guessing he called out to get Roger's attention in the postgame locker room commotion: "Hey, Rog, be a prince and let me get a shot of you holding up your hands to signify the number fifty-three. You know, five fingers of your right hand and three fingers of your left."

"Raise your hands a little higher."

"Yeah, that's it. Now, big smile."

"Let me get one more just to make sure."

As a result of those photos, I was able to peer into Roger's Yankee Stadium locker. In addition to seeing his uniform jersey, pants, underwear, glove, and bat, I could spot on the shelves miscellaneous items, such as large manila envelopes—which were probably fan mail—a glass ashtray, a Camel cigarettes package, an aerosol can of Right Guard deodorant, a Dobbs hat box, a folded towel with the letters L A U N D printed on it, a Budweiser beer can, a Robert Bruce shirt box, a bottle of eye drops, a small can of Ammens Medicated Powder, an official American League baseball box, and a snapshot taped to the side of his locker from the *LIFE Magazine* photo shoot that Rog did with Mantle.

I kept scouring the photo and noticed that on the inside edge of the locker were the words BAD DAY. They were underlined, and below the line was a single slash which probably represented the number one.

My assumption is that Rog didn't do well in a game and decided to keep track of how many bad days he had. Since it was his Yankee Stadium locker, I realized that his "bad day" happened during a home game after the July 31 All-Star break when his home run total was at forty.

After examining Yankee home-game box scores, here are my guesses as to the day he wrote it. There were three games in which Rog went hitless in four at-bats.

- August 17 vs. White Sox, 4 at-bats, no hits
- Sept 1 vs. Tigers, 4 at-bats, no hits
- Sept. 5 vs. Senators, 4 at-bats, no hits

Even worse, in a doubleheader on September 4 against the Washington Senators, Rog took the collar (no hits) in eight at-bats. Fortunately, the Yanks won.

But this day had to be it: the August 6 doubleheader nightmare against the Minnesota Twins. The total time to play the two games was almost seven hours. The Yanks won both games with Roger getting just two singles in twelve at-bats.

That was, indeed, a bad day for Rog.

November 17

As the days get colder and the nights shorter, I began collecting almost daily a number of unanswered questions about "life stuff," for which, unfortunately, the *Encyclopedia Britannica* didn't always provide answers.

Unanswered questions included: Did our alphabet start with only a few letters? What was the last letter added and when did that happen? Aren't we overdue for a new letter?

Why don't all human beings on earth speak one language? Does that mean that cavemen in Italy spoke a different language than the ones living in a New York cave?

Who discovered stuff that could be eaten like bacon, spaghetti, potato chips, and ice cream? What happened to those people who tried eating dirt, tree bark, and skunks?

Here's one that I'll probably never find the answer for: I've seen pictures of girls with their breasts exposed in *National Geographic* and wondered why guys who live with those girls don't have erections all the time. Why is that? Maybe the answer is, they do, but photographers don't include that in their photo frame.

While I'm at it, I've always wondered: Why don't girls fart?

November 25

Okay, I'm going to level with you.

Remember the 9 ½ Club I was a member of these past summer evenings? You know, two other guys, me and three girls. We'd meet inside the White Plains High School football field scoreboard to discuss sex.

Well, by November, my feelings had changed for one of the girls—the brunette. Honestly, I don't think they changed, but I just couldn't keep my desires to myself.

So I decided to ask her out on a date. This would be my first "go to the movies" date. My hope would be to wind up in the balcony of the darkened movie theater. I'm sure you get the picture.

But naturally, I wouldn't refer to it as a "date" to her.

I called her, hopefully right after she and her family were done with dinner, early on a Tuesday evening.

My prepared script in hand, I read the following when she answered:

"Hi, it's me, Andy," then for clarification, ad-libbed, "Andy Strasberg."

She said casually in a friendly tone, "Hi, Andy."

Since this was the first time I had ever called this girl, I decided to stick to my script with some small talk about school.

"How's school going?"

"Good," she said and asked, "How about you?"

"Good," I said.

Trying to keep the conversation moving, I asked, "Anything new with you?"

"No, not really," was her reply.

I delivered my next line, trying not to sound as if I was reading it. "Do you watch 'The Flintstones' on Friday nights at 8:30 on Channel 7?"

"No, why?"

I improvised with my corny reply, "Just wondering."

It was now painfully obvious to me and I'm sure to her that I had just asked a dumb-ass question with a lame response follow-up. I have no idea what I was thinking when I wrote it or why I said it.

I was running out of stuff to talk about because I had nothing else written down, except for popping the question. I decided to go for it. Once again, I carefully read my written script: "I was wondering if you would be interested in going to see 'Sink the Bismarck' at the RKO this Saturday afternoon."

She startled me and shot back quickly, "Let me ask my mom."

She put down the phone with a bang. I pressed my ear closer to the receiver so that I might be able to hear the conversation with her mother.

Silence. Couldn't hear a thing. Not even a mumble. I thought she might have broken the phone when she put it down.

While waiting, even though it was a cool November evening, I felt the perspiration from my forehead start to bead up. I wiped the wetness away with my right forearm, but didn't get all of it. As a result, I could feel the sweat run down my right temple.

Man, this is hard. How do other guys do this?

Then I panicked. What if she comes back and her answer is no? I hadn't thought that far ahead. My prepared script actually ends with the question about going to the movies. What do I say? Should I hang up? Where did she go? How long is this going to take? Next time, I'll be better prepared. I should have written out things if her response is no.

I was now confused and disoriented. Suddenly, she was back on the phone. "My mom said yes."

Oh, Lord, for a second I thought she misunderstood me and had asked her mother to go with me to the movies instead.

"Tell me what time and I'll meet you at the theater," she added.

Relieved, I stumbled with the answer, "Yeah, I'll let you know when I see you at school tomorrow."

"Great, see you then. Bye."

"Yeah, bye."

We both hung up. I stared at the phone. Even though she had said yes, I don't think it went all that well.

I should have told her it was a date. She's probably thinking that we're just going to the movies as, quote, *just friends*, unquote.

Oh, well.

A Double Date?—I couldn't believe my eyes when my afternoon movie companion's best friend showed up. *Artwork by Tom Dean.*

That Saturday afternoon, the mother of my date drove up in their family car, stopping right in the front of the theater. The passenger door opened and out stepped my afternoon movie companion. Then I noticed that the back door of the car also opened. Out stepped my movie companion's best friend, Bonnie.

They both walked toward me smiling. Her best friend? Shit, I'm sunk.

There's nothing I can do about this situation but try to weather the rough seas ahead.

After we greeted each other in a friendly but reserved way, I held up not three, but two tickets, announcing, "I've got them. Let's go in."

I glanced over at the surprise guest Bonnie, who, very business-like, walked over and bought her own ticket. Now if you're wondering why I selected this flick, it was because there's nothing like a good war movie that has a lot of action with the bad guys getting it in the end.

Shoot 'em up Westerns are okay, too. I also dig horror movies like *The Crawling Eye* from a few years ago. But when it comes to love stories, they don't float my boat.

Once inside the lobby, my plan was to buy a large popcorn that I would share with my date. But that plan has been blown out of the water since there were now three of us. Because I was outnumbered, I decided not to bring up the subject of refreshment treats and hold on to my money.

We passed through the lobby and entered the darkened theater. The three of us stood in back of the last row of seats, waiting for our eyes to adjust to the pitch blackness. After our eyes adjusted, the three of us walked down the aisle.

About halfway toward the screen, I asked both girls, "Is this okay?"

My date said, "Sure," and took a seat one in from the aisle. I sat in the aisle seat.

Bonnie immediately took a seat in the row behind the row where my date and I were sitting. She was off the aisle directly behind my date.

My God, this third-wheel thing is awkward.

The movie began. On the screen were scenes of Nazis marching, swastika flags flapping in the wind, and Hitler acknowledging his followers with that crazy salute of his that I'm sure he stole from the Indians' *how* palm greeting.

The movie announcer speaks in German. For crying out loud, what the hell was I thinking by selecting a movie in German? I'm an imbecile.

Thankfully, after a couple of minutes of hearing the German language, the American newsman Edward R. Murrow came on the screen speaking English. *Whoa*, that was a close one.

Most anytime I see a movie whose stars have a distinct accent or way of talking, immediately afterwards I take on their speech pattern.

That's how I was able to speak in French gibberish like Maurice Chevalier with my lower lip protruding after my parents took me to see the movie *Gigi* a couple of years ago. I'm not bragging, but I can also do voice impressions of Kirk Douglas and Georgie Jessel.

Most everyone in the movie spoke English, but with a German or British accent.

About halfway through the movie I decided that, since Bonnie was sitting directly behind us, putting my arm around the shoulders of my date was *verboten*.

The movie ended after ninety minutes with no surprises as the Brits sank the German boat.

As the movie credits begin rolling on the screen, my date and I got up and walked out to the street with Bonnie trailing us.

As the three of us stood in front of the theater, my date said, "Thanks," and then added, "See you in school."

Without realizing it, my British accent kicked in. In a cheerful, blustery, cockney voice, I said, "Well guv'nor, very good now. Cheerio. Fare thee well, fair maidens," and walked away.

THE END

November 29

By now I had almost forgotten about the baseball Rog hit for his fifty-ninth home run until I read an article by the *Baltimore Sun*'s Earl Shelby about how it had been turned over to the Baseball Hall of Fame. It happened at the annual Sports Headliner Banquet, attended by about six hundred fans, athletes, and civic leaders at the Lord Baltimore Hotel.

The home run baseball was caught by Bob Reitz in Memorial Stadium's right-field stands. In return for the baseball, the Sports Boosters contributed $500 to the Associated Catholic Charities. The check was received by retired Rt. David I. Dorsch, director of the organization, who then gave the ball to the director of the Hall of Fame, Sid Keener.

So after all the back and forth confusion, with Reitz changing his mind about what to do with the fifty-ninth home run ball he grabbed the evening of September 20, it turns out that everyone lived happily ever after.

Just like in the fairy tales.

Make Room—I decided to arrange my Roger Maris and Yankee souvenirs on display in my bedroom.

DECEMBER 1961

"The Polaroid Kid misses his last shot."

December 1

As everyone knows, baseball is best played when the environmental elements are most conducive.

With the temperature near or below freezing—while the days are shorter than the five-foot five-inch Angels outfielder Albie Pearson—December in New York provides ideal conditions to play baseball...That is, the Cadaco All-Star table-top board game version. I'm playing three games a week.

Once the top of the game box is removed, the contents resemble a baseball field. The game is played with a circular card the size of a beer coaster of each player. Each card has been cut out in the middle so that it fits neatly over a spinner. The possible outcomes of what the batter will do is determined by varying sized zones on the outer border of the card.

Action begins when the spinner is flicked with a finger to see what zone the arrow will point to.

At first glance, Maris's home run zone should be bigger, but then again this was based on last year's stats when Rog hit only thirty-nine round-trippers.

The game is less complicated than Monopoly, more active than Chutes and Ladders, but falls short of accuracy due to the fact that there are no pitching cards nor fielding cards.

I realize that playing a board game is not real baseball, but it's December and what alternatives do I have to keep busy before spring training?

Game Time—Playing baseball in the dead of winter in New York means a Cadaco All-Star tabletop baseball game.

I realize there's another baseball board game out there. It's APBA, which stands for "American Professional Baseball Association." But I am not a fan because it lacks the graphic sizzle of Cadaco All-Star Baseball. And I need sizzle. It's basically a boring and somewhat complicated card game with numbers and dice.

As if I was a baseball scribe, after every game I write a story similar to those articles that appear in the *Daily News*. I also write the headline, trying to be clever: BOMBERS BLAST BOSOX. In the story, I make sure to include quotes from my table-top players.

"I hit a fastball."

"I'm happy we won."

"I got the pitch I was looking for."

Pretty realistic, huh?

Hey, for those of you wondering why I didn't include the Coleco Electric Baseball Game, it's because baseball is not a game that is plugged into an electrical outlet.

December 9

An obscure note in an obscure Pennsylvania paper, the *Hazelton Standard-Speaker*, reads: "Time was when all boys wanted to grow up to be policemen, and all girls wanted to be nurses, but times have changed. Today's kids have a new set of heroes. The new idols are Roger Maris, President Kennedy, Mrs. Kennedy, and Alan Shepard."

December 10

On occasion, when I would not let go of a subject I was discussing with a family member, my mom would offer a descriptive suggestion in hopes I'd change the subject: "Stop beating your head against the wall."

Sometimes it worked. But not always.

With apologies to my mom, "the wall" in this situation is Ford Frick's 154-game-schedule as the deadline for the home run record.

I recall that in 1959, after the 154 regular-season games were completed in the National League, the Chicago Cubs' Ernie Banks and the Milwaukee Braves' Eddie Mathews were tied for the league lead in homers with forty-five each.

Yet because the Braves and the Dodgers ended the regular season tied for first place, Mathews' season continued with best-of-three extra games for the purpose of deciding a winner.

It took only two games for the Dodgers to win the pennant, but Mathews managed to hit one more home run, which ended his season with forty-six circuits.

So where was Frick on this? Why didn't he step in and use the 154 games as a defining measurement, explaining that Mathews' extra games weren't fair to Ernie Banks (aka "Mr. Cub")?

This "a season is a season" was accepted just a few years ago even though some seasons are longer for those teams that have the exact same record after 154 games. They had to play extra games to break the tie.

But Frick didn't say anything. Perhaps he was too busy dealing with the case of three unidentified Phillies for having what he referred to as an indiscretion in their private lives with an eighteen-year-old filly of the night.

Don't get me started again…for comparison's sake, it's not the number of games that matter but rather the number of plate appearances (Mathews had 682 plate appearances compared to Banks's 671)…because my head hurts and I'm running out of walls.

***

"You'll go to bed crying," and "Be careful what you wish for," are two of my mom's most used expressions.

The "crying" version was thrown in my face when it appeared to my mother that I was having too much fun in my everyday existence. She was warning me there's a price to pay for enjoyment.

As for the "wish for" saying, I suspect there's more to that, but my mother never finished it. Nor did she have to. It was understood. I knew that even if my wish did come true, I'd probably wind up disappointed anyway. Besides, I know you never end a sentence with a hanging preposition.

Those are the fatalistic, philosophical foundations to approaching life that infused my young mind.

Somehow, in my quest to methodically read every tidbit about what goes on in the privacy of a baseball player's life, I missed Dick Young's column, "Young Ideas," in the June 15 *Daily News*. That is, until today, December 10.

For some unexplained reason, the newspaper showed up in our cellar months after it was published. I'd normally read a newspaper that was, at most, only a couple days old. But this provided me with a hindsight point of view that I had never experienced before.

In this June edition, Young wrote about the Yankees' behavior in the clubhouse. To introduce his topic, he described in detail what happens when the official scorer makes a judgment not in favor of a player.

According to Young, the Yankee players want it in their favor both ways. When they are on the field they don't want to be charged with an error on a ball that's hit to them. Yet when they're at bat they don't want balls they hit to be errors committed by their opposition.

By the third sentence, Young flatly stated that the Yankees are "spoiled rotten."

He went on to call most of them selfish and self-centered. According to Young, they pout, they rage, they curse, they brood when they don't get things their own way.

He wrote how Mantle was not happy with the official scorer's ruling that his line drive was not ruled a base hit, but an error. To get back at the official scorer, Mantle hid in the trainer's room, off limits to newsmen, to avoid talking to a reporter.

Young wrote how Maris griped when he was given an error when attempting to field a bloop hit that he never touched. The official scorer explained that if, in his judgment, Maris should have caught it and didn't, it's an error—touched or not.

Young picked on a few others—Skowron, Boyer, and Kubek—explaining that many times they get over their exasperation quickly. Players like Ford, Richardson, Lopez, and Howard almost never complain about an official scorer's ruling.

Since I'm never going to be able to have a conversation with a major league player, I'm at the mercy of sportswriters like Young to provide their "insider" insight. I rely on their observations, hoping they are astute, objective, and communicate through their writing effectively so I can form my own opinions.

Or as Doris Day often sang, "*Que Sera, Sera*," (What will be, will be).

***

During the winter months I would handwrite letters to players, requesting them to autograph either an enclosed 3″ × 5″ index card, their baseball card, or a photo torn from a magazine.

I would mail the package to their home ballpark and always included an SASE, which is short for "self-addressed stamped envelope." It was my hope that once the season began they would autograph it and mail it back to me.

Unlike some of my friends, who were doing the same thing, I would never ever state in my request letter that the player was my favorite.

Why? Because I was afraid that Roger would find out and be disappointed because he thought *he* was my favorite player. Or maybe he'd start a fight between him and the player I sent the request to.

Made perfect sense to me.

December 11

The Eichmann trial concluded, finding him guilty on all fifteen counts.

The judge announced: "The court finds you guilty on charges of committing crimes against the Jewish people, crimes against humanity, war crimes and membership in hostile organizations."

Eichmann was sentenced to die by hanging. It's ironic that society finds it acceptable to kill a person to punish him for killing other persons.

December 12

At a crowded press conference at the Biltmore Hotel on December 12, Roger Maris and Mickey Mantle announced the launch of a new line of men's and boys' apparel carrying the name Mantle-Maris Wear. Similar to their previous endorsement contracts, their label would appear on such items as sweaters, pajamas, robes, dress shirts, sports shirts, sweat shirts, dress and play shoes, underwear...you name it.

***

Recently, I keep hearing on the radio "Please Mr. Postman" by the Marvelettes. It seems that my interest in music keeps growing with each passing hour. Every day, I hear a new song on the radio that is somehow better than the song that came out yesterday. Is it the words, the instruments, or an undetectable sound connection to my brain?

I may not be TV's Dr. Ben Casey, but my diagnosis is that you have no soul or heartbeat if you listen to that platter and don't get up and start dancing, man.

***

I just noticed that the movie version of the play *West Side Story* was released this past October.

Whoa, did that bring back memories!

I'm not one to brag, but during the summer of 1960 at Camp Kiowa we staged the 1957 Broadway play for the campers. I played A-rab and Chino in the production. Yes, I played both parts.

For the part of Chino I wore a white T-shirt and dungarees with my Garrison belt that my mom sent from home. Growing up in the Bronx, I knew that to look authentic the belt buckle should be worn off-center, close to my hip.

The highlight of the production had to be when I sang "America." Please don't confuse that song with "America the Beautiful." *West Side Story*'s "America" tune is saucy and best sung with a slight Puerto Rican accent.

Needless to say, I belted it out with a saucy accent.

December 13

The New York Times writer Peter Bart wrote on December 13 about the new business venture and the partnership between Mickey and Roger. Bart provided detailed information about potential earnings and what they described as their biggest endorsement venture to date.

"Each player will receive an advance check of $30,000 and then for the next three years are guaranteed $45,000 apiece plus royalties."

Frank Scott, the players' business manager, was quoted: "This is the biggest deal that I have ever signed for athletes." Scott also said he would try to work Whitey Ford, who also attended, into the deal.

The highlight of the event was when Whitey, Rog, and Mick stood up in front of the "Mantle and Maris" logo. It was a baseball and a silhouetted batter on each side swinging, with the name Mantle above the stitching and the name Maris below the stitching.

All of them were wearing standard business attire of shirt, tie, and slacks for the photo. They were to pose as if they were producing a garment when Whitey held up a large pair of scissors in his left hand near Roger's olive necktie, which prompted Rog to protest, "Don't do that, you'll cut it."

Whitey replied, "No, I won't," and then handed a $100 bill to Roger, saying, "Here, if I cut it, you can keep the hundred."

With that, Mickey, standing on the other side of Roger, picked up a pair of scissors with his right hand and snipped Roger's tie.

"Okay," said Roger, grinning. "I can buy a few of them with this," as he pocketed the $100 bill Whitey had just given him.

Whitey screamed, "I didn't do it."

"You gave him the idea," said Roger.

***

Babe Ruth was most likely the first player to be paid as much for what he did off the field as he did on it.

According to *The Sporting News*, Mantle earned an $80,000 income outside of his Yankee contract as a result of Frank Scott's efforts. Maris has made $110,000 from testimonials, merchandising gimmicks, and personal appearances.

That's a lot of moola for not having to try to hit a curveball from a sneaky lefty.

***

Shirley Povich of the *Washington Post* called Mantle and Maris "superstars," as reported in *The Sporting News*. I'm sure that the term originated in comic books and has been used before, but it's the first I ever saw it.

December 14

Roger attended the first meeting to negotiate his contract for 1962 with Roy Hamey. Afterward, both described the meeting as "amiable." According to United Press International, Maris was seeking $75,000.

December 15

After receiving the news that he had won the Associated Press Male Athlete of the Year award, Roger was photographed leaving a building with the doorman, Al Mechow, saluting him.

December 16

Traditionally, December is when I redecorate the walls of my bedroom.

This was relatively easy because I had a new 1961 Yankee pennant that included a photo of the team. I also had the oversized black-and-white photo of Mick and Rog that was included in the photo proof sheets my dad gave me.

To keep my baseball-themed wall display fresh, I also changed the framed pictures with new *Sport* magazine color photos of ball players I had cut out.

One of the most expensive baseball souvenir items I added since the season ended was a baseball rug. I saw it advertised in the October-November *Baseball Digest* magazine.

That issue's cover had a small photo of Mantle and Maris and the story headline: "WHAT M-M BOYS ARE LIKE OFF THE FIELD." So naturally I bought the magazine. Inside there was a half-page ad for a Baseball Fan's Rug from the RBI Shop in Highland Park, Illinois. The rug was white cotton chenille in the shape of a baseball, twenty-four inches in diameter.

The cost was an expensive $7.50, so I needed to ask my anonymous banker—who coincidentally gave birth to me in 1948—to gift it to me because I just had to have it.

My banker agreed. Easy.

The ad noted that the rug could be personalized with red lettering placed in the middle between where the red stitching formed a top-and-bottom border.

I specified that the wording in the center should be:

ROGER 61 MARIS

It arrived in the mail a few days ago. This rug, I am convinced, has to be a one of a kind because of the lettering I selected. This will be the centerpiece of my baseball wall display in my bedroom for 1962 and probably forever.

December 18

Starting in the late 1950s, my dad was a co-owner of 20th Century Lanes, a bowling alley in downtown Yonkers, New York, not far from Getty Square.

It had twelve lanes, ten with Brunswick automatic pin-setter machines and two with teen-age pinsetters—more commonly known as pin chasers—who would manually reset bowling pins, clear fallen pins, and return bowling balls to the bowlers.

My dad promised me that when I got a few years older I could earn money working as a pinsetter. It took me only a few seconds to realize how dangerous it was every time a bowling ball sent those heavy maple-wood pins flying in every direction.

No thanks.

The clientele was largely middle-class Italians who I thought were the nicest and friendliest people in the world. They loved to bowl, smoke cigarettes, and have a beer or two. Although I never saw the exchange of money, I knew they would make friendly wagers on everything from a roll of a frame to the "numbers game."

Trust me...at thirteen I knew.

My dad's work schedule started when he left home around three in the afternoon. Usually, he wouldn't return home until three in the morning. Understandably, my mother, sister, and I had to tippy-toe around our apartment in the morning so as not to wake him.

When I arrived home from school on Monday, December 18, my dad was still home in our den, sitting in his recliner watching TV, sipping a cup of black coffee and smoking a Camel cigarette.

As I walked by the den headed for the kitchen, I said hello. My dad responded by saying, "Andrew, I have something for you."

I walked in, sat on the edge of our sleeper sofa near his recliner. Without any ceremony or explanation, my dad handed me a large manila envelope that contained six 8″ × 10″ photo sheets with 141 minuscule black-and-white pictures printed on them. The pictures were the same size as 35 mm negatives.

Pointing to the photo sheets, he asked: "Do you know what that is?"

I looked closely and realized that the small photos were taken with a 35 mm motor-drive camera. They were shots of Roger Maris hitting his sixty-first homer at Yankee Stadium.

Incredulous, I asked, "Is this what I think it is, Pop?"

"It is."

In one corner of the sheets was written, "T. Triolo." In the other corner was "10/1/61." I squinted to see each tiny photo. But even without a magnifying glass I could see "moments in time" from that day, most of which I'm sure have never been published.

While I examined it, I asked, "Where did you get this?"

"It's a secret," he answered.

For whatever reason, my dad was always mysterious, never answering any of my questions about surprises like this so I knew not to ask again.

As I was examining each frame, he said, "I also have one other photo for you."

From behind the recliner, he pulled out a 16" × 20" photo portrait of Mantle and Maris with an out-of-focus photo of Babe Ruth in the background. It was the same image that had been on the cover of the August 18 edition of *LIFE* magazine, but this one was in black-and-white.

Since I had already asked once, I knew not to ask my dad how he got it. Except that, unable to control myself, these words spilled out in a raised voice as I asked, "How did you get this?"

I didn't wait for his response and quickly gushed, "It's incredible. I love it. I'm going to frame it and hang it in my room forever. Thanks, Pop."

Although my dad never revealed his source, I figured that "T. Triolo" was the photographer who took the photos. He must have lived in Yonkers or close by, loved to bowl, and was a regular at 20th Century Lanes.

Wanna bet I'm right?

December 20

Imagine a community filled with major league baseball players, including Roger Maris. Raytown, Missouri, is that place, according to an article in the December 20 edition of *The Sporting News*.

Sid Bordman, who wrote the article, names Bill Tuttle (Minnesota Twins), Norm Siebern (Kansas City Athletics), and Whitey Herzog (Baltimore Orioles) live just a good fungo shot from each other. Actually, Siebern lives across the street from Herzog.

Wait, there's more. Bob Cerv (New York Yankees) lives close by and so does Ed Rakow (Kansas City Athletics). Recently retired from the Baltimore Orioles, Arnold Portocarrero also resides in the area.

So there's a good chance that during the 1961 off-season you could bump into those guys if you went to the supermarket.

No, a better-than-good chance because those guys hang out at Consentino Brothers Super Market, located within a few blocks from where the players reside.

On occasion, the crew goes to the owner's hunting lodge at Mound City, Missouri. It's pointed out that Rog has the most staying power when it comes to hunting. I have no idea what "staying power" means, but I now know Rog has the most.

According to the article, Rog was in a bowling league last winter and "chucked" an impressive 175 average. Okay, I know what that means.

When it comes to golf, on his good days, Maris shoots around one hundred.

Rog was quoted in the story: "Right now, I think happiness is more important than money. Money isn't everything; maybe someday it will be. But I'd rather be with my family. I don't get to see my wife and children enough during the season."

***

The December 20 issue of *The Sporting News* ran a story about a special meeting of the Baseball Writers of New York to select their Sid Mercer Award for Player of the Year. The award is named in honor of New York baseball writer Sid Mercer, who died in 1945.

According to Dan Daniel, who wrote the article, it was the most violent (his word, not mine) and prolonged debate since the inception of the Sid Mercer Award in 1931. It was decided that both Mantle and Maris would share in the honor.

December 21

In a Christmas message from the Vatican, Pope John XXIII called upon world leaders to do their utmost to prevent war with all its possible horrendous consequences.

Utmost may not be enough.

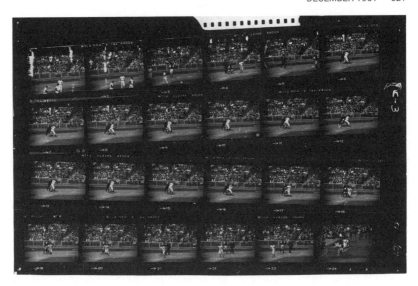

Contact 61—As is his custom, my dad was secretive as to how he obtained a number of photo contact sheets of Roger Maris hitting his 61st homer at Yankee Stadium on October 1, 1961. I think I figured out the how and where, but don't know the who.

December 26

It was the day after Christmas that I found the time to obsessively study the 8″ x 10″ black-and-white glossy photo contact sheets that my dad had given me.

The only way for me to scour these tiny photos that measured 1-7/16″ x 1″ was with a high-powered magnifying glass.

I was transfixed and held my breath as I began, like a police detective looking over a photo from a crime scene for a clue as to what happened.

One of the contact sheets was filled with photos of Yankee Stadium's home-plate area. From the vantage point, it appeared that the camera was set up just above Yankee Stadium's right-field stands, but below the upper deck.

It was obvious that the camera was locked into position, focusing on both sides of the batter's box.

With painstaking care, I slowly examined every Kodak Tri-X safety-film frame as shot by an unidentified photographer.

The first few frames appear to be random test photos.

Frames Nos. 1 and 2 are of the Yanks taking the field in the bottom of the first inning as Clete Boyer jogs in front of the batter's box toward third base. Also, in the lower left corner of the frame is a capless Yogi Berra, who just took off his batting helmet after popping out to Red Sox second baseman Chuck Schilling to end the inning.

In frame No. 3, Yankee backstop Elston Howard, in full catching gear with his mask on, is behind home plate, standing at attention. Yankee right-handed starting pitcher Bill Stafford has his head down, looking at the ground in mid-stride after crossing the first-base line as he's walking to the mound. His glove is resting on his chest and his right hand inserted into the pocket of the glove.

In frame No. 4, Yanks second baseman Bobby Richardson is getting set up in the batter's box for his at-bat in the bottom of the third.

Frame No. 5 shows umpire Bill Kinnamon alone at home plate, looking at the ball-and-strike counter in his left hand.

The at-bat sequence in which Maris hits his sixty-first homer begins with frame No. 6. Maris is standing in the left-hand batter's box as Red Sox catcher Russ Nixon and Kinnamon are in position, prepared for right-hander Tracy Stallard's first pitch.

The only noticeable difference in frame No. 7 is that Roger's right foot is lifted off the ground, taking his stride as the pitch heads to the plate.

In frame No. 8, Maris stops his motion with his bat behind his left ear as Nixon catches Stallard's first offering. The pitch appears to be outside the strike zone, but on the same plane as the interlocking "NY" logo on Maris's pinstriped jersey. Nixon's right hand covers the ball in his catcher's glove pocket so that it doesn't pop out.

Frames Nos. 9 and 10 show Maris standing upright once again, prepared for the next pitch as Nixon gives Stallard the sign for his next offering.

In frame No. 11, Maris lifts his right foot as he strides toward the thrown baseball again. In frame No. 12, Nixon catches the pitch low and inside near Roger's left foot before the ball hits the dirt as Maris stops once more so as not to swing at the pitch.

Frames Nos. 13 and 14 show the sequences of Maris preparing for the next pitch, just like in frames Nos. 6, 9, and 10.

In frame No. 15, Maris shifts his weight with his right-foot stride toward the pitch. In frame No. 16, his Louisville Slugger is now swung around and horizontal on the same plane as the incoming pitch, a fraction of a second before impact.

By frame No. 17, Maris's swing has followed through after connecting with the Spalding baseball. His left hand has released the bat above his right hand, which is near the bat's knob. His left arm is extended across his chest as if Rog was loosening up his left shoulder by stretching it out. While still holding the ash wood bat in his right hand, his right arm is fully extended behind his body after the bat meets the ball, producing that "tonk" sound that had rung out sixty times over the course of the 1961 season.

Maris's eyes look skyward following the batted ball. He is about to drop his serial A92 Louisville Slugger and begin to run out of the batter's box to first base, leading with his left leg in frame No. 18 as Nixon begins to rise out of his catcher's crouch.

Frame No. 19 shows Nixon standing upright with Kinnamon behind him, watching the flight of the rising baseball heading to right field. As Maris's body is turned toward first base, he shifts his weight to his right leg with his arms by his side beginning to form a 90-degree angle, bending them at the elbow and alternating each arm in a pumping motion like the wheels of an old-time steam locomotive.

The next four frames show Maris running to first base.

The last frame on the contact sheet of the Maris swing is frame No. 23. Maris appears to have taken only five running steps toward first base.

So I start over again, examining each frame in Maris's at-bat, but this time scrutinizing the faces of every fortunate fan sitting behind the plate watching the game as Maris hits No. 61.

Captured in the frames are ninety-four distinguishable fans' faces.

To begin with, I zero in on the group sitting to the third-base side of the backstop protective screen in the first row of Section 8 behind home plate in frame No. 6.

Sure enough, with the first game of the World Series to start on October 4 at Yankee Stadium, it appears that there are at least four members of the Cincinnati Reds sitting in the first two rows behind home plate. I'll bet they are taking notes about how to pitch to the Bronx Bombers.

I can make out pitchers Jim O'Toole—who's scheduled to pitch Game 1—plus Game 2 starter Joey Jay, along with Reds catcher Darrell Johnson and pitching coach Jim Turner.

In frame No. 6, as Rog awaits the first pitch, a well-dressed woman who I assume was the wife of one of the Reds' players is about to enter the row where they are sitting. She must've been a distraction, as a couple of people look at her as she makes her way to her seat in Row 2, probably saying, "Pardon me...pardon me...excuse me...pardon me."

Behind the Pardon Me woman entering the row is a somewhat obscured white-haired gentleman sipping a drink.

Four seats over to the right of Sipping Man and one row back is a fan who is evidently not close enough to the action because he is looking through binoculars. I name him Mr. Closer.

One row behind Mr. Closer and a couple of seats to his left is a kid not older than ten, who with both elbows on the pipe-bar box railing is holding his face in his hands. His facial expression appears to be bored. Behind Bored Kid is a man in a suit and tie wearing a smart-looking fedora.

Seated behind Smart Fedora is a bespectacled teenage boy leaning to his left so as not to miss the pitch. Sitting behind the Leaning Teen is a woman wearing dark cat-eye sunglasses looking out to the field.

It seems to me that Miss Cat-Eye Sunglasses is attending the game alone because no one is sitting next to her and certainly no one would get up to go to the bathroom as Maris came to bat. Sometimes in life you've just got to hold it.

Fourteen rows back, I spot a Yankee Stadium vendor dressed in white pants and shirt. There's no way to tell what White Pants Vendor is hawking as his back is to the field.

Polaroid Kid Exposed—As Maris connects for his 61st homer the Polaroid Kid (circled) loads his camera but momentarily looks up to see the record breaking baseball head toward the right-field stands.

Among the other spectators who stand out are Sailor Fan, Pipe Smoker, Yankee Jacket Boy, Coughing Man, and a kid, probably ten or eleven years old. He's standing in the first row of the aisle between sections, just to the left of the Reds players, and is snapping a photo with a Polaroid camera.

To the Polaroid Kid's immediate left in Section 10 is Scram Man, wearing a business suit, who's seated on the aisle in the first-row box seat as he shoots the kid a dirty look, no doubt wanting him to scram.

To me, it was obvious that Polaroid Kid had left his seat and then walked down the aisle of the home-plate box seats to the wire fence that separated the playing field from the seats. He stood there with his Polaroid J66 Land camera, hoping to capture a photo of Maris's historic record-breaking swing.

In that frame only one other fan has a camera that I can see. Camera Guy is holding a camera in front of his face, six rows back from Polaroid Kid. There's a good chance that Polaroid Kid was closer to Maris than anyone else who had a camera that day.

I now moved from frame to frame following Polaroid Kid snap a picture of Ball One that was outside, as called by home-plate umpire Bill Kinnamon.

Polaroid Kid then pulled out the tab of the two-minute self-developing photo so he could capture the second pitch that was low and inside, which resulted in Ball Two.

Again, he pulled the photo tab so he could shoot the third pitch. Apparently, that's when Polaroid Kid realized that was the last photo of the eight-shot pack of Polaroid film. He needed to reload.

The third pitch delivered from Boston Red Sox right-hander Tracy Stallard was a fastball that never reached catcher Russ Nixon.

In frame No. 13 Maris swings and sends the record-breaking homer on its way to the right-field stands.

Most fans can be seen with their mouths understandably agape. Sitting next to Scram Man is another older suit-and-tie gentleman who is beginning to stand with his right arm thrust into the air while his left hand holds the front-row railing.

By frame No. 21, Right Arm is now standing and somehow gets his arm even higher. Other fans are beginning to rise out of their seats, with some clapping in frame No. 22 while ump Bill Kinnamon takes a demonstrative step to Nixon's left to obtain an unobstructed view of the batted baseball in the air. Meanwhile, Nixon stands straight up, being the only person in the entire frame who hasn't moved since frame No. 19.

But, alas, when Maris connected, the Polaroid Kid is not in his previous prime location. My exhaustive search of the frame with a magnifying glass reveals that he was now ten rows back from the first row.

Polaroid Kid is in front of White Pants Vendor, who's squatted down with his back to home plate so as to not block the fans' view behind him.

Polaroid Kid is attempting to reload his camera while at the same time watching Maris's slight upper-cut swing. Oh, my God, Polaroid Kid missed capturing the momentous record on film.

For the first two pitches, no photographer was closer to Yankee Stadium's home plate than Polaroid Kid. He was right there. Then the all-powerful god of photography—"Kamera Obscura"—passed judgment. It was not meant to be for the juvenile shutterbug.

Interesting how things develop, wouldn't you agree?

December 29

There's a ton of talk about how much money Rog will make in 1962. Perhaps the most ingenious mathematical calculation I heard was from a friend who suggested that the Yanks pay Maris one cent for the first homer he hits and double it for the second homer, or two cents. Home run number three would be four cents.

By his tenth homer Maris would get $10.24, his twentieth homer would be $7,285, and by the time he gets to hitting his twenty-fifth homer he would earn $233,144 and so on.

So if you're thinking what I'm thinking, here's the answer: If Maris hit at least sixty-one homers again, his total would be somewhere in the vicinity of sixteen quadrillion bucks.

***

The Gallup poll results showing which men were most admired in the United States were printed in many newspapers around the country. JFK was No. 1. Dwight Eisenhower was No. 2. And No. 3 was Sir Winston Churchill. Thought for sure that either Maris or Mantle would be in the top twenty, but it didn't happen.

December 31

As a result of the last 364 days, I feel like I should be forty-five, not thirteen.

I may appear to be acting normal, but I'm anxious and concerned about what's going on in the world.

As a result of reading more than the sports sections in newspapers this past year, I learned about the Freedom Riders, the Eichmann trial, Fidel Castro, the threat of Russia led by Nikita Khrushchev, and the Berlin Wall.

Each news story had a similar, disturbing theme.

The commonality had to do with a combination of differences among peoples that results in distrust, which more than often causes hate, which manifests into violence and too often ends in death.

By far, the news stories that most upset me were the documented, horrific details of the Holocaust reported on a daily basis during the Eichmann trial.

I am trying to understand how and why this happened to six million Jews at the hands of Nazis. It is not logical.

If we all believe in a God, how could this happen?

Reading details of the ways in which Jews of all ages were tortured and murdered are hauntingly terrifying. Graphic images were published of skeleton-thin Jewish prisoners who hadn't committed any crimes yet wore striped prisoner pajamas, and the mounds of dead, many with bodies unrecognizable as human, at concentration camps such as Auschwitz and Krakow.

Had I been born a few years earlier and lived in the path of the Nazi terror machine, I, too, could have been tattooed on my arm with an identification number, resulting in the same catastrophic fate of being sent to a gas chamber that I was told was a shower.

I am overwhelmed with questions, and I don't know who to turn to for answers. Should I feel guilty because, until this year, I didn't know intimate details about the Holocaust and, as a result, didn't realize the severity of the tragedy? Is that a betrayal of my religion?

Are Nazis the most feared and hated group in the world? Are all Germans anti-Semitic? Was Hitler really Satan in disguise?

Should I despise Germans or does that perpetuate the problem of hate? Should I forgive those such as Eichmann who claim he was just following orders? After all, what is the difference between that and those American pilots who dropped atomic bombs on Japan's Hiroshima and Nagasaki, killing more than 100,000 citizens of all ages? Weren't those Americans just following orders? If the United States had lost the war, would those involved in the bombing have been tried for committing crimes against humanity?

While all that took place in faraway places before I was born, I am appalled that among our citizens this past year in the United States serious crimes are being committed against those people who are different or those who stand up for their rights.

Is it because I'm only thirteen that I can't comprehend, for example, why an angry group ambushed the bus carrying Freedom Riders in Anniston, Alabama, on May 14. The conscientious riders were testing the 1960 U.S. Supreme Court decision that segregation of interstate transportation facilities, including bus terminals, was unconstitutional in the deeply segregated South.

I read reports of the mob that attacked the Greyhound bus and set it on fire so the riders inside would be burned to death.

Fortunately, the occupants were able to flee the bus moments before the gas tank exploded.

I'm having difficulty understanding why this happens. Is hate an inborn universal human condition?

Does it eventually go away or get worse? Is it contagious?

Is it because we are all different? Our physical features, language, clothing, ethnic foods and religious beliefs? Is that what causes hate? Not understanding the differences or being envious? Aren't we more alike than we are different?

I'm convinced that if this intolerance of others keeps gaining momentum in a destructive manner, humans will ultimately annihilate themselves.

Look, I'm not a whiz kid, never won a game of Hi-Q, have barely read but a few pages of the *Encyclopedia Britannica*, and admittedly don't have all the answers in advance like Charles Van Doren. But I still have hope about the fate of all humanity.

If we don't self-destruct during the process of human evolution, then perhaps as a result of centuries of procreation between races and religions, the offspring around the world will become a society of indistinguishable citizens. They will not possess any apparent physical differences such as skin and hair color or unique facial characteristics. In other words, all humans will belong to a single race.

Perhaps all religious beliefs will merge and become united as one under a god. And listen to this—since I've heard about dead languages such as Latin, Sanskrit, and Old Norse, isn't it plausible that humans in the distant future will speak a universal language?

When? Well, don't hold me to it, but if I had to guess, wouldn't it be appropriate and ironic if all those things happened in 4,158 years in the year 6119, which is the reverse order of 19 and 61?

In any event, somebody has got to find a way to bring better understanding among all people living today.

Unfortunately, this past year I realized how naïve I am as I discovered that baseball is not exempt from problems of differences in people.

While I was aware that Jackie Robinson had broken the color line in 1947, I'm embarrassed to read about how Negro ballplayers are being treated now, not being allowed to stay in some of the same hotels as white players.

I'm proud that it was my Yankees who made headlines with their "One Roof" policy, proclaiming that every player on their team stays at the same hotel or they find another hotel.

How incredibly uninformed I am. Why? Because I thought discrimination was a thing of the past and was eliminated after Jackie Robinson began playing baseball in the major leagues. Yet that barrier still exists.

Now you may think I'm out of line, but it also appeared to me that not since those early years of desegregation in baseball has a player experienced the constant repetitious pressure of media attention and negative fan reaction that Roger Maris endured this past year.

Don't misunderstand me. Roger's experience doesn't come close to the severity of what those players of different skin color endured. But since then, I can't think of a player who went through what Rog faced, beginning in mid-July and increasing with each game.

Now, I'm not expecting Rog will hit sixty-two homers in 1962. But, man, I hope the 1962 Yankees repeat as World Champs. I'll bet that fans will expect a repeat of the home run derby from the M&M Boys, while anything short of that would be considered a failure.

Imagine if Mick and Rog hit significantly fewer homers in 1962. Let's say Mantle with thirty-four and Maris forty-one. I'm more than okay with those totals, especially if the Bombers win.

While I closely followed Roger's on-field exploits, I also paid particular attention to his personality and character this past year, as reported in newspapers and on broadcasts.

There are enough written accounts concluding that Maris is surly. He even admitted it when he said, "I was born surly."

"Surly" was not a word I was familiar with, so once again, as my vocabulary expands, I looked up the definition. Here it is: "ill-natured, abrupt, curt, blunt, crusty, irascible, grumpy."

However, if Rog was really all of those things he would have pissed off (my term, not his) every photographer and reporter who wanted his time. He was always accommodating, but only up to a certain point, as there were a couple of writers he could never please.

The other description I noticed was that he was often described as a "redneck," which, to me, means "poor white rural Southerner with little education."

That's not Roger Eugene Maris. Then I found out the term actually is off by approximately thirty-two inches below his neck. It's backasswards.

The term was used because writers couldn't use the baseball term "red *ass*," which means a player is intense and competitive, because it included the word "ass."

Unfortunately, that inappropriate term "red neck" has now been perpetuated by lazy writers who don't know Rog.

He was also described by some as an "angry young man," to which he replied, "If I'm mad, I act mad." Nothing wrong with that. If you're mad, aren't you mad? If you weren't, you'd be a phony.

What I found out about his personality greatly appealed to me. He is honest and forthright. He admits that he won't take criticism from anyone if it's undeserved, and he hates to lose. He speaks his mind but not in a rude way.

By no means is he a grand-stander, self-centered, or a pop-off, or even a know-it-all.

There are some traits that Rog is and I am not. He appears to be shy (okay, that's probably not me), not boastful (again, not me) but confident (that's not always me).

He seems to be uncomfortable being the center of attention, which I found interesting because this year he was, along with President John F. Kennedy and the astronauts, among the most prominent people in America.

One of his biggest bugaboos is when he is misquoted, which makes sense to me. Yet he is cooperative, talkative, literate, and sincere, almost to a fault.

As near as I know, he never says to reporters, "I'd rather not comment."

In 1961, Maris was vilified, glorified, ostracized, canonized, memorialized, and demonized. Yet he's the person I want to emulate.

So while I have Roger's personality traits to admire and try to mirror, I'm weary of being only 5' 2". It feels like I've been 5' 2" for the last ten years. I need to grow another foot, although right now I'd settle for nine inches by the time the Yanks open spring training in Fort Lauderdale next March.

It's also painfully apparent that I will be getting braces before puberty.

I'm afraid that my high-pitched voice won't change, and am resigned to the fact that for the rest of my life I'm going to sound like the soprano who sings the opening to "The Lion Sleeps Tonight." I'd prefer the voice of the guy who sings bass for the Coasters' "Mother In Law."

Now the real question is, could I be any funnier? I don't think so. Let's just agree that my sense of humor might have peaked in '61, although I'm working on a couple of new routines.

Quick half-turn, clear my throat, then quick turn back.

While overtly gesturing, I say in what I think is an adult, serious, middle-aged man's voice, "Look, Margaret, isn't that the Strasberg boy over there?" Then I make the sound of a door slowly opening...*kre-e-e-n*.

I take one step forward as if I walked through a door and continue with the portrayal of an older man, remarking, "Heard he does pretty good impressions of President Kennedy, Boris Karloff, and James Mason."

Then, in a woman's voice, I say, "But how do you know it's the Strasberg kid?"

I respond: "Short, crooked teeth, big nose, pot belly, kinky hair, wears glasses, and walks like a duck. Who else could it possibly be, Margaret?"

But, seriously, folks, I'm hoping the world continues to turn so that one day I can meet someone who was born June 1, 1961. Get it? 6/1/61. Perhaps I'll make the acquaintance of someone who was named after Roger Maris.

It's a long shot but maybe a baby was born in 1961 who will be a major league ballplayer, a famous actor, or an astronaut. Or maybe a scientist or even a future president of the United States.

It's more than obvious that with each passing moment, I feel baseball is taking on a bigger role in my life.

I couldn't help but compare myself to my dad, who was fourteen years old when Babe Ruth hit sixty home runs in 1927.

Now, thirty-four years later, Roger Maris hits sixty-one tonks and I'm a year younger than my dad was when Babe set the record in 1927.

Since it's the end of the year, I made some promises to myself.

To begin with, I am going to take full advantage of the fact that my parents lifted the restriction that I must be with an adult chaperone when going to Yankee games. My plan is to take the Central Avenue bus to the Woodlawn elevated train station to Yankee Stadium and attend at least twenty-five to thirty games in 1962. I'll arrive around 10 a.m. for a 2 p.m. game so I can meet the Yankee players as they enter the ballpark.

It probably won't happen, but I want to meet Maris. Fat chance. I'd like to talk to him and get his autograph. I'd also like one of his Louisville Slugger bats and to catch one of his homers. A guy can dream, right? I know I'm greedy, but I'm *honestly* greedy if there is such a thing.

Even though I'm not old enough to get a job as a Yankee ball boy, I'm still going to pursue the job and stick with my plan of mailing a letter once a year requesting an interview for the position. Hopefully, by the time I'm eighteen, the Yankees will write back to me, "All right, already, here's the date for your interview."

While I'm wishing and hoping, it would be nice to own a new record player—which in our house was still called a Victrola—that's not a hand-me-down from my sister, Bobbi, so I can listen to my records.

I recently saw an ad in *The Sporting News* for the Ted Williams Baseball Camp in Lakeville, Massachusetts. I'm going to write for a brochure to check out the possibility of attending over the summer. Cost is a factor, but I'm willing to work to earn the dough to go.

Corny as it sounds, I'm going to continue writing down thoughts about things I experience and my life observations, as I'm enjoying remembering those things through my notes.

And to my older self, I re-promise to get my Maris scrapbooks bound professionally, eventually. If I should ever get married, I have decided to have the ceremony performed on a baseball field at home plate. Also, I promise to return to Yankee Stadium in fifty years when I'm sixty-three years old on October 1, 2011, precisely at 2:43 p.m., which would be the exact moment Rog hit his sixty-first home run.

Knowing that I need to be more informed about events other than baseball, I will continue to make an effort to read more than the sports section. I'm embarrassed that until this year I never paid attention to grown-up things going on in the world.

These aren't resolutions. They are promises. My resolutions are to stop biting my nails, lose weight along with the nickname "Pot," clean up my room, and try to get better grades in school. Please note I used the word "try."

For me, 1961 was filled with many revelations, a few experimentations, some investigations, total preoccupations, growing transfigurations, and more often than not, dissatisfactions.

My world in 1961 seemed to be filled with an enormous amount of baseball, a lot of TV, more than a smattering of rock 'n ' roll, a few comics and cute girls, while the world was filled with a mixture of hate, promise, tragedy, hope, and adventure.

I go back to school in a couple of days. I'm convinced that when it comes to school, if you fit in, you're not gonna stand out. I need to stand out.

Speaking of standing out, I just read in the newspaper that snow flurries are expected in the New York area. Wouldn't it be great if that first day back, Tuesday, January 2, was a snow day and the schools were closed?

I will always cherish my yesterdays of 1961, but I'm kinda looking forward to tomorrow.

See you in '62.

THANKS

I would like this page to be last because now you have finished reading my auobiography. I would like to thank Miss Roberta Ellen Strasberg (my sister Bobbi) for her taking the time to type this and give suggestions. Thank you Bobbi. My thanks also go to a woman, I know pretty well, my mother, for giving me notes on the first few chapters. I thank her also for bringing me into this wonderful world. I would like to thank my father for letting me do it my way and not like when he was a boy. So with this message I would like to say thank you to the reader (who might even be me when I grow up) who had the patience to read my autobiography.

Sincerely yours,

Andy Strasberg

AFTERWORD

I've been asked to bring you up to date on some of those wishes, self-promises, and ambitions Andy Strasberg wrote about all those years ago when he turned thirteen. A post-game wrap-up of sorts.

Why me? You'll see.

To begin, that thirteen-year-old kid from New York is now seventy-one. He grew from 5′ 2″ to 5′ 10″ and, thanks to braces, he has straight teeth. He says he stopped biting his nails long ago.

But I'm getting ahead of myself.

Not surprisingly, given his persistence, Andy did meet Roger Maris. It happened during the 1962 baseball season, hours before a game outside Yankee Stadium on 157th Street.

I know this because Roger Maris was my father. I was born on August 21, 1961, or—as Andy refers to it—between home run Nos. 49 and 50.

After arriving Yankee players parked their cars across from Yankee Stadium, they'd be engulfed by admiring fans seeking autographs.

While other fans surrounded my father, Andy would hand him a short note he had written, praising the way No. 9 played baseball—hitting, fielding, and running the bases.

Andy would always sign the note, "Your faithful No. 1 fan."

The passing of a note in this way happened so often that I'm told my father would reach over the kids clamoring for his autograph to eagerly accept Andy's note.

As a result of those notes, my father soon realized Andy was a genuinely loyal fan.

One of my favorite Andy stories is how he asked my dad for a baseball during batting practice while he was shagging flies at Yankee Stadium.

According to Andy, everything happened suddenly. To his shock and delight, my father surprised him by casually flipping him a baseball. Andy was so startled that he froze. The ball softly hit Andy in his left shoulder, rolled away, and was quickly grabbed by another fan.

My father couldn't help but notice. Later, on his way to take a few swings in the batting cage, he asked teammate Phil Linz to deliver a baseball to

Andy with specific instructions about placing it securely in Andy's palm to ensure that the baseball stayed with the right person.

Andy still has that baseball.

In 1965, a year before Andy graduated from high school, he asked my father for one of his bats and one of his home run baseballs.

My dad responded by telling Andy that the next time he cracked a bat he would give it to him, but added, "You'll have to catch the homer on your own."

A couple of weeks later, moments before a game, just as he had promised, my father presented Andy with one of his Louisville Sluggers. Andy refers to that experience as the greatest day of his youth because it was the confirmation of a promise made by his childhood hero.

A Bat and a Ball—Prized possessions. Roger's first National League home run and a Maris Louisville Slugger.

Now hold on to your caps for this next story.

By far the most amazing of baseball circumstances one could imagine happened on May 9, 1967. That previous winter my father was traded from the New York Yankees to the St. Louis Cardinals. The Cardinals were playing the Pittsburgh Pirates in Forbes Field, a couple hours drive from Akron University where Andy was a freshman.

Andy assured his college buddies who made the trip with him that he'd introduce them to his childhood idol, Roger Maris. They were dubious.

When Andy spotted the new Cardinals outfielder, now wearing a jersey with the No. 9 on the back of his jersey, he tried to get his attention: "Hey, Rog!"

My dad turned and spotted his No. 1 fan. "Andy Strasberg, what the hell are you doing here in Pittsburgh?"

Andy took the cue and proudly stated, "Well, Rog, some of the guys from college wanted to meet you."

After introductions and a quick visit, Andy went to his seat in the right-field stands of Forbes Field as the game began. He sat in Row 9, Seat 9.

In the sixth inning, Pirates left-hander Woodie Fryman threw a pitch that my father hit for his first National League home run, sending it a few rows into the right-field bleachers.

Miraculously, Andy caught the ball.

Really.

Although, as you'll have read in *My 1961*, Andy might have struggled in junior high, he more than made up for it as in 1971 he graduated from Long Island University cum laude with a degree in English.

A few days after graduating college, Andy began his quest to find a front-office job in baseball by traveling around the country. He didn't have immediate success.

As a result of his laser focus, four years later, in 1975, Andy was hired to work for the San Diego Padres and eventually was promoted to Vice President of Marketing.

In 1976, immediately after the Padres season ended, Andy married the smart and very attractive Patti Hampson in a small home-plate wedding ceremony at San Diego Stadium.

From the time my father retired from baseball after the 1968 season, he and my mother kept in contact with Andy.

Sadly, in 1985 at the age of fifty-one, my father passed away from lymphatic cancer. The funeral service was held at Saint Mary's Cathedral in Fargo, North Dakota.

The temperature that December day in 1985 did not rise higher than two degrees with wind-driven snow flurries. After the service, Andy approached my mother to offer his condolences. They hugged and talked briefly.

Then my mother turned to me, my three brothers and two sisters, and said, "Kids, I want to introduce you to Andy Strasberg."

Instantaneously, my older brother, Roger Jr., recognized Andy's name. "I know you," he said. "You were Dad's No. 1 fan."

Andy responded, "You'll never know how much your dad meant to me growing up."

My brother countered: "And you'll never know how much you meant to our father."

That was the beginning of Andy's friendship with the next Maris generation.

In 1989, Andy's story of catching my father's first National League home run appeared in a number of publications, including *Sports Illustrated* and *Reader's Digest.*

Andy received hundreds of complimentary letters, one of which was written by Steven Jager, who pointed out that growing up he too was a fan of Roger Maris and that his daughter's first name is Maris.

Thanks to the cooperation of Jim Healey of the Red Sox, Andy has the October 1, 1961, radio play-by-play of my father's sixty-first home run as called by Ned Martin.

In 2000, Andy was hired as a technical consultant for the HBO movie *61**, directed by Billy Crystal. In addition to working behind the scenes, Andy was given a cameo role.

Let Andy explain: "Halfway through shooting the movie, Billy Crystal offered me an opportunity to get on screen, asking if I wanted to be an umpire in one of the scenes. I said no and explained that after Roger hit his sixty-first home run, one fan came out of the stands to congratulate him a few steps before he reached the Yankee dugout. I told Billy that I wanted to be that fan when I was thirteen and still wanted to be that fan at fifty-two."

Billy told him, "Then that's the role you'll have."

At the age of sixty-three, on October 1, 2011, keeping the promise he had made to himself at age thirteen, Andy went back to the site of old Yankee Stadium, which is now a public baseball field. Precisely at 2:43 p.m., he played the audio recording of Phil Rizzuto broadcasting the at-bat when my dad hit his sixty-first home run.

Ironically, it was that day that Andy met Roger Bow at the Yogi Berra Museum. Bow mentioned that he was born September 9, 1961, the day Maris hit his fifty-sixth homer. Yes, Roger Bow was named after my father.

After spending twenty-two years with the Padres, then eighteen years as a consultant for numerous Major League teams, legendary players, and the National Baseball Hall of Fame—roles which included assisting a few inductees with their acceptance speeches—Andy finally retired.

But not from his love of baseball.

Relying on notes he made throughout his career, Andy now spends much of his time writing of his life experiences. He is currently working on a book about working for the San Diego Padres.

Andy is often invited to share those experiences with audiences around the country. He has spoken before groups at the National Baseball Hall of Fame and Museum, the Yogi Berra Museum, the Smithsonian's National Postal Museum, a brunch for the volunteer umpires at the Little League

World Series, Lincoln Center in Manhattan, Fenway Park, Coors Field, Fordham University, and Stanford University.

Ten years ago, Andy wrote and performed a one-man, one-act theater production, *That's Baseball*. It includes vignettes based on his friendship with my father and our family.

In 1999, Andy represented our family for the ceremony when the U.S. Postal Service issued a commemorative stamp that acknowledged my father hitting sixty-one home runs.

On a personal note, when our oldest son turned thirteen in 2003, Andy took him to his first Yankee game at Yankee Stadium. He also invited the fan who caught my father's sixty-first homer, Sal Durante, and his wife, Rosemarie, to join us. We had a great and memorable time.

For that past thirty-five years, Andy has attended and helped organize the annual Fargo charity fundraiser my father started in 1984. To this day, our family continues the Roger Maris Celebrity Golf Tournament, which benefits several charities, including The Roger Maris Cancer Center.

Clearly, our family's relationship with Andy that began when he was a fan of my father has blossomed into much more. He is considered more than a friend and fan. He has become part of our extended family.

But of all the magical things that have happened to Andy, the one experience that most stands out for me is deeply personal. It happened on August 3, 1990, the day our first son was born.

On that day, my wife, Fran, and I called Andy from a Florida hospital to tell him that Fran had just given birth to a baby boy. We told him that we were naming our son Andrew and wanted to know if Andy would be his godfather.

Of course, Andy said yes.

I'm confident Andy never imagined back in 1961 that his childhood hero's grandson would be his namesake and godson.

Randy Maris
December 11, 2019

No Introduction Necessary—Andrew Maris, born August 3, 1990, meets Andy Strasberg.

ACKNOWLEDGMENTS

It Was a Snap—After graduating high school in June of 1966, I arranged with Roger to have our photo taken by my buddy Arnie Cardillo before a Yankee game.

With the very real possibility that I will unintentionally forget someone, this is my opportunity to extend my appreciation to those wonderful people who assisted me with this project.

First, let me respectfully acknowledge my deceased father, mother, and sister who lived with me and put up with me every day, including holidays, in 1961.

To my wife, Patti, who played a significant role in allowing me to spend an inordinate amount of time compiling those things that happened to me in 1961. Fortunately, it is Patti who every day provides love, encouragement, and inspiration to me while our canine daughter, Hazel, patiently listens to me proofreading aloud.

Due to my good fortune, I proudly acknowledge my ongoing friendship with the Roger Maris family that began with Roger himself outside Yankee Stadium in 1962 and then in 1968 when I first met his wife, Pat.

Later, I met the next generation of the Maris family in 1985 when I was introduced to their children: Susan, Roger Jr., Sandra, Kevin, Richard, and Randy and eventually their spouses and children.

Also, I could not overstate the investment of time and talent that John Freeman and Dave Wright provided. They lent their sharp writing and editing skills when I often needed wording enhanced, sentences reconstructed, and paragraphs moved around and gently edited so there was more continuity and clarity in my written thoughts.

My cleanup hitter was Pete Rowe, who proofread every sentence once the manuscript was completed.

I'm honored that Todd Radom, the very talented graphic designer, was able to bring to life my visual descriptions and create a cover that far exceeds anything I could have imagined.

Very much appreciated for this endeavor is the artistry of Rich Kee, Chuck Beebe, Russ Opdahl, Bob Inwood, Ben Valley, and Jeff Crispell.

Great thanks, as well, to Marty Appel, who never hesitated to provide guidance on everything having to do with the Yankees whenever I needed it.

Sadly, but not surprisingly, I have lost touch over the years with my orthodontist's sensitive, caring nurse and my ultra-understanding Rabbi Schwartz.

Then there's my foundation of ongoing dear friendships that I have enjoyed, in some cases, dating back to 1961.

Those include: Jim Gold, Jim and Janice Healy, Duane Dimock, Susan Mendolia, Peter and Joyce Briante, Arnie and Debra Cardillo, Tom Larwin, Tim Wiles, Bret Moutaw, Dave Greene, Lloyd Kuritsky, Terry Cannon, Kevin Baskin, Peter Stolpe, R. C. Stolpe, Mike and Jeanette McDuffee, Phil Cuzzi, Andy McCue, Amanda Hamels, Belinda Bird, Jeff and Li-An

Merideth, Dick and Susan Dent, Tom Shieber, the Sal Durante family, Matt Dahlgren, John Hampson, Scott Keene, Greg Howell, David Kramer, John Miley, Andy Holden, Brian Richards, Danny Cohen, Kirk Kenney, Bob Costas, Billy Crystal, Keith Olbermann, Mark Chiarello, Rob Johnson, Steve Montgomery, Phil Gries of Archival Television Audio, Inc. and my adorable niece Julie Kappers and her children Jefferson and Sydney.

Photographically, I'm indebted to the National Baseball Hall of Fame and the Cleveland State University photo department.

I also wish to thank two people with whom I am still very much in touch—Mr. Clements, my Highlands Junior High School "boss" homeroom teacher in 1961, and my best friend that year, Ray Simons.

Original art by Mark Chiarello.